"Sarah Palin Out of Nowhere"

Mr Frank A Aquila

CHRISTY! YOU ARE A GREAT AMERICAN! - GOD BLESS! FRANK

Dedication

Dedicated to each patriot, who has the spirit to fight for freedom, to speak the truth, and holds the passion in their heart to return America to the land of opportunity to pursue happiness and the blessings and grace God has provided in America.

Table of Contents

Acknowledgement

Since January 2011, I have dedicated myself to writing "Sarah Palin Out of Nowhere," and it is only by the grace of God that I was able to write it. Even though I had "great influence" on Senator John McCain's 2008 vice-presidential selection of Governor Sarah Palin, who has become one of the most famous and influential political figures in American political history, I had never thought of writing this book until after the shooting of Congresswoman Gabrielle Giffords in Tucson, Arizona on January 8, 2011. The liberal media continued their assault against conservatives and Governor Palin, with their first reports assuming that a right-wing conservative was responsible for the shooting. After they realized the shooter was not a right-wing conservative, they immediately placed their attention on Governor Palin, finding some way to use this tragic event to blame Governor Palin for the shooting. The continual assault of false accusations against Governor Palin by the liberal mainstream media disturbed me, and I was persuaded by two of my friends, Elliott Serrano and Israel Carrero, to write "Sarah Palin Out of Nowhere."

With so much time consumed to writing "Sarah Palin Out of Nowhere," I had to sacrifice much time with my family. I want to thank my parents, Louis and Ruth Aquila, who assisted me with my two boys, Louis and Steven. I also thank my boys for understanding the time I needed to write, while they played quietly.

I want to thank everyone who worked with me on the long journey of this project. Don Moyer was the first to assist me in explaining the process of writing a book. He assisted me on the guidelines and answered many of my questions. He introduced Heather Visser, who owns a website design company, and assisted me in the original website design for "Sarah Palin Out of Nowhere." I also must thank my good friend, David Marks, who patiently assisted me with all my computer technical difficulties.

I want to thank Teresa Whitaker, Evelyn Bowser, and Mary Lou Neufer, who spent many long hours reviewing, editing and revising each chapter. I also want to thank Jeffrey Lemasters Tahir, who as an attorney spent many hours reviewing, fact checking, and referencing "Sarah Palin Out of Nowhere." These four incredible and patient people assisted me in making "Sarah Palin Out of Nowhere" a fabulous story. There were also many other people who contributed their time, ideas and assistance to "Sarah Palin Out of Nowhere," including Ron Devito, David Harmer, Phyllis Wohlferd, and my mother, Ruth Aquila.

I want to thank Rollan Ross and Sarah Palin News for supplying and approving the beautiful photograph of Governor Palin for the cover and Kristi Honas, who gave me the idea of "Sarah Palin Out of Nowhere" as the title for the book.

I want to thank Revolutionary Media for marketing "Sarah Palin Out of Nowhere." The team of Daria DiGiovanni, Kimberly Foster Moore, and Beverly Pipes did an outstanding job providing information and press releases to the media, coordinating media events and interviews, reorganizing the website, and coordinating social media networking outlets, such as Twitter, Linkedin, and Face book.

I want to thank all my friends from and around South San Joaquin County, who assisted me in developing the South San Joaquin Republicans, including Carl and Lois Neaterous, who were the original people to assist me in the beginning of the organization. I want to thank Bob Busser for being my mentor and encouraging me to get involved in the political process. I want to thank Don Parsons for all the individual insight he gave me on San Joaquin County politics. I want to thank Congressman Richard Pombo for recognizing my effort in the community and introducing me to President George W. Bush. I want to thank Laura Gadke, who recommended me as a county chairman for Senator John McCain's campaign in 2008. I want to acknowledge Senator McCain and his staff, including Brian Forrest and Bob Pacheco, who worked directly with me and passed on my recommendations about Governor Sarah Palin to the McCain advisers.

Lastly, I want to acknowledge Governor Sarah Palin for being a true American patriot and an example of what America would expect from a politician and president. She is an inspirational lady, who is honest, courageous, humble and of impeccable character. She has shown the strength to lead with grace while under pressure. She has earned everything she has achieved in life and provides a vision of hope and excitement for Americans to once again proclaim America as the greatest nation in the world.

Testimonial

Sarah Palin Out of Nowhere! This book is the quintessential book about Sarah Palin's rapid rise to the forefront on the political stage. Frank Aquila takes the reader through not only his influence on Sarah Palin being picked as John McCain's running mate, but also through the media attacks that Governor Palin faced, and still faces, the problems that America faces today, the causes of those problems and why Sarah Palin is the perfect solution. In a sea of books about Sarah, Sarah Palin Out of Nowhere is a refreshing, honest and well written read. You will not be disappointed!

~ TL Whitaker

Frank Aquila has "connected the dots" so we can comprehend the left-wing agenda which has caused many logically thinking Americans to be baffled. He also reveals the integrity, grit, love of country, and many wonderful accomplishments of Governor Sarah Palin, which were somehow kept from public view during the 2008 election bid! Sarah Palin Out of Nowhere is important reading for those desiring to understand what lies beneath the façade of modern Democratic politics.

~ Evelyn Bowser

Sarah Palin Out of Nowhere is truly a one of a kind work. The story of the author mirrors the story of the subject. Through his unusual entry into the political world, Frank Aquila tells the story of Governor Palin's unusual rise to the top. He takes the time to explain where the United States has gotten off track and, most importantly, how to get back. A must read for anyone who wants to understand the future of America.

~ Jeffrey Lemasters Tahir

It has been an honor to be a part of the "Sarah Palin Out of No-where" team. Frank Aquila is a public servant who sacrificed much to research and explain, in a common-sense manner to "busy grassroots people'" exactly where OUR America is at this critical crossroad in time. WE must also unite and come "out of nowhere," no longer remain silent, and work boldly to restore our liberties for future American generations.

"I was raised to believe that you don't retreat when you're on solid ground; so even though it often seems like I'm armed with just a few stones and a sling against a media giant, I'll use those small resources to do what I can to set the record straight. The truth is always worth fighting for....Let's just acknowledge that commonsense conservatives must be stronger and work that much harder because of the obvious bias." Sarah Palin

After reading each chapter in this book, we will collectively realize We are ALL here for "such a time as this." May God continue to bless America and the new Patriots battling, in truth, for her!

~ Mary Lou Neufer

Preface

Six months before Governor Sarah Palin stepped into the national spotlight on August 29, 2008, Frank Aquila, as Senator John McCain's campaign chairman from San Joaquin County, California, had his own spotlight shining on her. Now, Frank Aquila reveals an amazing and intriguing story of how he lobbied for Governor Palin to be on the presidential ticket and provides the actual emails he sent which greatly influenced the selection of Governor Palin as Senator McCain's vice-presidential running mate in the 2008 run for the White House.

In his book, Frank Aquila relates how he undertook a non-traditional journey to become Senator McCain's San Joaquin County's campaign chairman while living in the liberal San Francisco Bay Area, working as a peace officer, and raising two young boys as a single father. A political outsider, Frank Aquila was rejected by the Republican Party when he attempted to provide a new strategy for reaching and informing voters of California. He recounts how that rejection stirred him to form his own grassroots political organization, the South San Joaquin Republicans (SSJRs), and how its success allowed him to meet President George W. Bush, become a delegate for the Republican Party, and eventually become Senator McCain's Chairman of San Joaquin County.

Frank Aquila tells how he influenced the selection of Governor Palin and why he lobbied for her to be on the presidential ticket before anyone noticed her as a possible choice. He explains how and why the liberal mainstream media used their bias against Palin as a vice-presidential candidate compared to their unwavering support for then-Senator Barack Obama as a presidential candidate and how she enlivened both the presidential ticket and the conservative movement.

Finally, Frank Aquila makes his prediction for the next presidential election, lists his solutions for America, and what we must do to re-establish America as the greatest nation in the world.

Chapter 1
Out of Nowhere

"Better to fight for something than live for nothing" ~ General
George S. Patton

Lobbying for Sarah

Governor Sarah Palin really did come "Out of Nowhere." Alaskan
politics is not front and center for most of America, and most of America had either not heard of or knew very little about Sarah. This included the mainstream media. I had heard her name a couple of times
as I became more involved in politics; however, all I really knew about
Sarah was she was the attractive governor of Alaska.

As Senator John McCain's campaign chairman for my county, San
Joaquin, in California, I wanted to assist and make the right recommendation to those advising Senator McCain. I felt this was not only my obligation, but also my opportunity to inject my own thoughts into these
political circles of influence. Due to the fact that California was not a
"battleground state," I felt this may be my only opportunity to make a
real difference in the campaign. Sarah was not initially at the forefront
of my mind, nor was she mentioned on various sites as a possible running mate. I read the various names of potential vice-presidential candidates, including those published by Newsmax, which named 24 possible vice-presidential candidates. None of these websites mentioned
Sarah Palin. As I was driving to work early one morning in late March
2008, I heard Sarah's name mentioned as "a rising star in the Republican party with the guts to stand up for what is right" and that "someone in the Republican Party should take a look at her." I immediately
researched her and located a website put together by Adam Brickley,
who had also been lobbying for Sarah on his website. In my research,

I also came across a few articles encouraging the McCain campaign to select Sarah. While there were actually a few "unheard or unnoticed" people supporting Sarah's selection by the McCain's campaign, I realized that my position as his San Joaquin County chairman and the connections it allowed to his campaign, I may be able to make a real case for his staff to seriously consider and select Sarah. The more I uncovered as to who she was and what she stood for, the more I realized I had truly found an exceptional lady and leader who would exceed all expectations to be Senator McCain's vice-presidential running mate. She truly came "Out of Nowhere."

However, even I underestimated Sarah. She was everything I would have hoped for in a vice-presidential candidate, but then a possible problem came to light. Sarah was pregnant with her fifth child. I immediately became non-committal and unsure of my own recommendation. I thought to myself, "How difficult would it be for Sarah to deliver a baby and then shortly thereafter enter a gruesome nationwide campaign as a vice-presidential candidate?" I thought I may be wasting my time and that McCain would not choose her.

I returned to step one and again began looking at the various websites which included many recommendations and reasons for various candidates. I was even drawn into the "vote for your favorite candidate," where you are asked to list your email address to subscribe to the website newsletter. I simply could not find myself excited for any of the candidates being proposed by the mainstream media. It was not that I did not like the other candidates. I just continually felt each individual potential candidate came up short in adding true energy, excitement and experience to the McCain presidential ticket. There were also many whom I felt may bring a potential problem for the McCain ticket.

One interesting person was then-Secretary of State Condoleezza Rice, and I really considered her as a possible selection for McCain. I felt that, although she may not be able to help with the black vote, she would attract women to support and vote for her. However, she was Secretary of State for President George W. Bush and would draw problems for McCain as President Bush's popularity had fallen drastically toward the end of his second term. McCain really needed to distance himself from the unpopular Bush administration. Other women McCain could be interested in would be Meg Whitman, who ran eBay, and Carly Fiorina, who ran Hewlett-Packard and was one of McCain's economic advisers.

Governor Mitt Romney was a serious choice. I had even voted for him in the California primaries. I really appreciated his business experience, and he always presented himself as presidential. However, the Romney health care plan he enacted in Massachusetts was going to hurt him, as both Senators Hillary Clinton and Barack Obama, who were still fighting for the nomination at the time, were also in favor of government health care.

McCain's good friend Senator Joseph Lieberman was also an interesting choice. He had just recently been the vice-presidential nominee in the 2000 election with Vice President Al Gore. However, McCain would struggle to excite the conservative base of the Republican Party since Lieberman was considered a moderate and had, until recently, been a Democrat. As McCain was also considered a moderate, many conservatives would struggle to support and vote for him. Other moderates reported to be considered by McCain were Florida's Governor Charlie Crist, New York Mayor Michael Bloomberg, Senator Chuck Hagel and New York Mayor Rudy Giuliani.

Former Arkansas Governor Mike Huckabee and Minnesota Governor Tim Pawlenty would each be a respectable choice, but how much would they add to the ticket to draw the excitement McCain would need to win the election? Although South Dakota Senator John Thune and Ohio Congressman Rob Portman were also being mentioned, I felt they were fairly unknown nationally and would just not add anything extra to assist the McCain ticket. The longer I sat there researching on my computer screen, the more my mind continued to return to Sarah. She appeared to be the perfect choice.

Within days of my research of Governor Palin, and my consideration of other possible candidates as choices for the McCain ticket, Trig Palin was born on April 18, 2008. Sarah had been in Texas as the keynote speaker at an energy conference. She began to experience labor pains, but continued to finish her important speech. She contacted her current doctor, who had also delivered her daughter Piper. Sarah caught an Alaska Airlines flight from Dallas to Anchorage, with a stop in Seattle, where she was examined by doctors before returning to Alaska to deliver Trig. Sarah would later say, "I am not a glutton for pain and punishment. I would have never wanted to travel had I been fully engaged in labor." Either way, Sarah has always taken the unconventional road and, even if she does not admit it herself, she is one tough lady. For the next two days, I would think back and forth in my mind about Sarah and how perfect a choice she would be for this vital role. I thought to myself, "Sarah Palin has been underestimated her entire life! Am I underestimating her myself"? I was! Sarah is exceptional.

I had been in contact, both by phone and email, with Brian Forrest, Senator McCain's California Regional Chairman, for a little more than a month discussing issues about Senator McCain. On April 20, 2008, at 7:33 a.m., I took my first step to lobby for Sarah to be Senator McCain's vice-presidential nominee by sending an email to Brian, but I am sure this particular email caught him by surprise. The email was also copied to Ron Nehring, Chairman of the California Republican Party; Tom Del Baccaro, Vice Chairman of the California Republican Party; Laura Gadke, Regional Chairwoman for the Central Valley Region of the California Republican Party; and Dale Fritchen, Chairman of the San Joaquin County Republican Party.

My emails, with the responses from the McCain campaign, are listed below in the original unedited format. The phone numbers and email addresses were deleted for privacy purposes.

"From: Frank Aquila [mailto:xxxxxxxxxxxxxxxxxxx]
Sent: Sunday, April 20, 2008 7:33 AM
To: Brian Forrest

Cc: Ron zz- Nehring; Ron zz- Nehring; Tom zz- Del Baccaro; Tom zz- Del Beccaro; Laura zz- Gadke; Dale zz- Fritchen; Dale C. zz- Fritchen
Subject: Hello Brian

Hello Brian,
Since you are the Regional Chairman for Senator John McCain's campaign, I would like to see if you could pass along some information of who ever is working with Senator McCain on his list of possible Vice Presidential Candidates.

I would like to make the brief case for Alaskan Governor Sarah Palin. She governs a state. She is young, attractive. She is Conservative. Her nomination as Vice President would be the Worst news for the Democrats.

The Democrats will try to paint McCain as too old and at the same time, paint her as too young. So you take out the age factor.

In recent polls, I see McCain's weakest support among women. With Obama the likely Democrat nominee against Hillary, women would flock to McCain with Palin on the ticket as many women I have heard stated they were voting for Hillary since she was a woman.

Sarah Palin is also a rising star in the party. She is very favorable in her state where she is the governor. She would be able to point to her Executive experience in running the largest state in our nation.

She is Conservative. Some of those who have been upset with McCain point to not being Conservative. She could balance this out and bring in conservatives.

She is attractive. Although that may seen sexist, in reality it is true as I have heard many people, including on the radio where men would be interested in having an attractive woman to look at in politics.

There are so many advantages to Sarah Palin being on the ticket with Senator McCain. This would be awful for the Democrats as this would eventually set up the Republican Party to have the first woman President, something the Democrats would like to mantle.

I hope you can pass this along to the right people.

Thanks,
Frank A. Aquila"

On April 21, 2008, I received the following email response from Brian:

"Brian Forrest <XXXXXXXX> wrote:
Frank,

Thanks for the info. I will pass this along to the appropiate campaign folks. Thank you.

Brian Forrest"

Later that day, I sent this confirmation email response to Brian:

"—- On Mon, 4/21/08, Frank Aquila <*xxxxxxxxxxxxxxxxxx*> wrote:

From: Frank Aquila <xxxxxxxxxxxxxxxxxx>
Subject: RE: Hello Brian
To: "Brian Forrest" <XXXXXXXX>
Date: Monday, April 21, 2008, 9:28 AM
Brian,

I appreciate it. I hope it is considered

Frank"

I explained to Brian that I wanted to make a brief case for Sarah. I pointed out to him that she was currently a state governor. I wanted to make that point to him, since she would be the only person on either presidential ticket to have any legitimate executive governing experience. I also pointed out that Sarah was a conservative. I wanted to make this issue known since McCain was going to have a difficult time attracting conservatives of the base to support and vote for him. I really felt that Sarah could excite the conservative base to vote for McCain. I also wanted to dilute the age factor. I knew there were those within the media, as well as in the Democrat Party, who would try to paint McCain's age as too advanced. McCain also had a generation gap with the younger generation. Sarah was only 2-1/2 years younger than Obama. I felt Sarah could attract the younger voters. I also pointed out to Brian that Sarah would greatly assist McCain with attracting women to support the ticket, especially since Obama was edging Hillary Clinton for the Democrat nomination. I pointed out to Brian that Sarah was not only a rapidly rising star in the Republican Party but, as Alaska's governor, she had the highest approval ratings of all 50 U.S. governors. I pointed out the fact that Sarah was also an attractive candidate. I suggested that adding Sarah to the ticket would allow the Republican Party an opportunity to set up the first potential woman president.

Having taken these steps with regard to Governor Palin, I felt I had fulfilled my obligation to express my opinion and then began to work on other issues for the McCain campaign. As chairman from San Joaquin County, I soon began to have email exchanges with other county chairmen, as well as with Bob Pacheco, the California State Co-Chairman for Senator John McCain. At that time, gasoline prices had risen, and Bob suggested that I locate Latino-owned, small businesses that were affected by those rising costs. I was able to provide Bob the names of a couple businesses in my area, including F I Granite and Marble, based in Hayward, California. Fernando Ugarte, the owner and one of the original people to join and support my county organization, the South San Joaquin Republicans, was also interested in informing more Hispanics about the conservative values of the Republican Party.

I wanted people to understand the differences between John McCain and Barack Obama. I wrote a series of letters that summer for the South San Joaquin Republicans and timed their release prior to the election in my local newspaper. My first letter addressed the qualifications of John McCain.

"Who is John Sidney McCain?"

In our upcoming election, America will choose a president who will determine the direction of America for future generations.

Our next president should be experienced, knowing how to make sound decisions in a crisis. He should be nonpartisan, with a proven record to reach past party lines to accomplish the will of the people on difficult issues. He should honor the Constitutional principles of limited government, strong national defense, and individual freedom.

Senator John McCain has the proven leadership and experience to lead and protect America.

As a young man, John McCain followed the tradition of his father and grandfather in serving his country as a Naval Aviator in the Vietnam War. He was given the option to return home early during the Vietnam War, as his father was an admiral in the U.S. Navy; however, John refused to return because he wanted to continue to serve his country first. On October 26, 1967, during his 23rd bombing mission, a missile struck John's plane and forced him to eject, resulting in the breaking of both of his arms and his leg. He was taken as a prisoner of war, denied medical treatment, and beaten and tortured by the North Vietnamese for more than five years. After his release, John continued his Navy service until his retirement in 1981, at which time he received several Naval honors for his courageous service.

In 1982, John began his political career in the House of Representatives before being elected, in 1986, to the United States Senate, where he quickly established himself as a reformer in reducing wasteful government spending by closing loopholes of special interests to limit government debt and keep taxes low. He believes in a strong military and that the most sacred responsibility vested in a president—the Commander-in-Chief of our military—is to "preserve and protect" America. Senator McCain has also been an advocate for giving our veterans the full benefits they deserve. Senator McCain has established himself as a senator who is willing to act in a nonpartisan manner, working with both political parties to get issues accomplished, even if this causes irritation within his own party.

For the record, Senator McCain and Senator Obama are polar opposites on partial-birth abortion, parental notification of abortion, marriage protection on the ballot, homosexual indoctrination of school children, gay adoptions, gun-owner rights, activist judges, and raising taxes.

Senator McCain believes it is important to be a servant of the people where issues are debated and solved in Washington to better America. In a recent letter, Senator McCain wrote, "I am running to keep America safe, prosperous and proud. I am running to restore the trust of the American people in their government. I am running so that our children and grandchildren will have even greater opportunities than the ones we were blessed with. And I am running so that every person in this country, now and in generations to come, will know the same sublime honor that has been the treasure of my life: to be proud to be an American."

Our next president should be a patriot and a proven, experienced leader, who has served his country and spent his entire life placing America first. Our next president should be John McCain.

Frank Aquila, October 2008

My next letter, I addressed Barack Hussein Obama. I believed it was relevant to include a person's whole name, which is why I included

John McCain's middle name in my previous letter. McCain denounced comments by those who used Obama's middle name, including talk show host Bill Cunningham, who used it to address a crowd and referred to Obama as a "hack" and "Chicago-style Daley politician." Cunningham stated the time would come when the media would "peel the bark off Barack Hussein Obama." However, the media had yet to delve deeply into or reveal who the real Barack Hussein Obama was. They had sheltered him and even stated he should be proud of his middle name. Senator John Kerry of Massachusetts referred to Obama, using his middle name, stating he should be proud of his past and Muslim heritage. In essence, conservatives were being told by McCain that they were making "disparaging remarks" and that he would "repudiate" any such comments that would associate Obama with his Muslim past at the very same time liberals and the media stated how Obama should be proud of his name. Regardless, when we are electing a president or any politician, we should not be "politically correct," hide or outright ignore the truth. The American people have a right to know the history and the person they may be voting for in any election, which is why I wrote the following letter to a newspaper editor:

"Who is Barack Hussein Obama?"

Should the President of the United States of American have a "friendly" relationship with terrorists who bombed the U.S Capitol, the Pentagon and the San Francisco Police Headquarters, killing an officer? Barack Obama does. His rite of passage into politics came through the home of William Ayres, the organizer of the Weather Underground, who declared war on America in the 1970s with such terrorist action and was ironically quoted on September 11, 2001 in the New York Times, stating, "I don't regret setting those bombs. I feel we didn't do enough."

Obama also has an admittedly close relationship of "social conferences" with Frank Marshall Davis, a member of the Communist Party USA (CPUSA), who mentored Obama at the beginning of his political career, which led him to the endorsement of the Democratic Socialists of America (DSA), of which William Ayers is a member. The DSA is the largest socialist organization in America, which might explain why many of Obama's campaign workers display a flag featuring Communist hero Che Guevara and Obama's refusal to wear a pin of the American Flag or place his hand over his heart during the playing of the National Anthem.

Obama's mother and grandparents were atheists, while his father and step-father were devout Muslims. His step-father, Lolo Soetoro had a great impact on Obama's upbringing, raising him Muslim while he attended school in Indonesia. He was also registered as a Muslim while attending an affluent Catholic school in Hawaii. He joined a radical church in the black community developing a close relationship with his racist pastor and "mentor," who blames America for 9/11, calling America the U.S."KKK"A and named racist Louis Farrakhan, who is head of the Nation of Islam, its "Person of the Year."

Obama worked as an organizer and lawyer for ACORN, a group widely recognized for its association with voter fraud. He also sat on the board of a non-profit organization called Arab American Action Network, which supported Muslim terrorist organizations and boasted about destroying Israel and opposing all U.S. immigration laws.

While running for public office, Obama also received financial support from Iraqi Billionaire Nadhimi Auchi, who was convicted of corruption in France and ripped off the food for oil program related to Iraq. Auchi assisted Obama in the purchase of his million dollar mansion in a suspicious real estate deal with political fundraiser Antoin "Tony" Rezko, who also assisted Obama with $250,000 in campaign fund raising. Rezko is from Syria, a known terrorist nation bordering Iraq. Rezko also used Obama's state senate office and was recently convicted on 16 federal corruption charges.

Hamas, an identified terrorist organization, has endorsed Obama. Ahmed Yousef, chief political adviser to the Hamas Prime Minister, said, "We like Mr. Obama, and we hope he will win the election."

Obama has the most liberal voting record in the U.S. Senate, although he has minimal experience, not even completing one full term. He has endorsed homosexual marriage and supports partial-birth abortion. He voted against parental notification for abortions on teenage girls. He supports affirmative action in colleges and government. He opposes the Patriot Act while supporting Constitutional rights to terrorists at Guantanamo Bay. He supports granting driver's licenses to illegal immigrants while extending welfare and social security benefits to illegal immigrants. He has also promised a massive tax increase to enable a government takeover of our health care system and other new government bureaucracies. Obama has also indicated he wants to appoint judges who make social policy instead of properly applying the law as it related to the Constitution. This theory of presidential power of judicial appointments would have an enormous negative impact on the moral fabric of our country for decades to come.

Obama also lacks the experience to fight terrorism. He voted against funding the military with the supplies they needed to obtain victory in war. He also stated he would invade Pakistan, a country that is an ally in the fight against terrorism, while also stating he would meet, without preconditions, with other foreign leaders who support terrorism, including Iranian President Mahmoud Ahmadinejad. Ahmadinejad is linked to the terrorists fighting against our military in Iraq and vows to destroy Israel. Obama even stated to the media that Ahmadinejad would be a guest at the White House in his first month in office.

Does America really know Barack Hussein Obama or the people who have molded his mind? Sadly, most Americans do not know much about him except that he is for change. However, this is not the change America can risk to take.

Frank Aquila, July 2008

Throughout the summer of 2008, I had not given up on Sarah being McCain's vice-presidential selection. I had not sent any further emails to the McCain advisors; however, I did talk on the phone a few times with Brian about Sarah, and he seemed to agree with my position on her. Since Newsmax did not list her as one of its 24 potential selections, I wrote to them several times between May and June. To my relief, Newsmax finally listed her in July 2008. At that time, I felt Sarah was beginning to get some recognition, as I was beginning to find more information about her now listed as a potential running mate for McCain. I felt it was an appropriate time to send another email to lobby for Sarah.

Several years later, according to a March 13, 2011 article published in the Washington Post by Emi Kolawole, who was former campaign manager for McCain's 2008 presidential campaign, I learned that in August 2008, Sarah was added to the vice-presidential "short list" because McCain requested a woman to be considered for the vice-presidency. (1) According to a Washingtonian magazine profile of A.B. Culvahouse, an attorney who oversaw the vetting of the potential vice presidents, the short list included former Massachusetts Governor Mitt Romney, Minnesota Governor Tim Pawlenty, Florida Governor Charlie Crist, New York City Mayor Michael Bloomberg, and Senator Joseph Lieberman. The article went on to state that Sarah's name came up occasionally, but not as a serious choice. But Governor Palin was very much under the consideration of McCain from the beginning of the selection process.

August 2, 2008 was the date I would send my next email to the McCain advisers, which coincided with the McCain advisers listing Sarah on the "short list" for McCain. This time I had the email address to Bob Pacheco, the California State Chairman for McCain. I used this opportunity to send both Bob and Brian my email, as I continued to lobby for Sarah, and included a poll conducted by Rasmussen Reports showing McCain polling low among women and pointing out Sarah's selection would energize McCain's campaign while, at the same time, removing the enthusiasm from of the Obama campaign.

"—- On **Sat, 8/2/08, Frank Aquila <_xxxxxxxxxxxxxxxxx_>** wrote:

From: Frank Aquila <xxxxxxxxxxxxxxxxx>
Subject: McCains VP Choice..please pass along to McCain campaign
To: "Brian zz- Forrest (*)" <XXXXXXXX>, "Bob Pacheco (*)" <XXXXXXXX>
Date: Saturday, August 2, 2008, 8:22 AM
Brian,

As we have spoken in the past about this subject, here is the latest number quote from Rasmussen Reports today, August 2, 2008

Among men, 34% are Democrats, 33% Republican. Forty-four percent (44%) of women are Democrats, and just 30% claim the GOP as their party.

This is all the more reason for McCain to pick Sarah Palin. He will attract women, she is Conservative, she is attractive, she is a governor, she is near the same age as Obama (so they can not use that against her)

She is the Democrat's *Worst* Nightmare!!!

I hope you and Bob can both pass this note along. I have friends who will not be attracted to the ticket with the posibilities being discused, especially Romney. As unfair as it is, they will not vote for a Mormon. Palin will shake up that ticket and she favors drilling in Alaska. Her nominee will take life out of Obama and present a young look to the ticket, which is what we need.

Frank Aquila"

It was assumed Obama would select Senator Hillary Clinton as his choice for vice president. When the announcement came that Obama selected Senator Joseph Biden, I sent another email, on August 22,

2008, to the McCain campaign. I referenced that this was an opportunity for McCain and that Biden was arrogant and his style would not be attractive to female voters who were unhappy about Hillary not being selected.

    "—- On **Fri, 8/22/08, Frank Aquila <xxxxxxxxxxxxxxxxx>** wrote:

    From: Frank Aquila <xxxxxxxxxxxxxxxxx>
    Subject: For McCain
    To: "Bob Pacheco (*)" <XXXXXXXX>, "Brian zz- Forrest (*)" <XXXXXXXX>
    Date: Friday, August 22, 2008, 11:40 PM

    Hello Bob and Brian,

    Again, I would like to have my thoughts forwarded to the McCain campaign.

    I feel the pick by Obama of Joe Biden makes it even more essential that John McCain pick Sarah Palin for his VP. Biden is arrogant and talks tough in a demeaning style. He will be their attack dog for Obama; but in a VP debate, Biden will not score points with the average American with that style against a woman. I believe his demeaning and arrogant style will push more women toward McCain or the pick of Palin will at least neutralize Biden where the Dems would not want to have him come across to rough on a lady. I believe the youthful attractive appearance is what the Republican ticket needs. With Hillary not on the ticket, women will definitely cross over to a McCain Palin ticket.

    Frank Aquila
    San Joaquin County McCain Chairman"

    On August 23, 2008, I read an article entitled, "Why Sarah Palin," which had been written on August 4, 2008 by New Conservative.

I wanted to pass along this additional information, as I knew there would be a selection soon, so I sent another email forwarding the article.

"—- On **Sat, 8/23/08, Frank Aquila <_xxxxxxxxxxxxxxxxxx_>** wrote:

From: Frank Aquila <xxxxxxxxxxxxxxxxxx>
Subject: For McCain
To: "Bob Pacheco (*)" <XXXXXXXX>, "Brian zz- Forrest (*)" <XXXXXXXX>
Date: Saturday, August 23, 2008, 12:02 AM

Hello Bob and Brian,

Just some other food for thought to pass along:
Why Sarah Palin?
Email
Written by newconservative on Aug-4-08 6:22pm
From: thenewconservatives.blogspot.com
If you like this article go to http://readerarticles.realclearpolitics.com/?period=all and vote for it.

As we go into the second of four possible VP choices I have chosen to highlight Alaska Governor Sarah Palin. Elected in 2006 Sarah Palin is the first woman, and the youngest person at 44 years of age, to hold the office of governor in Alaska. Nicknamed "Sarah Barracuda," while she was leading her High School basketball team to the State title. She has gone after corrupt politicans on both sides, supported drilling in ANWR and drilling off-shore, is a strong fiscal conservative, and a devout Christian. She currently has around a 90% approval rating. Let's start with looking at how she has attacked corrpution in her state.

Governor Palin has passed ethics reforms in her state and is ethical to the point where it almost cost her a political career. She is ref-ered to as, "A crusading corruption buster." She has gone after corrupt Republicans as well as Democrats in Alaska. "The landscape is littered with the bodies of those who crossed Sarah," says pollster Dave Dittman, who worked for her gubernatorial campaign. It includes Ruedrich, Renkes, Murkowski, gubernatorial contenders John Binkley and Andrew Halcro, the three big oil companies in Alaska, and a section of the Daily News called "Voice of the Times," which was highly critical of Palin and is now defunct. (Hard to sell papers critizing someone with a 90% approval rating.) It is now a crime in Alaska for public servants not to report bribery that they know about. http://weeklystandard.com/Content/Public/Articles/000/000/013/851orcjq.asp?pg=1

Another issue where she would be a plus is on Coastal drilling as well as drilling in ANWR. With high energy prices and American's screaming for congress to act Palin will help highlight one of Obama's biggest weaknesses. Also being from Alaska Americans may be more interested in her opinion about drilling there than they would a politican who may have visited once or twice in their lifetime.

Governor Palin also has a record has a strong fiscal conservative. She believes that people can handle their money better than government, an overriding conservative principle. Palin cut property taxes while at the same time increasing services as a Council Member/Mayor of Wasilla, Alaska. As Governer she has vetoed 1/3 of earmarks put into legislation, including several put in by Republicans. http://www.pittsburghlive.com/x/pittsburghtrib/opinion/columnists/vassilaros/s_517252.html

Governor Palin is a devout Christian. This can only help McCain with the social conservative base of the party. Who, for whatever reasons, do not believe he shares their values. Palin is pro-life and believes that marriage should be between a man and a woman. However, she failed to sign a bill outlawing Gay Marriage due to the fact the Alaskan Supreme Court had said the law would be unconstitutional. She refers to her State Constitution as "my bible in governing."

Let's see did I forget anything why else would this young woman be a good pick for VP? That's right, because she's a young woman. Having an energetic young woman on the ticket would help McCain with the women's vote and Palin could also do a great job on energizing the base. Also with a nickname like "Sarah Barracuda" you have to believe she could fill out the traditional role of the VP has an attack dog very well. I would not want to be on the other side of a debate with her.

http://www.realclearpolitics.com/articles/2008/06/the_vp_case_for_gov_sarah_pali.html"

On August 25, 2008, I forwarded an additional excellent article I had come across on the internet, entitled "Biden, Check Palin, Checkmate," written by Josh Painter. Even though I had sent four previous emails, I knew the decision would come any day and wanted to give one more final push to the McCain advisers.

Therefore, on August 25, 2008 1:11:59 P.M. Pacific Daylight Time, xxxxxxxxxxxxxxxxxxxx I sent the following email:

"Hello Brian and Bob,

You are both the only people I know with connection to the McCain campaign. I was just going to wait to see what happens; but I decided to contact you once more as this is critical to a McCain Victory. I am going to attach an article that sums it up the best. Please pass along to the McCain people. Senator McCain has an opportunity to bring in Hillary voters (the women vote, which our party has lost over the years) and he has an opportunity to bring in the Evangelical vote with Sarah Palin, who is a favorable Conservative.

Frank Aquila

[Attachment]

Biden, check. Palin, checkmate.

Sarah Palin would be an even better VP pick than Mitt Romney

Posted by: Josh_Painter

Saturday, August 23, 2008 at 03:48 PM

I've already shown how Sarah Palin would be a smart pick by John McCain to be his running mate. In light of recent events, she's looking like a smarter selection.

The announcement made early this morning by the Obama camp that Delaware Senator Joe Biden is Obama's choice to share the Democrat presidential ticket with him sets the stage for McCain to name his own vice presidential nominee. The conventional wisdom seems to be that it will be former Massachusetts Governor Mitt Romney. Although I think Romney would be a strong selection, the Biden pick would make Gov. Palin an even stronger one.

Within three hours of news of the Biden selection being aired, Team McCain produced and released this hard-hitting ad with video clips of Biden dissing Obama's inexperience and praising his old friend and Senate colleague, John McCain:
There's no shortage of similar clips from the GOP primariy season depicting Romney attacking McCain and McCain returning fire. A Romney pick would guarantee that the Democrats would use it and effectively cancel out the impact of the McCain ad. But Palin wasn't involved in that fight, so there's no such ammunition for the Obama campaign to use against her. McCain's ad could run from now through election day, and the Democrats would be denied the opportunity to reply in kind. Instead, Biden would be forced to explain his criticism of his own running mate.

One of Romney's strongest assets is economics. He was very successful in the private sector and has won acclaim for turning the Winter Olympics in his home state of Utah around. But to most Americans today, "economics" is translated as "oil." The price of gasoline at the pump and food at the grocery store is what's on their minds. The financial markets and corporate arenas where Romney earned his creds might as well be on a distant planet. Sarah Palin knows all about oil. She's an avid proponent of drilling in ANWR and makes a strong case for it.

But Palin is no stooge of Big Oil. She stood up to the oil companies in her state and pushed through a modest 2.5% increase on the state taxes they pay for their access to Alaska's bountiful oil deposits. That raised the tax from 22.5% to 25%, an amount the companies can pay and still enjoy considerable profits. The oil companies and some of her fellow Republicans had fought against the bill, arguing that the extra 2.5% would would put a damper on future Alaskan oil exploration. That has not been the case. Conservatives don't like tax-raising, but Palin justified the increase by pointing out that the previous 22.5% tax was passed in 2006 under suspicious circumstances. Several members of the legislature that set the amount of that tax were convicted or indicted on federal bribery charges related to the bill. Palin also explained that the '06 tax did not perform as advertised, and she offered as evidence an $800 million shortfall in expected revenue. Whether you agree or disagree with Palin's actions, you have to admit that the Democrats can't paint her as being in the pocket of Big Oil.

Gov. Sarah Palin has also pushed through her legislature a gas pipeline project which will bring a fresh supply and lower prices to those of us in the lower 48: The legislature had been trying for 30 years to authorize something like this and, up until now, had blown it. Palin got it through. Getting it off the ground, the state says, will be the biggest construction project in U.S. history.

Palin considers the $26 billion project her biggest accomplishment as governor. "It was not easy," she told IBD. "Alaska has been hoping and dreaming for a natural gas pipeline for decades. What it took was getting off the dime and creating a competitive market in Alaska."

The 1,715-mile gas line would stretch from Alaska's North Slope to Fairbanks and down to Alberta, Canada. Then it would take existing gas lines to Idaho. In 10 years, Palin says, the lower 48 states would receive 4.5 million cubic feet of natural gas a day. By 2030, according to Energy Department estimates, Alaska's annual natgas production would quintuple to 2 trillion cubic feet.

In light of the inablity of the U.S. Congress to do anything about our energy problem, voters will be favorably impressed with this "can-do" governor and her determination to move the ball downfield on energy. While others talk the problem to death, Sarah Palin has been doing plenty about it.

A McCain-Palin ticket would offer hope to Americans angry over our energy dependence on foreign—and often hostile—sources. It would stand in stark contrast to Obama and Biden, both of whom opposed increased domestic drilling. McCain is for drilling offshore, but has yet to be convinced to embrace drilling in ANWR. Sarah Palin is perhaps the only person who could convince him. McCain-Palin could even adopt a variation on the "Energy for Alaska" theme used by Sarah in her contest for Alaska's governorship—"Energy for America." It's a good one, and it should resonate with American voters who have been strapped for cash by high pump prices, as well as those concerned about America's energy security. Romney, as good as he is on economic matters, just can't relate to American voters on energy issues the way Palin can.

Biden is going to be Obama's attack dog, a role vice-presidential picks are usually given so that the presidential candidate's hands don't have to be washed. Can Sarah Palin stand up to the crusty old Senator in a fight? It would be a mistake to write her off. Alaska is a tough place, and it demands much of those who choose to live there. Palin has taken on her own party by fighting corruption and using the line item veto to cut the budget, angering Democrats and entrenched Republicans alike. In a piece for the Weekly Standard last year, Fred Barnes wrote:

In the roughly three years since she quit as the state's chief regulator of the oil industry, Palin has crushed the Republican hierarchy (virtually all male) and nearly every other foe or critic. Political analysts in Alaska refer to the "body count" of Palin's rivals. "The landscape is littered with the bodies of those who crossed Sarah," says pollster Dave Dittman, who worked for her gubernatorial campaign.

Gov. Palin grew up in Wasilla, where as star of her high school basketball team she got the nickname "Sarah Barracuda" for her fierce competitiveness. She led her underdog team to the state basketball championship. Palin also won the Miss Wasilla beauty contest, in which she was named Miss Congeniality, and went on to compete in the Miss Alaska pageant.

Don't let that pretty face fool you. She's tough. I'll wager that because she was tough enough to take on Alaska's corrupt pols, she should have no problem with Biden in the VP debate or with bringing the elite Obama down a peg or two.

Palin has another appeal that Mitt Romney just can't match, and it's through no fault of his. It's a matter of gender. Recent polling shows a problem for Obama:

Perhaps the biggest factor keeping the presidential race close has been Obama's inability to close the deal with some of Hillary Clinton's supporters. According to the poll, 52 percent of them say they will vote for Obama, but 21 percent are backing McCain, with an additional 27 percent who are undecided or want to vote for someone else.

What's more, those who backed Clinton in the primaries—but aren't supporting Obama right now—tend to view McCain in a better light than Obama and have more confidence in McCain's ability to be commander-in-chief. Obama's decision to choose Biden and <u>stiff</u> Hillary has her supporters even angrier right now. By selecting Sarah Palin as his running mate, McCain would show them that he, unlike Obama, doesn't take women's votes for granted.

The Democrats are touting Joe Biden's blue collar roots, which they will exploit to try to continue to define McCain as so out of touch with the average American that "he doesn't even know how many houses he owns"—nevermind that all members of the Senate are rich, and Biden's compound is not your average American crib. They will tell us how he had to take second and third mortgages on his house to send his kids to college, and they will have many more stories of Biden as the average Joe.

If McCain chooses him, Romney will be portrayed by the Dems, rightly or wrongly, as a zillionaire who's out of touch with average Americans. They can't define Palin that way. Her parents were school teachers. Her husband Todd actually worked for a living in a blue-collar production job for BP on the North Slope for 20 years. And he's a commercial fisherman in the summer. Todd is also something of an Alaska sports legend, having won the gruelling 2,000-mile Iron Dog snowmobile race four times. Oh, and he raises the kids while mom is working as Alaska's CEO. The couple's youngest child has Down's syndrome, a condition the doctors made them aware of before his birth. Yet they never even considered abortion, and they say the baby is "a blessing." The story marks a stunning contrast to the pro-abortion positions of Obama and Biden. Palin is also a lifetime member of the NRA, an organization which has given Biden an F-rating. He even <u>boasted</u> that he wrote the language contained in the assault weapons bill. Romney's record on gun control is shaky, while Palin's is rock solid. America's 80 million gun owners will love her.

The Palin family is a great story waiting to be told to the lower 48 if McCain is wise enough to pick Sarah. Even the drive-by media will be fascinated by it and eager to tell it. As good as Mitt Romney is as a vice-presidential choice, Palin is even better."

To my surprise, I received a response back from the campaign. Bob Pacheco, as the California Campaign Chairman for McCain, wrote back to me, stating:

"—- On **Mon, 8/25/08, XXXXXXXX <*XXXXXXXX*>** wrote:
From: XXXXXXXX <XXXXXXXX>
Subject: Re: For McCain
To: xxxxxxxxxxxxxxxxxx
Date: Monday, August 25, 2008, 1:30 PM
Frank, I have previously passed on your comments. They are aware of your position on the issue.

Bob Pacheco
California Statewide Co-Chair
Latino Coalition, McCain 2008

UNIDOS CON McCAIN"

For the first time, I knew my emails and my attempts to lobby for Sarah had made it to those who would make the final decision. I wrote back to Bob to thank him and that we would know soon.

"—- On **Mon, 8/25/08, Frank Aquila <*xxxxxxxxxxxxxxxxxx*>** wrote:

From: Frank Aquila <xxxxxxxxxxxxxxxxxxx>
Subject: Re: For McCain
To: XXXXXXXX
Date: Monday, August 25, 2008, 1:52 PM

Thanks Bob,

We will know soon

Frank"

I felt that I had done everything I could do. It was now time to wait and see what would happen. For four more days, I would have to wait for their announcement.

During those next four days, this issue continued to play on my mind. If only McCain would choose Sarah. I had thought, even if the ticket did not win, it would immediately place Sarah as a front runner for 2012. I knew America would love who she was, as well as her qualities as a genuine lady and honest politician.

On August 28, 2008, I left work in the early evening and listened to the radio on the way home. I was disappointed to hear pundits on the radio discuss that it was either Governor Romney or Governor Pawlenty who McCain would choose as his vice-presidential running mate. Both men would be fine picks, but I had pushed hard for Sarah. I had even heard that McCain wanted his long-time friend Joseph Lieberman on the ticket, but his advisers seemed to have talked him out of that. There was no mention of Sarah. I began to feel one of the more popular names would be chosen by McCain, since Sarah really did not get the full attention as a possible choice from the media or from the various websites which speculated about McCain's potential vice-presidential selection. She continued to remain "Out of Nowhere."

Electrifying the Ticket

On the morning of Friday, August 29, 2008, I woke up knowing Senator McCain had made his selection. I didn't even want to turn on the television. I was fully expecting McCain to have picked former Massachusetts Governor Mitt Romney or Minnesota Governor Tim Pawlenty. My curiosity won over my expected disappointment that

Sarah would not be selected. As I turned the television on, I saw the news reports of a plane at the Hook Airfield in Ohio which was registered out of Alaska. There was no official news; but there was speculation that Sarah may be McCain's vice-presidential selection. I was in a state of disbelief, not wanting to get too excited for a potential let down; but this was unexpected! Then, "out of nowhere" a photograph of Sarah appeared on the television screen, and I nearly fell out of bed to listen more closely to the news reports. As I stumbled to catch myself, another news report announced that there was confirmation that Romney was not selected, and he was still home in Massachusetts. I went downstairs to turn on the television with a smile on my face. I was almost positive that Sarah had been selected, but there was not yet any official confirmation. The news reports announced that Pawlenty was also not the nominee, and that he was still in Minnesota. The news reports continued to show a video of the small plane at the airport registered from Alaska. Again, there was speculation and reports about Sarah Palin, the Governor of Alaska. The news reports stated there were no official statements, and that there were still possibilities that someone else may be the nominee. At that point, a photograph of Carly Fiorina, who was McCain's economic adviser, appeared on the screen as others who may have been selected by McCain.

As I remained glued to my television waiting for an official word, my phone rang. I have caller identification on my phone, and my phone tells me audibly from the speaker where the call is originating. I did not want to be interrupted at that moment, and often I do not answer my phone if I do not know who is calling. The phone speaker stated "Los Angeles." I did not know anyone from Los Angeles. However, I answered the phone, and this is my recollection of that conversation:

"Hello," I answered.

"Can I speak to Frank Aquila?" a male voice asked.

"This is him," I responded.

"Frank, this is Bob Pacheco," Bob introduced himself.

"Yes, Bob," I replied, immediately aware this was not an ordinary phone call with all the current unfolding speculation on the news about Sarah. After all, Bob was the California Chairman for McCain 2008. I recognized his name from our email correspondence, although we had never spoken to each other until that moment.

"I just want to be the first to say congratulations! You got your girl!" Bob informed me.

"Sarah Palin!?" I began to feel goose bumps on my skin, but I still asked that questioned with great excitement.

"Yes!" Bob answered.

"Sarah is a great choice and the American people will fall in love with her," I responded, filled with absolute joy and happiness.

"Well, I know you had been lobbying for her for quite a while, and your emails did it," Bob responded, agreeing.

"I don't know how much [of an effect] my emails had on her selection," I humbly added.

"It had a great effect. Your emails went directly to the people who made the final decision and had great influence on her selection," Bob confirmed.

"I know John McCain and served in the Navy with John McCain," Bob continued, and spoke with me about his experience with McCain and their relationship as close friends.

"Well, I think she will do great for the ticket!" I told him, excitedly.

"I think she will and just wanted to call you and tell you myself," Bob stated.

I thanked Bob Pacheco for his call and promised to work hard on the campaign!!

I continued to watch the television and, soon afterward, there was an official announcement that Sarah Palin, the Governor of Alaska, had been selected as the vice-presidential nominee for Senator John McCain. I felt excited, although not to the point of a "thrill going up my leg," but, rather, experienced goose bumps of happiness and excitement. I was anticipating watching the introduction of Sarah and hearing her address the 12,000 people who had shown up in Dayton, Ohio, to greet the new vice-presidential nominee. Now the stage was set for McCain to introduce Sarah Palin.

On August 29, 2008, Senator McCain's birthday, he not only received a great birthday gift in the selection of a fine lady as his running mate, but he gave America a great gift. McCain explained to the crowd why he was running for president and further explained he was looking for a candidate who would shake up Washington. McCain went on to state he had found someone with an outstanding reputation who would stand up to the special interests and entrenched bureaucracies in Washington. He explained he had found someone who had successfully fought against corruption, failed policies, and government waste. She was someone who had executive experience to tackle tough problems. He described Sarah as someone with strong principles, a fighting spirit, deep compassion, decent, and hardworking who came from a middle-class family. McCain went on to describe the background of Governor Sarah Louise Palin.

McCain also described what Sarah was not. She was not part of Washington; but she had the grit, integrity, good sense, and fierce devotion which were needed in Washington. He described her as doing what is right and putting the interests of the people before the special interests. Senator McCain stated that Governor Palin was who he needed and who the country needed to make America first. He introduced Governor Sarah Palin, of the great state of Alaska, then, "out of nowhere," she appeared, and the crowd roared with excitement.

Everything that I had anticipated in her selection was coming true. I could see the energy and excitement in the crowd before she was even announced to the world. I have seen rallies of excitement before; but this crowd was there to see Sarah, the first female candidate ever on the Republican ticket. Sarah made her way to the podium, and I could feel the energy in my living room 1,500 miles away.

Sarah thanked Senator McCain and his wife, expressed the honor and privilege to be selected, and promised to give nothing less than her best. She introduced her family and shared the history of her and Todd. She let people know she was an average "hockey mom" from Alaska, who got involved in politics to put people first. She provided background of her public service as one who stood against "politics as usual." Sarah pointed out some of the legislation she signed into law in Alaska, the ethics reform, as well as working together with both Republicans and Democrats. Sarah pointed out that politicians are expected to govern with integrity, good will, clear convictions, and a servant's heart. She then expressed that was how McCain served in Washington, as a man who served his country and not just his party.

Sarah went on to express the many accomplishments of McCain and her desire to serve with him. She recalled that it was nearly 88 years to the day that women were granted the privilege to vote in America. Sarah took a moment to reflect on two other women who broke the glass ceiling of political accomplishments, as she recognized the achievements of Representative Geraldine Ferraro and Senator Hillary Clinton in the 1984 and 2008 presidential primaries, respectively.

Sarah stated the mission was clear to take their message to the voters to change Washington for a better America. The crowd loved her through the chants of "USA! USA! USA!" Sarah had excited the ticket! The conservative base of the Republican party was equally excited with a boost of energy that had previously been lukewarm with McCain. They had sent a warning to McCain that if he did not place a conservative on the ticket with him, it would be disastrous. There was now a wave of emotion and excitement throughout the conservative base.

Sarah had it all. She was intelligent, articulate, attractive, and represented those conservative values that brought optimism to conservatives. According to a statement from Phil Burress, of Citizens for Community Values, the selection of Sarah was historic for both social and fiscal conservatives and a great day for Americans! He went on to say, "Sarah Palin is a working mom; a woman who is unabashedly and personally pro-life; a life-time member of the NRA; a true frontierswoman who, while challenging the influence of big oil companies and while being environmentally conscientious, is in favor of oil drilling in her own state as part of a program to achieve energy independence. And, like McCain, she is a maverick—a woman who is in no way attached to Washington bureaucracy. What more could conservative voters ask for?"

The McCain campaign immediately raised $7 million on-line. Conservatives were in love with Sarah. There were hugs, tears and those who were jumping with joy. People appreciated her as they began to hear her incredible life story as an ordinary lady who had integrity, values, and stood for the will of the people over the will of the government. Even sportsmen became overjoyed, as Michael Bane, who has a show on the Outdoor Channel stated on his blog, "FINALLY, we get 100 percent behind the Republican ticket...change we can believe in!" He continued, "You know I've had my problems with McCain, but he has reached out a hand to us both at the NRA Annual Meeting and with the amazing selection of Sarah Palin as his running mate."

Conservatives who originally were not planning to attend the Republican convention in Minneapolis were now making plans. The wave of electricity was built up for Sarah, the governor who came "out of nowhere" to excite and intrigue America. The focus was now set for her acceptance speech at the Republican National Convention in Minnesota on September 3, 2008, where 20,000 Republicans waited to see Sarah at the packed-out Xcel Energy Arena with delegates waving signs saying "Palin Power."

The anticipation was growing, and America came to see who this incredible lady was, who came "out of nowhere" to energize the political process. Over 40 million viewers tuned in to see her, which was approximately the same number of viewers who tuned in to see Obama give his acceptance speech.

Sarah's entrance was thunderous with repeated chants of "Sarah! Sarah!" Others screamed out their love and support for her. Sarah introduced herself to America as "just your average hockey mom" and a small town outsider who seeks "to serve the people" rather than the "Washington elites." She was as qualified to be president of the United States as Senator Obama through her years of executive experience as a mayor and governor.

Sarah quickly responded to questions about her experience to serve, pointing to Obama's inexperience, stating, "And since our opponents in this presidential election seem to look down on that experience, let me explain to them what the job involves. I guess a small town mayor is sort of like a 'community organizer,' except that you have actual responsibilities," referring to Obama's experience as a community organizer in Chicago.

Sarah then went after the media stating, "And I've learned quickly, these past few days, that if you're not a member in good standing of the Washington elites, then some in the media consider a candidate unqualified for that reason alone. But here's a little news flash for all those reporters and commentators: I'm not going to Washington to seek good opinion—I'm going to Washington to serve the people of this country."

Sarah spent time in her speech talking about her husband, Todd, and her children.

Sarah spent time talking about issues, including foreign policy and national security, which Sarah has tied to energy in the past. Sarah reinforced the thought to "drill now," stating "our opponents say, again and again, that drilling will not solve all of America's energy problems, as if we didn't know that already, but the fact that drilling won't solve every problem is no excuse to do nothing at all."

Sarah made a great case for McCain through her brilliant, forceful, and articulate speech to the delegates and to the American people. The delegates loved her and appreciated her fighting spirit to strike back against the media and the Democrats for the many things they stated about her, leading up to the convention.

Sarah represented everything America once was. She is strong, determined, and unapologetic. She has energy, confidence, and is full of faith. She is humble, honest, and real. She was a pioneer of the land, who appreciated the gifts from God. Sarah is a leader the liberals have not feared since the days when Ronald Reagan was president. Sarah did not just talk the talk. She led by example and earned the respect of those she led, applying those principles to her own life.

America got to meet Sarah, and she immediately brought a breath of fresh air to the presidential ticket as an honest, middle-class American, who was a Washington outsider.

Reaganese

Great leaders are very rare to come by. President Ronald Reagan is often mentioned as one of the greatest leaders of America. His son, Michael Reagan, had become convinced there would be no other leader like him to emerge and lead America again until he saw Sarah. In an article in Human Events on September 4, 2008, Michael Reagan reflected his thoughts of the 2008 Republican National Convention as Sarah accepted the vice-presidential nomination.

Michael Reagan immediately recognized Sarah Palin as someone who had the similar qualities as his father. In his own words, as he watched Sarah speak to America, he stated "there, before my very eyes, I saw my Dad reborn; only this time he's a she." Michael was stunned to see the magnitude of electricity and inspiration that had not been seen in the conservative movement since his father. Michael stated Sarah had "resurrected my Dad's indomitable spirit and sent it soaring above the convention center," the same way President Reagan did when he was at his best.

Michael described Sarah as "un-intimidated by either the savage onslaught to which the left-leaning media had subjected her, or the incredible challenge she faced." Sarah was "oozing with confidence," and she stood at the podium as a fighter, knowing she had her moment to fight back against those who had unmercifully attacked her. Sarah proved she was much more than a woman who had achieved the highest accomplishment of any Republican woman. She was a "red-blooded American with that rare, God-given ability to rally her dispirited fellow Republicans and take up the daunting task of leading them—and all her fellow Americans—on a pilgrimage to that shining city on the hill my father envisioned as our nation's real destination."

Michael pointed out that Sarah needed only a few words to reveal her Democrat rivals as "old-fashioned liberals making promises that cannot be kept without bankrupting the nation and reducing most Americans to the status of mendicants begging for their daily bread at the feet of all-powerful government." Sarah was able to show herself as an American, who was "one of us" in the small town status, while showing the record of Obama for the "sham that he is" "without any solid accomplishments beyond conspicuous self-aggrandizement." Sarah was not part of the elite Harvard crowd or a community organizer of "leftist activism," or someone embedded with the "nation's most corrupt political machines," as Obama was. Sarah confronted corruption in Alaska and defeated it. Obama never challenged the corruption that occurred in Chicago but went "along to get along."

Michael concluded "Welcome back, Dad, even if you're wearing a dress."

There were many similarities between President Reagan and Sarah Palin. Both had become gifted public speakers and were sports broadcasters; both began a career in front of the camera. Both also had strong faith in God. Reagan had a sense of destiny, while Sarah would call her pursuit of public service as a call of a "servant's heart."

Sarah states she was inspired by President Reagan, remembering his era while she was in high school and college. She called him "my inspiration" for his patriotic vision of America. Sarah remembers him as the "Great Communicator."

Both Sarah and President Reagan had come under similar attacks and media bias from the liberal media and the movie industry. Journalists, editors, producers, and anchormen fought against Reagan and his policies. They tried to portray Reagan as someone who was going to bring America into a nuclear war and attempted to rebut him whenever and wherever they could as a dangerous and ignorant man who should stay in Hollywood as a "B" movie actor and cowboy. They portrayed him as an "idiot" and uneducated "dunce." Reagan was also called a racist, homophobe, hard-hearted, extremist, hater, Neanderthal, and ideologue.

Hollywood worked anti-Reagan jokes into their sitcoms. In June 1989, Actor John Cusack called Reagan "a criminal who used the Constitution as toilet paper." Larry Gelbart, the creator of MASH wrote that Reagan had "a dim notion of reality" in a November 6, 1989 New York Times op-ed. John Singleton, who was director for "Boyz n the Hood," stated in the September 1993 edition of Playboy, "I was 12 years old. Children in junior high school thought [Reagan] was going to drop a bomb. During the 1981 assassination attempt, the news came over the school intercom. Here in the ghetto everybody clapped. I clapped.... At 12 years old, I already had contempt for fascist politics. He was more of a monster than I could imagine at 12 years old."

With all this contempt and hatred, Reagan never hated anyone. He loved people and freedom. He loved America. What he hated was communism, big government, poverty, and taxes. Reagan understood that government was not the solution, government was the problem. He understood that big government and taxes destroyed a free economic society. He never promised to cut government programs, but he restrained their growth in giving power back to the people. Reagan defeated communism and won his second term as president with a landslide victory of 49 states.

Ronald Reagan is regarded as one of America's finest presidents, even though the left, the media, and Hollywood tried to influence the American people from voting for someone they portrayed as an "amiable dunce."

Michael Reagan knew his dad. He understood that Sarah was made of the same mold as President Reagan. That is why the left continues to fear her. If she were really unqualified to be president, they would not feel the need to continually attack her. They would be elevating her to be on the next national ticket to assure an easy victory for Obama. They realize she represents Middle America unlike any other leader America has had since President Reagan. This is the real reason Sarah is attacked by Democrats and the left-leaning mainstream media.

Chapter 2
Grassroots Politics

"If you are not a liberal at twenty, you have no heart. If you are not a conservative at forty, you have no brain." ~ Winston Churchill

The Formation of My Conservative Thought

Most people would not expect someone living an hour outside of the liberal San Francisco Bay Area to have a "great influence" on the selection of then-Governor Sarah Palin as Senator John McCain's vice-presidential running mate in the 2008 election.

To understand how such a seeming contradiction could happen, one must first understand who I am. After my grandparents immigrated to the United States from Italy, my father was born and raised in Richmond, California. He was a registered Democrat and a union man who worked in a local grocery store. My mother was raised in Berkeley, arguably one of the most liberal cities in the nation. She was a registered Republican, who stayed home most of my childhood, until she later decided to work as a seamstress at a local cleaner's shop. My parents were both conservative and Christian. My father usually worked on the weekends, so I usually attended church with my mother. My parents moved from Richmond to Martinez before settling in the farming community of Knightsen, located just outside of Brentwood, near the Bay Area. This should not be confused with the Brentwood that is famously known for movie stars or O.J. Simpson's infamous police chase.

My first interest in politics began while I was young and in school. I did not often discuss politics with my parents when I was younger, but I frequently watched the television news. I still remember my interest in watching the inauguration of President Ronald Reagan, when I was merely ten years old, and how impressed I was by him. However, I can also remember being influenced by one of my liberal teachers in grammar school, as he taught us that we had too many bombs in America and should get rid of them. Even at that early age, my mind was being molded in two different directions—liberal and conservative.

School was not easy for me. My father could not read or write throughout most of my school years. It was not until I entered high school that he learned to read, and it was still a struggle for him. Because of my poor reading and writing skills, I had to be enrolled in special education classes. It is only by the grace of God that I have now overcome these obstacles and am able to write this book. I remember crying many times, as I struggled to understand my school work. I would often get sick to my stomach because of my struggles, yet I was a diligent student and always completed my assignments. My mother would help me when she could, and she always told me that I would become someone important. She would tell me that I needed to go to college, but I had a strong fear that I was not smart enough to attend college.

At the beginning of my high school years, my parents placed me in a Christian school, Heritage Baptist Academy. The school helped me advance in my reading and writing skills, but I was still behind everyone else. They placed me on a reading machine and taught me how to study. I also learned more about God in two years than I had learned in all of the other years of my life combined. After two years at Heritage, I returned to public school so I could become involved in baseball.

When I returned to Liberty Union High School in Brentwood for my junior and senior years, my counselor, Ms. Arce, also encouraged me to attend the community college. She recommended that I attend an orientation at Los Medanos College. This orientation was set up for many of the Hispanic students who also had special needs. Many people thought I was Hispanic, mistaking my last name "Aquila" with the Hispanic last name "Aguila."

The day I was scheduled to visit the college, I checked in with the bus driver and took a seat. I was quickly called back to the front of the bus, and the driver asked me why I was on the list to attend the college orientation. I tried to explain to her that my counselor had recommended me; but she told me I could not go because the tour was only for "Hispanic students" and not "white students." This was my first encounter with affirmative action, which I feel is glorified racism against poor, white children. Many of my friends were Hispanic, and most were better off than me. Yet, I was discriminated against due to my ethnicity. I believed "all" people should be treated equally and given an equal opportunity. Unfortunately, after such difficulties, I gave up. I was not going to attend college. I felt I had achieved enough just by being a high school graduate.

At this time, I was employed at the city's recreation department as a baseball umpire. My boss, Frank Acebo, asked me if I was going to college, to which I responded I was not. When he asked me why, I told him the other kids were smarter than me. He gave me some advice that I will never forget: College is not about how smart you are, but about how hard you work. He said that the key to getting a college degree is to attend each class, do the best you can and, if you do that, you will earn a "B." He was correct. I started college in 1987 at Los Medanos College. For the next 11 consecutive years, I remained in school, taking at least one class per semester. I received my Associate of Arts Degree from Diablo Valley College before obtaining my Bachelor's Degree in Criminal Justice, in 1998, from California State University, Hayward, now known as California State University, East Bay. I graduated with a 3.3 GPA.

During this time, I began working with the Concord Police Department as an intern, before being hired by Contra Costa County as a probation counselor at a nearby juvenile rehabilitation facility. While I originally wanted to be a police officer and worked as a reserve officer in Brentwood, I also wanted to do something to change the moral direction of our country and guide teens who were struggling with the destructive influence of their surroundings.

While working at a youth rehabilitation facility for incarcerated boys, I began to work on my teaching credentials at Chapman University. Although I was able to get an emergency teaching credential, I never completed the program. I dropped out after completing five classes. Most of my professors were good, but I was disturbed by what I was being taught by one in particular. A professor from Berkeley explained to the class how to teach homosexuality to elementary students. She believed that second grade was the most appropriate time to introduce this concept. The professor then explained that she would begin by reading the class a story about a two girls who met, liked each other, and eventually kissed. When the children responded by saying, "eew" or "yuk," the teacher would then explain to them that it is "okay for two people to like each other." This was the teacher's opportunity to indoctrinate the children with the liberal influence of homosexuality.

I was not liked by some in the class, as I often challenged their liberal positions. I knew this professor did not like me, when I received the lowest grade in the class for not conforming to what she expected from me. As I challenged this instructor, telling her that I felt second grade was too young and asking if the parents were given an opportunity to remove their children from the class, she responded that this age was not too young. She went on to say that, during the first year of her instruction of this curriculum, notices were sent to the parents. However, when some students were excused from the class, other students began to ask why they were excused. As a result, it became easier if the parents did not know about the objectionable material beforehand in order to avoid this "distraction" altogether.

Changing Politics

When I registered to vote, I asked my father why he was a Democrat. He told me because his parents were Democrats, and they were told to vote Democrat, so he also registered as one. He went on to tell me, however, that he believed we should vote for the person and not the party. He later admitted to me that Ronald Reagan was the first

Republican for whom he had voted. I told him that, as a Christian, I could not vote for a Democrat, and I would register as a Republican. My father listened to my reasoning but remained a Democrat.

Prior to September 11, 2001, I married and moved to Manteca in San Joaquin County, the city famously known for the first water slides in the nation. My house was actually completed and final papers processed on September 11, 2001. My parents also sold their small farm and moved to Manteca. My father wanted to re-register as a Democrat, not because he wanted to be a Democrat, but he wanted to say to the Democrats who would call to remind him to vote that he was going to vote Republican. While the thought put a smile on my face, he registered as a Republican for the first time.

When my sons, Louis and Steven, were born in 2002 and 2004, I started to become more serious about politics. I became interested in the political process after watching the 2000 election battle between George W. Bush and Al Gore. I had been fascinated by politics before that but never volunteered or expressed my opinions.

There were also other issues that caused me to become interested in politics. Prior to Louis bang born, I found out I would have a boy from an ultrasound. My friend, who worked in a building where ultrasounds were performed, told me a story which truly disturbed me. A couple had come in to find out the sex of their baby. When the couple found out it was a girl, they left. The same couple returned approximately six months later. Again, they were told, "it's a girl." This cycle repeated itself two more times until, on the fourth time, the couple was told, "it's a boy." Three times the babies were aborted for being the wrong sex—a girl. I knew in my heart that abortion should never be a means of birth control or determining the gender make-up of a family.

As a new father, I felt the need to become proactive and involve myself in the political process. I felt there were a lot of problems in our country, and I was not happy with the marketing techniques or policies within the Republican Party, especially the California Republican

Party. I also saw the failures of both political parties to do anything in controlling the problem of illegal immigration due to the fear of alienating the Hispanic voters. I believe we are a nation of laws, and we should not undermine those people, such as my grandparents, who went through the immigration process legally. I also felt the Republican Party had missed a golden opportunity to protect our borders for national security reasons after September 11, 2001. To me, it is a primary responsibility of our government to protect our borders and our citizens.

During this period of time I wrote several letters to various California Republican state senators and assemblymen. I also made recommendations to the National Republican Party and each state party chairman about how to reach out and inform voters on the issues and positions of the Republican Party. I remember listening to former New York Mayor Ed Koch, who is a Democrat and voted for President George W. Bush. Mayor Koch once made an interesting point, explaining that no one will agree with a candidate on every issue, but if one agrees with a candidate on the majority of issues, that person is most likely the right candidate.

I like to point this out to people who are one-issue voters. I suggest that people look at their own family. No one in a family is going to agree on every single issue, so how can we expect a party of 100 million voters to agree on every issue? I explained in my letters to the various Republican leaders that, if voters were to look beyond party labels and focused on the individual issues, many people would realize they are conservative and would most likely vote Republican. I felt many of the voters were uninformed about the issues, and it is in our best interest as a party and a nation to inform the voters about the issues and the candidates. I suggested the Republican Party inform the voters about various issues and the difference between the Democrat and Republican Party platforms. Through a survey of the issues, a person can find out where he stands politically. I developed my own survey and used it on my Godfather, who is a hard-line Democrat. At the end of the survey, he saw he was more conservative than he thought and was in line with President Bush.

I was frustrated that out of so many letters sent to Republican leaders, I received only three replies. These were from Brian P. Eastin, Executive Director in Tennessee; Michael Myers, Executive Director in Michigan; and Republican National Committee Chairman, Jim Nicholson, who each thanked me for my recommendations. All the other letters went unanswered until I received a call from a retired state senator from Bakersfield, California, whose name I can't recall. He expressed appreciation for my letter and suggestions, and directed me to the San Joaquin Republican Party (SJRP) in Stockton.

Soon after that, I was contacted by their representative, Bob Busser. Bob met with me to discuss my ideas for reform, which he really seemed to like. I suggested that we should set up a website, which was eventually created, and that the Central Committee should provide an atmosphere of family activities to encourage families to become involved as well as small city organizations. When Bob invited me to speak briefly to the San Joaquin County Republican Central Committee (SJRCC), I knew I was an outsider with no political experience, but maybe that is what the Republican Party needed. I was honest, and I had a strategy to make the party better. In many ways, that is how Sarah Palin got started—as an outsider who was honest and wanted to make a difference in getting things done.

We met at a Mexican restaurant in Stockton. There was a small group of about 15 people. I was introduced by the chairman as a guest speaker and offered a few minutes to speak. I was excited to present my ideas to the Central Committee and could tell many members were interested. I spoke to them about getting more people involved by having "fun days" so we could discuss politics. Another suggestion I had was to have city captains in each city who would be the leaders within their community. They would be responsible for organizing local meetings and events and personally reaching out to people. However, I was quietly and politely interrupted by the chairman. While my ideas and enthusiasm were appreciated by the SJRCC, it was not the plan the chairman desired. I believe he allowed me to speak only as a courtesy, and then he wanted to move on to his own agenda.

Despite these obstacles, I did not give up. I continued to meet with Bob Busser on a regular basis, discussing with him how we should accomplish my ideas and who he might know to assist me, since I felt my ideas were being ignored. At that point, I decided to call the chairman to explain my ideas, which I discussed on the phone with him for an hour. Eventually, it got fairly heated between us, with him telling me, "I cannot believe I wasted an hour of my time talking to you about this. You are not going to do it, and if you want to do anything, you will be a precinct captain." A precinct captain is a person in charge of a voting precinct who meets the voters, gathers information about them and acts as a liaison if they have questions.

Although San Joaquin County had 518 voting precincts, there weren't 518 precinct captains. Actually, there were only a few precinct captains, and some of those people were in name only. Very few people actually went out and walked their voting precinct. I could have easily given up and decided to do nothing. I was disappointed that my ideas were ignored, but I went through the training and did what I was supposed to do as a precinct captain just to show the chairman he was not going to drive me away or accuse me of not doing what he asked me to do. I also attended the central committee meetings. After I completed the training, I was allowed to have access to those in my voting precinct through a system called Voter Vault, which provided voting history on the voters in a particular area.

During the summer of 2004, I did what every good precinct captain was supposed to do. I met the voters in my voting precinct. When I got off work, I would put my son in his stroller and walk with my father in various parts of the neighborhood, throughout the entire summer, covering all parts of the voting precinct, introducing myself to voters. Often, I felt I was wasting my time and continued to be disappointed that my suggestions were being ignored by the central committee. It was a frustrating time, but I was committed to follow through on my position as precinct captain, even if I felt I was a one-man-army walking the battle lines of this precinct.

The precinct captain is a great idea for most areas of the United States, where people are more engaged in the political process. However, in California, people are not as motivated or involved in politics. Therefore, a different strategy is needed to bring together and form a coalition of those interested individuals who are conservative and frequently feel isolated in various parts of the community. Ideally, that strategy would help those individuals work together in various areas to inform their neighbors, friends, and family to make a difference in their community.

After watching the 2004 election, I wanted to do more than be a precinct captain. I still had a plan to develop my ideas and start an organization in Manteca. At the same time, I was busy as a single father of two young boys and working full time. I wanted to change politics and begin a strategy that would allow the busy person to get involved in the political process.

The Birth of the South San Joaquin Republicans

The South San Joaquin Republicans (SSJRs) was the fuse that ultimately allowed me to help get Sarah Palin on the presidential ticket with Senator John McCain, but the formation of this organization was initially met with much resistance. The chairman of the San Joaquin County Republican Central Committee (SJCRCC) had ignored all my ideas. After following his direction as a precinct captain, I realized there needed to be changes in the way things were being done. I began to think of a way to organize the people who also had conservative views in Manteca.

In May 2005, I called Ken Vogel, the Executive Director for the SJCRCC. Ken was one person who really appreciated and listened to my ideas. I told him I was going to personally organize my home city of Manteca, and I was going to hold just three meetings a year—January, May, and September—with my first meeting scheduled for September 2005. I planned to call my organization the Manteca Republicans. I asked him to provide me the names of those people from Manteca who had expressed interest in volunteering during the 2004 election. Ken provided me with about 50 names; and during that summer, I spoke to each of those people on the phone. People were skeptical about such an organization and did not know who I was. Many vented their frustration with the SJCRCC, while others told me they just wanted to find a way to get involved but really did not know how to do it. Due to my frustration, I could relate to each of these people. My entire purpose was to provide the bridge for those people who wanted to get involved.

I spent that summer setting up the first Manteca Republicans meeting to be held at the Perko's Cafe Banquet Room for a September evening. My neighbor, Carl Neaterous, told me he could get Willie Weatherford, the Mayor of Manteca, to appear as a guest speaker for the first meeting. I also made several calls to people who wrote conservative letters to the editor in the local newspapers. With access to Voter Vault, I looked up their political leanings and invited them to the meeting.

David Marks became the first city captain in Manteca and my original partner in forming the organization. We had met while registering people to vote in 2004, and he became an instant friend and supporter of the Manteca Republicans in addition to showing me how to use the computer.

I also spent that summer writing the first of many letters to the editor of the Manteca Bulletin. My first letter to the editor was titled, "Why I am a Republican." In it, I explained to the readers why I was a Republican and introduced myself as the city captain for Manteca.

"Why am I a Republican?"

When I am asked why I am a Republican, I reply that I became a Republican because I am a Christian. Christianity has been under attack for many years. It has become an obsession of the American left. Their goal is to silence Christians, using diversity and tolerance as a means to advance their agenda, yet take away the rights and liberties we have as Christian Americans.

Our Founding Fathers would have been blasted by the American left as right-wing extremists. The phrase "Under God" is offensive to atheists, so some suggest we remove it from the Pledge of Allegiance, even though 86% of Americans believe in God. The phrase most often abused is the term "separation of church and state." This phrase is not even found in the U.S. Constitution, but it is quoted as gospel by the American left. This phrase was used so the government could not establish a government-sponsored religion, such as the Church of England.

Now, Christmas is under attack! No longer can some employees say, "Merry Christmas;" they must say "Happy Holidays." A Christmas tree is now referred to as a ""holiday tree" in Massachusetts. "Christmas vacation" has been replaced by "winter recess" on the school calendar. Have you noticed that the American Civil Liberties Union (ACLU) is searching America for nativity scenes, religious displays and ornaments, Christmas carols or any Biblical references or prayer that might be "offensive," thus violating their bizarre interpretation of the term "separation of church and state"?

I could go on with numerous examples, but I am a Republican because I believe in limited government, low taxes, support for a strong military and preserving the Bill of Rights for our individual freedoms of life, liberty, and the pursuit of happiness. For my children, I want to protect those rights granted to me through the blood of many brave Americans, to whom I wish I could say, "thank you for your sacrifice and service." Therefore, I align myself with the Republican Party.

The liberal wing of the Democratic Party has aligned itself with the anti-Christian movement. The left wing realizes it will have a difficult time advancing their homosexual agenda for gay rights, gay marriage, legalized drugs, the redistribution of wealth through taxation, or the rights of a terrorist rather than the rights of an unborn child, as long as the Christian right of the Republican Party stands in opposition.

I don't expect everyone to agree with me 100%, just as I don't agree with today's Republican Party 100%. I believe both parties have failed us in protecting our borders, and the Republicans have tried at times to compromise with the Democrats, rather than fight for their basic principles.

With their alliance with the Democratic Party, the media has tried to characterize the right wing of the Republican Party as "extreme," but you never hear of an "extreme left wing." I'll stand with what the Bible says in Ecclesiastes 10:2, "A wise man's heart is at his right hand, but a fool's heart is at his left."

I am glad I am in the RIGHT party; that is why I am a Republican.

Frank Aquila
City Captain, Manteca

The letter was read by Pastor Michael Dillman of the Assembly of God in Manteca. He sent me an email and invited me to speak at his church, because Pastor Dillman liked to involve people in the community to speak in his church. I was nervous, so I requested the questions he was going to ask so I could be prepared. I hated to speak in front of others, but if I was going to put together this organization, I had to learn to speak about it. I spoke to the church for about ten minutes. Pastor Dillman became one of my most avid supporters, providing the invocation for my first meeting; and he has given several invocations since then. As a veteran himself, he had a large following and was involved in making sure our veterans and those who have fallen while fighting for liberty were never forgotten.

The editor of the *Manteca Bulletin*, Dennis Wyatt, published most of my letters to the editor. Dennis, who likes to focus on the people of the city, wrote a story about me after I organized the South San Joaquin Republicans, and he later wrote an entire editorial about me on September 15, 2010, titled, "Aquila & Associates practicing pure grassroots politics." Most of the letters created a firestorm in the editorial section between local Democrats and Republicans. I am sure all the attention to the editorial page brought interest to the paper. Many people have emailed me thanking me for being a conservative voice in the city, but I occasionally received emails from local Democrats expressing their frustration with my beliefs. One person loved to ramble on against any letter I wrote. Although I rarely responded to his war of words in the paper, I enjoyed our battle of expression and thought.

Some people from the smaller towns around Manteca, such as Lathrop, Escalon, and Ripon, also heard about the upcoming meeting and expressed interest. One such lady was Kristy Sayles, who was running for the Lathrop City Council. When I told Kristy about my idea to form these city meetings and establish city captains, she expressed interest in being the first city captain for Lathrop. I offered the position to her and she accepted. She went on to win her city council seat, and she eventually became Mayor of Lathrop.

Everything came together for the first meeting. Over 30 people had come to an early-September meeting, at which I laid out the goals and mission of the Manteca Republicans: to bring Republican and conservative organizations together from the community in an interchange where each person could get involved in order to make a difference in the community and have an opportunity to know those who were our elected representatives.

Attending this initial meeting were Mary Park and Suzanne Tucker, two ladies who were both from Tracy, a larger city near Manteca.

Both Mary and Suzanne were part of the SJCRCC and expressed an interest in being part of this new organization. Soon Mary became the city captain from Tracy and a huge supporter of what was now developing into the South San Joaquin Republicans (SSJRs), which included the cities of Manteca, Tracy, Lathrop, Escalon, Ripon, and Mountain House.

Conflicts between Elephants

The SSJRs became a unique organization for the busy conservative, who did not know how to get involved in politics or did not have the time to get involved, but wanted to make a difference. I often referred to our organization as the Baskin Robbins of politics. People could come to the meeting to meet the representatives of various Republican and conservative organizations and choose the organization that interested them. Since we met only three times a year, there was an incentive for people to come to the meetings; otherwise, if they missed a meeting, they would have to wait eight months for the next meeting. People could easily attend three meetings a year. It also provided a platform for the candidates to have an audience and meet with their constituents.

My neighbor, Carl Neaterous, suggested I move the meeting location to Chez Shari, a restaurant located on the Manteca Golf Course. Carl knew the father-son team of owners, Frank and John Guinta. They were delighted to have the organization meet at their beautiful facility overlooking the grass and lakes of the golf course. They even donated hors d'oeuvres for anyone attending the meeting. Frank told me it was his donation to the Republican Party, and later John told me the meetings provided the best advertisement for their business, as people knew about their facility from the newsletter I sent to the organization and the meeting briefs in the newspaper. However, getting the media to provide the meeting information was a difficult task.

Several people also asked if I could get Congressman Richard Pombo to come to the next meeting. I was intimidated at the thought of even asking a congressman to come to the meeting, but I knew it would be an opportunity to attract more people. The only other congressman I had met was Congressman George Miller, who showed up to the Contra Costa County Fair when I was in Knightsen 4-H and Brentwood FFA (Future Farmers of America). Congressman Miller stood next to me and asked me about my animals. Honestly, at the time, I did not know the difference between a senator, congressman, or assemblyman; but I knew he was an important man because of all the staff around him. At the time, I had no idea about his liberal politics, but it was an opportunity to talk to him about my animals and an opportunity for him to get a photograph in the newspaper.

When I called Congressman Pombo's office, they were very friendly with me. I provided the information for the January 2006 meeting. Congressman Pombo accepted my invitation and would be at the meeting with the stipulation that he did not want any media to be aware of his attendance. Although I was excited to have Congressman Pombo as a guest speaker, I was disappointed that I could not use this opportunity to let the community know about the new SSJR meeting with Congressman Richard Pombo.

The meeting still brought in a good crowd. We had double the number of people from the previous meeting. Everyone appreciated the new building and the hors d'oeuvres. The Navy Sea Cadets brought in the American flag, and we had someone play the National Anthem at the beginning of the meeting. This became a regular routine at the beginning of each meeting.

Congressman Pombo was at the beginning of a tough campaign because many environmental organizations had targeted him due to his position as the Chairman of the House Resource Committee, his support of off-shore oil drilling, water rights for farmers, and reforms to the Endangered Species Act. Congressman Pombo just wanted to meet and talk to his supporters without the media misrepresenting his words.

I was very impressed with Congressman Pombo, and I think he was equally impressed by our organization. His chief of staff, Steve Ding, invited me to dinner over the summer and told me that Congressman Pombo wanted to work with me to expand a Northern San Joaquin Republican organization once he won re-election. I was also invited as his guest to many of his events.

I did not know it at the time, but many of Congressman Pombo's staff had conflicts with those on the San Joaquin County Republican Central Committee. I could not understand why they were not working with each other during the election. Each was working out of separate buildings, with a group of volunteers calling the same voters and walking the same precincts during the 2006 election. As an observer, I just tried to get along with everyone and avoid personal conflicts.

As I continued to have meetings, more and more people came, and my email list grew to the point I had to create separate email accounts by the name of the individual cities. People were getting to know me, and those who were originally skeptical began to come to the meetings. One of those people was Carlon Perry, who was born and raised in Manteca and had been Mayor of Manteca. He lost a bitterly-fought race for re-election against Mayor Willie Weatherford. Carlon also had problems with the Republican Central Committee during his campaign, when they refused to endorse him as a Republican and he, as well as several others, told me how the South San Joaquin Republicans had "put some fear" into the SJCRCC. He told me, as well as others, that I was doing the work they should have been doing all along, and that they did not think the SSJRs would succeed.

The success of the SSJRs also led to endorsements. I never thought my endorsement would be worth much, but Carl Fogliani, Congressman Pombo's campaign manager, asked me to sign a card endorsing Congressman Richard Pombo. It was the first time I was ever referred to as a president. I did not know what my title would be since I was not elected to the position. I often referred to myself as a founder or chairman, but the title of president was special to me.

Now that I was providing endorsements, I offered an endorsement to Samuel Anderson, who was running for one of two city council seats in Manteca against two incumbents, Democrat John Harris and Republican Vince Hernandez. This upset the establishment of the SJCRCC, who told Anderson he could not use the endorsement. There was some confusion because Anderson was not endorsed by the SJCRCC. I later found out that a candidate could purchase an endorsement from them, which is what John Harris did. Anderson threatened a lawsuit, and Dennis Wyatt wrote an editorial in the *Manteca Bulletin* telling Anderson to accept the SSJR endorsement and drop the conflict he had with the SJCRCC. I was stunned by the conflicts that could be created with a few personal endorsements, but I had the right to provide any endorsement I wanted for any candidate.

One person who became a great friend and source of information was Don Parsons. He had a story about any person who had run for any office in San Joaquin County. As a political consultant, he knew the blueprints of every area of San Joaquin County. He knew about each person and the personal relationships each person had with other people, whether it was good or bad. I had Don come to one meeting to talk to people about the process of running for office. Don was also very generous to me personally. My boys had won a pageant for being the best looking boys in their age category. I put them into the competition so they could win a trophy, but had no idea they would win the title. The boys were offered the opportunity to travel to Southern California to compete against all the other winners from Nevada, Hawaii, Arizona, and throughout California, but I could not afford the $1,000 cost. Don wrote a check to me and told me to enjoy myself with the boys. I have never seen such generosity from someone, and it felt special to have made such extraordinary contacts with so many important people.

One unusual contact that I did not expect was a message from Congressman Pombo's office on my answering machine in September 2006. I called back to talk to one of his staffers, who told me that Congressman Pombo had asked if I would be interested in meeting

President Bush. I was speechless and stunned. When I told the staffer, "Yes!" she went on to tell me that Congressman Pombo was very impressed with the work I had done in organizing the SSJRs and wanted to reward me for my work to be a greeter for President George W. Bush when he arrived in Stockton, California, the following Monday.

Greeting the President

One of the most inspirational moments anyone could have is to meet the President of the United States of America, the leader of the greatest and most powerful nation in the entire world. Congressman Richard Pombo provided me this opportunity, after he selected me as one of seven people to greet President George W. Bush on a fall evening in 2006. Congressman Pombo was a seven-term congressman and Chairman of the House Resource Committee. I knew he had many friends and associates he could have chosen to greet the President, but he chose me.

Congressman Pombo provided me this opportunity as a reward for my work in putting together the South San Joaquin Republicans, an organization designed to provide access to our political leaders as well as provide opportunities to get voters involved with the political process and with conservative and Republican organizations in the area. Congressman Pombo and his staff did not have a great relationship with the San Joaquin County Republican Central Committee, so I believed it was possible he also used this opportunity to let a few people on the SJCRCC see that he was not pleased with the conflicts and lack of support they provided him.

Meeting President Bush was a great honor because I had great admiration for him. I had never met a president, and I really liked President Bush. As a Christian, I remember his answer to a question in the 1999 Republican primary debate in Iowa, when he was asked, "Who is your favorite political philosopher?" and he responded, "Jesus Christ, because he changed my life." Whether people agree or disagree about Jesus Christ being a political philosopher, I admire President Bush for using the opportunity to acknowledge Jesus Christ as the one who changed his life. I had read a story about President Bush's faith and how he accepted Jesus Christ as his Savior. I often felt the liberal media was against him because of his faith, just like the media was often biased against Christians. President Bush was never ashamed of his faith and brought both honor and dignity to the presidency. He often mentioned God in his public discourse, and he began each morning with Bible devotion and prayer.

President Bush also did not get credit from the liberal media for the accomplishments he achieved as president. He came into the presidency during a time when the economy was entering a recession. Despite the shock to the nation as a result of the attacks on September 11, 2001, and two wars being fought at the same time, his tax cuts allowed the United States to regain economic prosperity. He was blamed for the recession at the end of his presidency, but the media failed to inform the public who really caused the economic crisis. I wrote an article about this entitled, "Who Caused this Economic Crisis?"

"Who Caused this Economic Crisis?"

How did this worldwide economic crisis begin, and who is responsible for it? In 1996, a bipartisan Congressional Bill, H.R. 3019, was promoted and approved by President Bill Clinton to make changes to the 1977 Community Reinvestment Act, signed into law by President Jimmy Carter. H.R. 3019 allowed Freddie Mac and Fannie Mae (originally formed by the government to facilitate mortgage loans to homeowners) to accept mortgages from poor, low-income home buyers. The new requirement lowered the previous 25% down-payment to zero money down-payment. In 1999, the requirements for approval of a mortgage by Freddie Mac and Fannie Mae were reduced even further to allow home buyers to obtain adjustable rate mortgages (ARMs) based on the Federal Fund interest rate. There were some further changes as a result of the Gramm-Leach-Bliley Act, a deregulation of the financial services industry.

As President Bush took office in 2001, the economy began to enter into a recession. With the terrorist attack on September 11, 2001, the federal government lowered the Federal Fund interest rate to fight off the recession in 2001-2002. The lowered interest rates made the low-cost adjustable rate mortgages accessible to more people, spurring many people to purchase homes. Through supply and demand, combined with low interest rates, the real estate boom began. As a result, home prices soared in value.

In April 2001, the Bush administration warned that Freddie Mac and Fannie Mae were too large, over- leveraged, and their failure "could cause strong repercussions in financial markets." By September 2003, Republicans began to question Democrats about stronger oversight needed for Freddie and Fannie. The issue was opposed by Congressional Democrats. "These two entities—Fannie Mae and Freddie Mac—are not facing any kind of financial crisis," said Representative Barney Frank of Massachusetts, the ranking Democrat on the Financial Services Committee. "The more people exaggerate these problems, the more pressure there is on these companies, the less we will see in terms of affordable housing," Representative Melvin L. Watt, Democrat of North Carolina, agreed, adding, "I don't see much other than a shell game going on here, moving something from one agency to another and in the process weakening the bargaining power of poorer families and their ability to get affordable housing."

As the economy recovered into 2003-2004, interest rates began to go up to combat inflation. As interest rates increased, adjustable mortgage rates were also adjusted, causing adjustable rate loan mortgage payments to increase. As these loans became expensive, many people began to sell their homes, resulting in home prices reaching their peak in 2004.

In 2005, the Senate Banking Committee, then chaired by Republican Richard Shelby, tried to rein in the two organizations by passing some strong new regulations. Democrat Senator Chris Dodd of Connecticut successfully threatened a filibuster. Barney Frank continued to defend Fannie and Freddie as "fundamentally sound" and labeled the President's proposals as "insane." Senator Thomas Carper of Delaware stated, "If it ain't broke, don't fix it." Maxine Waters of California accused Republicans of being racially motivated, and Gregory Meeks of New York stated, "I am just pissed off."

All the Republicans on the committee voted for the Housing Reform Act. All the Democrats, including the current Chairman, Senator Chris Dodd, voted against it. Both he and Frank blocked the Housing Reform Act, which would have forced oversight and audits of Fannie Mae and Freddie Mac. Since Democrats blocked it, those new regulations never got consideration by the full Senate, and the bill proposing new regulations died.

Why would Democrats block the reform? Follow the money. Chris Dodd and Barack Obama were the top two recipients of campaign donations from Fannie Mae. Franklin Raines, the former CEO of Fannie Mae, then became an operator for the Democratic Party, after he received $90 million in salary and bonuses at Fannie Mae, where the financial records were manipulated to meet earning targets so he could get his bonuses at the expense of the people. Meanwhile, Barney Frank received more than $40,000 in campaign donations while he was involved in a sexual relationship with a Fannie Mae executive.

Meanwhile, by 2005, too many homes were on the market. The supply and demand of too many homes caused home values to fall. With the inability to sell their homes, many homeowners began to refinance their mortgages. However, as home values continued to decline, many home owners could not refinance their homes because they owed more on their homes than they were worth. Many of those homeowners began to walk away from their homes, which avalanched into a huge economic crisis, as banks were left to cover the costs of loans, forcing them to declare bankruptcy. Many states, county governments, and cities were forced to declare bankruptcy with defaults on municipal bonds and a lack of revenue from projected property taxes. With the economic slowdown, people have lost their jobs and more people are watching how much they spend as we sink into what may be a bigger depression than the Great Depression of the 1930s.

Nevertheless, the Democrats successfully politicized this as the Republican's fault. On October 14, 2008, Senator Hillary Clinton said, It breaks my heart to see the U.S. in an economic crisis eight years after Democrats left the nation in sound fiscal shape." Wow! What a cover-up! Many people may blame President Bush just because he was President during this time, but this economic storm began to brew long before he took office.

Frank Aquila, January 2009

While I did not agree with everything President Bush did as President, I don't think anyone agrees on everything. I felt the Republican-controlled Congress under President Bush should have controlled spending and limited government growth. While I also agree with free trade, I believe it must be fair trade before we do business with other nations. I also feel both political parties have turned a blind eye towards illegal immigration, our southern border, and that all of our borders should be protected. September 11, 2001 provided the perfect opportunity for President Bush to announce enforcement of border protection. No one should be able to come into America from Canada, Mexico, or through our shores without our government knowing who they are.

One of the most overlooked issues is the presidential authority to appoint judges. I was very pleased with President Bush's judicial appointments. He appointed several great conservative pro-constitutional judges. Justices John Roberts and Samuel Alito, Jr. were two great selections for the United States Supreme Court. A president has considerable ability to shape the future of this country with the selection of judges, who often have the power to rule on the constitutionality of specific laws and are not beholden to an electorate.

Of course, a major issue during the presidency of George W. Bush was the Iraq War. Prior to the beginning of the war in 2003, more than 110 Democrats supported the war, and the entire national security team of the Clinton administration backed the war in Iraq. President Bush, many people from the Clinton administration, and other prominent Democrats each made statements about the serious threat from Iraqi President Saddam Hussein, his unwillingness to cooperate with United Nations inspections, and the acute threat of weapons of mass destruction (WMDs). President Bush mentioned it would be a long and difficult war.

Public perception changed as the war went on and no weapons of mass destruction were found. The media ignored reports that Saddam's Air Force officer, Georges Sada, stated the WMDs were moved into Syria six weeks before the war started. (1) Many Iraqi prisoners reported the same information. President Bush was accused of lying to the American people even though Saddam Hussein was already known to have used weapons of mass destruction to kill millions of the Kurds living in northern Iraq. (2)

Many argued that the al-Qaeda terrorist network was not in Iraq, but it was. The al-Qaeda commander in Iraq, Ayman al-Zawahiri, stated in December 2005, "You have set the timetable for the withdrawal a long time ago and Bush, you have to admit that you were defeated in Iraq...." (3) On November 10, 2006, al-Muhajir, who took over leadership of al-Qaeda in Iraq when Abu Musab al-Zarqawi was killed in a U.S. air strike, stated, "Remain steadfast on the battlefield you coward. We will not rest from our Jihad until we are under the olive trees of Rumieh and we have blown up the filthiest house—which is called the White House."(4) It certainly seemed that Democrats knew the serious threat posed by al-Qaeda in Iraq. Despite that fact, they were using the political winds as a masquerade for their own political power.

Many of our finest American service members sacrificed their lives liberating Iraq, while those same Democrats who once supported the war waved the white flag of retreat and defeat, announcing, "We lost the war." The Democrats preferred the grim picture of the war, created by al-Qaeda, for their own political gain. Democrat Congressman James Clyburn even admitted that a good report about the war would be "a real big problem for us." (5) The Democrats rolled out their new campaign slogan in 2006 titled, "A New Direction." It has become a sad day in America, when politics would become more important than a victory from our military.

Democrat leader Senator Dick Durbin even went so far as to compare the United States troops to Nazis, Soviets, and Pol Pot. (6) Others were calling our troops criminals and demanding our troops give rights to the enemy they were fighting. Many of our fine soldiers were thrown in jail for performing their jobs and protecting liberty. The war was treated like a "police action," although we were fighting against an enemy who wanted to destroy us.

Most disturbing to me is that President Bush received no credit or acknowledgement for the victories in Iraq. The world and the United States were safer as a result of the removal of Saddam Hussein. Democratic elections of an Iraqi Parliament were put together, and life in Iraq was better than it was in 2006. The people had more recognized rights, and the Iraqi armed forces took over major military operations while the American military now is tasked with supporting and training the Iraqi troops. And yet, Vice President Joe Biden stated that victory in Iraq was President Obama's great achievement. (7) This, despite the fact that Obama was an outspoken critic of the war, declaring defeat before he was elected President.

One thing that angers me is seeing our military personnel treated poorly by our government. These troops placed their lives on the line to protect and defend our liberty. One mother told me about her son who was arrested along with seven other soldiers in Hamdania, Iraq. These soldiers were arrested after they killed an Iraqi "civilian," who had been placing roadside bombs, attempting to kill the very soldiers who killed him. These soldiers were interrogated without counsel and incarcerated at Camp Pendleton near San Diego, California. Later, they were offered plea deals.

I informed this mother that I would be greeting President Bush and asked if she would like to have me deliver a message to the president. Often, these parents grieve, not knowing what our own military is doing to their sons or daughters. Many of them do not understand what is happening, and many of their letters go unanswered. I wanted to ease the mind of this mother that her letter would be received by the Commander-in-Chief himself. She immediately composed a letter and brought it to my home.

As I prepared to meet President Bush, I drove out to the Stockton Airport near my home. I met Bob Busser there who, along with his wife, Sharon, were also greeters for the president, and we met some of the Secret Service who were already there. I had the letter to give to President Bush in my back pocket, which was covered by my dress coat. However, when we met with Secret Service, we went through an extensive scan and orientation. I began to feel nervous about handing the letter to the president, thinking that if they saw me pull something out of my back pocket, there could be a problem, and I did not want to make a scene. I spoke to one of the Secret Service agents and told him about the letter. I asked if he could make sure President Bush got this letter from a mother whose son was locked up while serving his country. The Secret Service agent agreed and was very friendly to me.

All the Secret Service agents that I met were friendly. They all seemed to be young, and most were former military members. I was able to talk to them about their job and their qualifications. I was intrigued by the assignments they carry out and what they have to do to prepare for the president's arrival. Obviously, they did not reveal their identities, but the Secret Service agents I spoke with were regular men with the dark glasses, wearing ear pieces to talk with each other. This was a whole new experience for me.

As we walked out to the tarmac, I got chills throughout my body, because I knew this was going to be one of the most incredible moments of my life. The weather was perfect as the sun was beginning to set. I would be the last in line to greet the president. Bob and Sharon Busser were just in front of me. We could hear the Secret Service talking about the location of Air Force One. As I looked around, I could see the Secret Service in various positions on rooftops, each of them looking at different views to detect any dangers.

Within minutes, I could see Air Force One descending on the airport like an enormous, graceful bird coming in for a landing. I was amazed at the tremendous size of Air Force One. Immediately after landing, several black-tinted limousines pulled up, lining themselves up in two different motorcades so that no one would know in which vehicle President Bush would ride. The door to Air Force One swung open. In a few moments, President Bush stood there in a dark suit with a yellow tie, waving to the people below. Behind him was Congressman Pombo coming down to meet the greeters. I did not know Congressman Pombo would be accompanying the president, but I was grateful that I would have my first opportunity to thank him while at the same time meeting and greeting the president.

President Bush took a few moments with each greeter. He was very personable and amiable, and had a smile for each of us. I became speechless even before he reached me. He had just finished shaking Bob Busser's hand and giving Sharon a hug when he was in front of me saying, "How you doing, partner?" I felt as nervous and speechless as I was on my first date, struggling to utter a word. I told him that I really appreciated everything he was doing for our country and was glad for him to visit us. He responded that he hoped the people here would welcome him. I told him we did and we were very glad he came. We were shaking hands during that exchange while Congressman Pombo stood behind him.

As our hands parted, I reached out to Congressman Pombo and told him how stunned I was to have such a wonderful opportunity. I shook his hand and thanked him. We began to have a conversation as he also thanked me for everything I was doing. During the exchange, the Secret Service was attempting to move us away because television cameras and reporters had swarmed the greeters. Since the other greeters were out of the way first, I actually stood for a moment by myself. A man nearby was being interviewed since he had witnessed everything. To my surprise he pointed to me, stating, "He is the one to talk to; he just shook hands with the president." Immediately, news reporters were asking about my meeting with President Bush and if I felt it was good that he came. I acknowledged that it was not every day you are privileged to meet a president and said, "Anytime a president comes to your community, it is a good thing."

Unfortunately, Congressman Pombo lost his re-election bid one month later when the Democrats claimed control of the House of Representatives. In one year, I had gone from starting an organization, to a close relationship with my congressman, to meeting the President of the United States of America. Now, I felt unsure of the direction of the SSJRs and delivered a letter a month later to Congressman Pombo, thanking him for his service and telling him that I wished I could have done more to assist him to victory.

As for the letter from the mother of the soldier, President Bush did reply with a letter from the White House. He explained that the investigation must take its course. The mother later informed me that seven of the eight soldiers were released after 18 months of incarceration, while the one remaining was still fighting for his freedom. Many of the soldiers accepted plea deals. I personally feel our military men should be given every benefit of the doubt and presumed innocent until proven guilty. Even then, we must realize they go through training to fight an enemy in war. They should be provided those circumstances to justify their duty. It is not a "police action" as some may think. It is war, and our military deserves support on every level!

California Republican Convention

My relationship with the San Joaquin County Republican Central Committee began to improve when a new county chairman was elected—Dale Fritchen. I did not know Dale at the time, but he had been on the school board in Stockton and eventually won an election to be on the Stockton City Council. He was soft-spoken, intelligent, and helpful in unifying those who had conflicts within the SJCRCC. He began to repair the problems that had occurred. Although I did not attend many SJCRCC meetings, I was there the night he was elected. Dale made a point to let me know he was going to work with me, and he was true to his word.

One of the first things he did was to offer me a position as a delegate from San Joaquin County for the State Republican Party, a position that allows certain members to vote for leadership and rules at the California Republican Convention. While I would have accepted this position from Dale, I had just been offered a position as delegate from Assemblyman Greg Agazarian's office. Carl Fogliani ran Assemblyman

Agazarian's campaign, as well as Congressman Pombo's campaign, so Carl wanted to have me as a delegate under Assemblyman Agazarian. Each county has a certain number of delegates, and the more elected politicians from your county, the more delegates you receive. Being new to the political atmosphere, this was a different experience for me. I did not understand the significance of this position until my phone began to ring off the hook. Every person who was running for a leadership position on the California State Republican Executive Committee called me, lobbying me for my vote. I did not know any of these people or their positions. I did not even know I was going to be receiving these calls. I was instantly popular and now know what a politician must go through before voting for legislation. I spoke to many people, and each person sounded good to me. I told each person I would consider them for my vote, as this would be my first time going to a Republican State Convention, which was being held in Sacramento.

Bob Busser was also a delegate, and I relied a lot on what Bob had to say. We rode together to the Republican State Convention. I was taken aback by the size of the convention. I have never seen so many Republicans in one place. There were many booths and training centers, and people were lined up to meet with other delegates. Bob was my mentor. I would have been lost without him.

I met several people who were running for the state offices of the California Republican Party, who were interested in my vote. I was not convinced who would receive my vote, but I made up my mind immediately when I heard Laura Gadke's speech. From Tulare County, she was running for chairwoman of the Central Valley Region. When she had called me earlier, I told her how I called many people who volunteered during the elections and also about my use of Voter Vault. I would scan the newspapers for other conservative-minded people who wrote letters to the editor, then call them. I figured if they took the time to write a letter, they wanted to get involved and make a difference in our society. Laura spoke to the delegates about me and my organization, saying that we needed to reach out to others who also want to get involved and show them opportunities where they can make a difference on the local, county, and state levels. She told them how I scan the letters to the editor and that we needed to be pro-active in informing people about the issues. Laura won the position as regional chairwoman of the California Central Valley Region. She was also a significant bridge to my future relationship with the McCain campaign.

Another person I met was Tom Del Bacarro, who was running for vice chairman of the California Republican Party. I was intrigued by Tom since he is from my home county and sounded very sharp. However, I had a conflict with my vote, since Congressman Pombo had endorsed the gentleman who was running against Tom. I talked to Congressman Pombo, who was gracious and told me to vote for the person I thought would do the best job. Tom had provided me his phone number and told me to call him if I had any questions. Since the convention lasted another day, I talked to Bob on the way home and spoke to Tom that night. He laid out his plan for California and promised he would also work with me.

When I returned the next day, Bob and I had training together with Ron Nehring, who became the Chairman of the California Repub-lican Party. While Ron spoke, he took some questions from the crowd. I used this opportunity to voice my opinion of problems I saw within the Republican Party and how we needed to reintroduce the Republi-can Party to the people. I told Ron the Republican Party needs to put out an advertisement letting people know Republicans are the party of both Abraham Lincoln and Martin Luther King, Jr. We need to let people know about our conservative issues and our party platform. I told him too many people vote for Democrats but do not know why they vote that way. I knew I was off topic from the training, but felt it might be my only opportunity to speak my mind to the man who was going to be chairman of the state. I felt my question was deflected, but also felt my point was made clear. Bob acknowledged after the train-ing that I put Ron in a tight spot. I questioned myself and wondered if I should have waited for a better environment or opportunity, but did not know if there would have ever been a better one.

Bob and I saw Dale Fritchen, chairman of the SJCRCC, who invited us to come to a luncheon at which New York Mayor Rudy Giuliani was the guest speaker. Dale invited both Bob and me to sit at his table. It was great to feel welcomed by the new county chairman. During lunch, Mayor Giuliani came in to a standing ovation. It was exciting to stand next to him as he made his way to the front of the room. On that afternoon, he made his announcement that he was running for President. He did not do it in the traditional way in a press conference, but in a serious and often humorous speech to the crowd attending the sold-out event. Again, I took in the moment, looking around the room to see all the camera crews from the various news outlets. I was very impressed with Mayor Giuliani and the stories he had to tell from his time as mayor of New York City and his time as an attorney in the Reagan administration.

After lunch, it was near the time to vote for the new officers. I saw Ron Nehring and apologized for speaking my thoughts at an inappropriate time. He was fine with it but was obviously busy as he was preparing for the voting that was going to take place shortly. He provided me with his email address and told me to send him a letter with my recommendations. I also saw Tom Del Bacarro and told him I would be voting for him. He thanked me. Tom won the position of vice chairman, while Ron won the position as chairman. I felt I had accomplished a lot in just two days.

As Bob and I were preparing to leave, I saw Mayor Giuliani walk by with four men in dark suits who were escorting him. I felt this was an opportunity to perhaps meet the mayor, so I quickly joined the other men in the dark suits. Since I also had on a dark suit, I blended in perfectly and soon found myself walking side-by-side with Mayor Giuliani. His security men didn't notice until a lady stepped in front of the mayor and asked him for his autograph. When the mayor stopped and actually turned, bumping his shoulder into mine, I was noticed by his security men, who quickly pushed their bodies between mine and the mayor before moving on. I still smile when I think of standing next to Mayor Giuliani, who was known as "America's Mayor" after the September 11, 2001 terrorist attacks in New York. I looked back to see Bob Busser trying to catch up to me and told Bob, "I did not meet Rudy, but I got bumped by him." Bob and I had a good laugh.

Marketing Success and Managing Failures

After the California Republican State Convention, I continued to build the South San Joaquin Republicans. California politics in itself is challenging, and the marketing of the SSJRs allowed me to put together entertaining and informative meetings that drew people's interest. From my great team of city captains, I selected a few people who were active in their area to work with me in the development of our organization. Some of the city captains took an active role while others were a contact for their city if anyone wanted to ask questions. I often told the city captains that I understood their busy schedules. I told them they could do as little or as much as they wanted based on their ability and time. I just asked for them to come and support the meetings. This was also a great way for people to get involved and position themselves within their city to begin a political career, making themselves known to the public if they chose. That is what was unique about the SSJRs. It was designed for busy and working people who wanted to make a difference in their community. I often compared it to both Wal-Mart and Baskin Robbins. We were like a distribution center, providing various choices for those people who wanted to get involved but did not know how to do so or what they could do based on their schedules. Therefore, setting up the meeting was quite easy, and sometimes I scheduled an event to take the place of a meeting, such as a dinner honoring the Gold Star Families or a Congressional Forum.

During this same time, I had the honor of meeting families of those who lost a loved one in Iraq. These were the Gold Star Families. I wanted to do something special for them, and we always gave special recognition to our Gold Star Families at all meetings. Two fathers, with whom I became very close, were Michael Anderson, who lost his son, Michael Anderson, in Iraq; and Scott Conover, who lost his stepson, Brandon Dewey, in Iraq. Both supported me while I also supported them.

At this time, I scheduled a meeting called "Mayors' Night with our Veterans," to which I invited all the military organizations, such as The American Legion and Veterans of Foreign War, from South San Joaquin County. I also invited all of the five Republican mayors from South San Joaquin County. I don't know how many of the mayors wanted to attend, but I know none of them wanted to be the only one who did not attend. I was told this may have been the first time all the mayors were together and, obviously, the first time all the mayors spoke to the various veteran organizations.

Pastor Michael Dillman, who had performed the invocation of the first South San Joaquin Republican meeting and was also a veteran, gave the invocation for this meeting. Each of the mayors spoke, as did the Gold Star Families. Chairman Dale Fritchen, whose son was also serving in our military, spoke, as did the Military Moms, who talked about how we can support our troops overseas. I felt it was important to provide each and every one of our veterans the respect and acknowledgment they deserve and to show our Gold Star Families that their loved ones will never be forgotten.

Wanting to pay special tribute to our Gold Star Families, I undertook one of the most difficult responsibilities I have ever attempted. I organized a dinner called "Never Forgotten ~ A Tribute to Our Gold Star Families." It was like organizing a large wedding. I wish I could say that I received substantial contributions for the event, but that was not easy due to the poor economy. People had to be very conservative with their money. I was fortunate to receive a $1,000 donation from an individual who wished to remain anonymous. The dinner was free to the Gold Star Families. Pastor Dillman offered his church, the Assembly of God, as a location for the function. His wife, Jan, worked with me to arrange the dinner. I worked on the advertising, and Karl Geletich, who was a city captain in nearby Escalon, assisted in obtaining flowers for the Gold Star Mothers. Cheryl Dodge-Milligan assisted in obtaining donations of wine for the Gold Star Fathers. The event took a year to plan. There were several meetings between me, Deborah Johns, a Blue Star Mother (a mother of an active soldier) and Gold Star Father,

Michael Anderson. In the end, $1,500 in donations remained. These funds were donated to a fund called the Vet Fund, which funded the Gold Star Project under the California Department of Veterans Affairs. This project financed the cost to provide special vehicle license plates as recognition for the Gold Star Families.

As the new chairman of the California Republican Party, Ron Nehring was going to be in Stockton for the San Joaquin County Republican Central Committee meeting. I had sent him an email with my suggestions and wanted to follow through with him. I went to the meeting and listened. After the meeting, I asked him if he had read my ideas. He told me he had the email, but had not read it yet. He asked to remain on my newsletter and said he would get back to me.

I also continued to stay in touch with Tom Del Bacarro, since he was vice chairman of the state and lived nearby. We spoke occasionally. I once called him just after he proposed to his girlfriend, and he told me I was the first to know about their engagement. Tom and I became friends and eventually spoke together at a dinner at the Discovery Bay Women Federated.

Ron and Tom both asked to be speakers at one of the South San Joaquin Republican meetings. It was great to have the chairman and vice chairman of the California Republican Party at our meeting, even though we were not an official Republican organization.

Since Congressman Pombo had lost his seat in Congress in 2006, the district remained a district of interest for both political parties. The registration affiliation was nearly evenly divided between Democrats and Republicans. Dean Andal, a local businessman, went unopposed in the primary in 2008, but lost in the general election. We always held the last meeting prior to the election as "Congressional Night," which allowed voters in the area to meet and ask questions of the congressional candidates. In 2010, many in the district were interested in the seat. We decided to use one meeting to schedule a congressional forum at Crossroads Community Church. Pastor Mike Moore, of Crossroads

Community Church, had given the invocation at several of our meetings and opened his church as a service to the community for people to get to know the candidates. Several Democrats complained about a church holding a congressional forum, but Pastor Moore stated he was doing it for the community and would open it in the future for the Democrats if they wished.

The forum attracted over 500 people as six congressional candidates took questions that I had prepared. With the assistance of Mary Park, a city captain from Tracy and volunteer church staff, I moderated the forum, which was the first forum I had ever moderated. The entire forum was a great success. Later, the TEA Party Patriots of Eastern Contra Costa County and the Discovery Bay Women Federated teamed together to hold another congressional forum, asking me to moderate the event.

Although I had a great relationship with all the candidates, I was disappointed by the infighting between them. They lost focus on defeating the incumbent and were politically assassinating each other. This may work in a district that is 80% Republican but not in a district that is evenly divided. In the end, David Harmer won the primary, but lost the general election by less that one-half of one percent, largely because he was outspent by a wide margin by the incumbent.

Through the process, I was able to meet David Bowman, from our local radio station, who is better known as "Dave Diamond." He had a conservative talk show called "Afternoon Live with Dave Diamond" out of nearby Modesto. I originally spoke to him when I attempted to obtain advertising for the "Never Forgotten Dinner" for the Gold Star Families. We regularly talked about politics, and he attended both the congressional forum and our meetings. His "On the Air" endorsement of the South San Joaquin Republicans assisted in drawing more people and attention to the organization.

I did not achieve all the successes I aspired to achieve as president of the South San Joaquin Republicans. I had desired to put together a Republican Hispanic Assembly in the area as well as a Manteca Republican Women Federated and a Young Republican Federation. It is always difficult to start any organization. You have to have a core group of people who are willing to stay and work together to establish it. There were many great people who wanted to assist in putting these important organizations together, but the organization would fail. There would be attempts to restart the organization again, but the effort was fruitless. It is very difficult to bring people back after an organization dies. Once you are able to find new people who share the same interests and goals together, those who were previously involved may return if the organization has strong leadership.

I tried to keep those in South San Joaquin Republicans informed about various issues by submitting letters to the editors to various papers and sending weekly newsletters to those on the email list.

One area of local politics that I enjoyed was meeting and interacting with the local voters. I had volunteered to work with Mary Park, who was a coordinator from the San Joaquin County Republican Central Committee. Mary's job was to organize and schedule volunteers for the registration booth at the various city functions throughout the county. Manteca had two city functions—the Manteca Street Fair in April and the Manteca Pumpkin Faire in October. David Marks and Scott Herman were two city captains who assisted me at these functions.

We were handing out stickers for the assemblyman, but it was not an interesting item for people to wear. I spoke with Laura Gadke, who was the Central Valley Regional Chairman in California, and told her we needed stickers that said, "Vote Republican" to hand out at these functions. This is the type of sticker we needed to get people to wear. People would see their friends wearing one and then they would do the same. I told Laura we needed to be marketing ourselves better. I think she spent her own money to have some made. The next function turned into a Republican rally with several people wearing "Vote Republican" stickers.

One day while Scott Hermann was working with me, he said that we needed to do something more to attract people to our booth, like maybe a dunk tank. I loved the marketing idea and rented a space next to the Republican booth the following year at the Manteca Pumpkin Fair. The dunk tank was an instant success. I had put a tarp around the backside and placed the booth in a grassy area near the sidewalk with a large sign, "Dunk the Democrat." The weather was great that year, and the water was warm, so I had no problem getting some local teens to volunteer to sit in the dunk tank with either a Bill or Hillary Clinton mask. One year we had cool weather, so I loaded the bottom of the dunk tank with blankets and sleeping bags and the top with a thousand plastic balls for the "Democrat" to fall into. I charged $5, and people would move closer and closer until they "Dunked the Democrat," guaranteed. Each person received an American flag as a prize. I had a line of people who enjoyed seeing the "Democrat" being dunked. I even had Democrats throw the ball for their children. Once, I had a Democrat volunteer to sit in the dunk tank.

The local Democrat chapter hated the dunk tank. They went to the officials running the festival and tried to have it shut down for harassment. The officials disagreed with their complaint, so the local chapter tried to issue a complaint to the police chief alleging it was threatening. The police chief disagreed. Both the festival officials and the police chief told the Democrat Club that it was freedom of speech, and if they wanted to get their own "Dunk the Republican" dunk tank, they had every right to do so. When you can boil the blood of your rival, you know you have succeeded.

Many have asked me to run for political office or for the San Joaquin County Republican Central Committee, but I have chosen to remain president of the South San Joaquin Republicans. It has allowed me to assist the candidates and develop some great relationships. If I were a politician, I would not be able to run my own political organization. If I were on the SSCRCC, I would have to abide by the rules that govern such a committee. With my own organization, I have the freedom and luxury to do what I feel is best for the county and the conservative movement. I have no one who governs me or controls what I do. I can endorse those people I feel are the best for a position. I have also told people that I am a single father of two young boys, and a father's priority has to be for his children and to provide them every opportunity to succeed in life. That truly is a measurement of real success. One day I may decide to enter into another role as a servant to the people; but I will trust God to direct my path, if that opportunity should one day arise.

Chapter 3
Underestimating Sarah

"Government exists to protect us from each other. Where government has gone beyond its limits is in deciding to protect us from ourselves." ~ Ronald Reagan

County Chairman for Senator John McCain 2008

During the 2008 Republican presidential primaries, I enjoyed watching all the candidates, polling of various match-ups, and public perception. I would often listen intensely to the candidates, who were guests on the Sean Hannity Show. I really like Sean Hannity, who is a person knowledgeable about politics and humble about himself. I think if Sean were to ever run for office, he could easily be a politician the people could trust. I have never seen him lose a debate and, with his honesty and humility, I think he would relate well with most voters. Often, radio callers, who had previously claimed to be liberal, became "Hannitized," a term used on his show for those who disgard their liberal thought and became conservative.

As a public service, Sean brought all the candidates on his show. The exception was Texas Congressman Ron Paul. He had previously appeared; but I do not recall him being a guest of Sean during the presidential primary. Although I did not agree with Congressman Paul about his Iraq war position, he was a candidate who offered great ideas for the Republican ticket, including an audit of the Federal Reserve.

One candidate whom I really liked, but no one really noticed, was California Congressman Duncan Hunter. When I attended the California Republican State Convention a year earlier, I met some people who were trying to promote him. He simply lacked the finances to develop name recognition, making himself a virtual unknown to the American people. I also really liked Tennessee Senator Fred Thompson, who was then out of politics and working as an actor. I think he carried the persona of a president more than anyone else. The liberal media immediately lost focus of his qualifications to be president and, instead, was focused with news reports about him having a "trophy wife." The liberal media has often attempted to divert public perception away from the issues in its attempt to influence the minds of the voters. Senator Thompson was a solid conservative, who would have been a strong presidential nominee. Unfortunately, his campaign never really came together.

I liked New York City Mayor Rudy Giuliani. He spoke well, as candidates often do in order to attract the conservative vote. Since I had the opportunity to "bump" into him earlier at the California Republican State Convention and heard him speak, I felt he could win the presidency if matched against any Democrat. He also had respect as "America's Mayor," after he led New York City following the September 11, 2001 terrorist attack. Unfortunately, his campaign never gained footing, and many thought he would be too liberal. I thought Massachusetts Governor Mitt Romney appeared presidential and was very good at speaking to a crowd; but I was concerned that his Mormon religion could be a factor. It is very unfortunate that some people I knew would not vote for him because of his faith. My other concern, however, was his support of government-run health care while governor. I was also intrigued by Arkansas Governor Mike Huckabee. Governor Huckabee, a former Baptist minister, was very likable; but I had some concerns about his tax policies.

Then there was Arizona Senator John McCain, whom I respected for his service in Vietnam. However, as a conservative, I had been irritated with some of his political positions in the U.S. Senate. Senator McCain marched to a different drum, marketed himself as a "maverick" and a moderate, and was known to go against the grain of his own party. While I respect those with different opinions, I strongly disagree on compromising principles, including undermining or compromising the U.S. Constitution. Senator McCain was a member of the "Gang of 14," a group of seven Democrats and seven Republicans, who met to compromise within the Senate on the selection process of President Bush's judicial nominees.

President Bush's judicial nominees were being filibustered by the Democrats, who were in the minority, in the Senate. The minority party has the option of using a filibuster to force the cloture rule that a super-majority of 60 votes of the 100 senators were needed to end a filibuster. This rule had previously been applied on legislation; but it had neither been created for, nor has it ever previously been applied to, confirmation of presidential judicial nominees. Several judicial nominees were filibustered, preventing President Bush from exercising his right to place his choice of conservative judges on the federal bench.

Senate Republicans had threatened to change and clarify the filibuster rule by using the "nuclear option" or "constitutional option," which would prevent a filibuster from being used against a judicial nominee. The role of the Senate is to confirm or deny a nominee, based upon qualifications, through a straight up or down vote, not to play parliamentary games based on political ideology. As the Republicans were then in the majority, they had the power to end this controversial, unprecedented procedure.

The "Gang of 14" compromise stopped the "nuclear option" by the Republicans and the filibuster by the Democrats. Only five of the judicial nominees were confirmed while others, who were equally qualified, were not confirmed. The filibuster still remains an issue today because of the "Gang of 14" compromise, even though it was clearly not the intent of the framers of the U.S. Constitution to allow a minority of patricians to block the confirmation desired by the majority of the Senators.

By the time the 2008 Republican presidential primaries reached California, Congressman Hunter, Senator Thompson and Mayor Giuliani were no longer in the race. There were a number of people taking notice of Congressman Paul's campaign, which I respected. I felt Governor Romney and Governor Huckabee were splitting the conservative vote. This allowed Senator McCain, a moderate, to perform very well. My final vote was cast for Governor Romney, but I knew that I would support any of the candidates against the Democrat nominee. I would not agree with any candidate on every issue, but I wanted a candidate with whom I knew I could agree on most of the issues. Therefore, when Senator McCain won the Republican presidential primary, I knew I would provide him my full support.

Since I was not an original supporter of Senator McCain, I was shocked to receive a call from his campaign in March 2008. Brian Forrest, who was the regional chairman for Senator McCain, told me that he had heard great things about me. He asked if I would be interested in serving as Senator McCain's San Joaquin County campaign chairman. After a moment of confusion, I asked, "Why me"? Brian advised they were looking for influential, organizational people. The McCain campaign staff had spoken with Laura Gadke, the California Republican Party Central Valley regional chairwoman, and she recommended me. I accepted the position, telling Brian to keep me informed of my required duties as chairman.

Although Brian and I spoke throughout the week, it appeared that he seemed uncertain of my responsibilities. I received campaign update emails, mostly from him, with names of those involved in Senator McCain's staff, including Bob Pacheco, who was Senator McCain's California campaign chairman. We discussed possible locations for large McCain signs. I called on Steve Ding, ex-Congressman Pombo's chief of staff, as he would be very familiar with the best locations. I spoke with Steve's wife, Shannon, and asked if she would be interested in working with me on the campaign. Sharon agreed, and I reported back to Brian that she was going to assist me.

Brian was also looking for someone willing to serve as Stanislaus County chairman and asked if I could recommend anyone. I thought of Darren Johnson. Darren was an articulate man and former marine. He had assisted in several political campaigns in both Stanislaus and San Joaquin Counties and was actively registering people into the Republican Party. Darren was exactly what the Republican Party needed. As a black man, he felt it was his obligation and duty to inform the black community how the Democrat Party's liberal policies had failed Black America. In no time, Darren was the Senator's Stanislaus County chairman.

I had also written about the Democrats' Failure in Black America in one of my letters to a newspaper editor:

"Democrats' Failure in Black America"

Martin Luther King, unknown to most, was a Republican. He believed Black America should strive to achieve the most of each opportunity through a dream of equality.

Most in Black America aligned themselves as Democrats through the social programs of the New Deal created by President Franklin D. Roosevelt, although he appointed a life member of the Ku Klux Klan, Senator Hugo Black, Democrat of Alabama, to the Supreme Court. In 1944, FDR chose as his vice president Harry Truman, who had joined the Ku Klux Klan in Kansas City in 1922. Prior to Roosevelt's New Deal, a majority of Black America had been Republican, thanks in part to President Abraham Lincoln's yeoman efforts to end slavery.

While Black America has been loyal to the Democrat Party, Black America has been taken for granted by the Democrat Party, using racial divisions and pandering from social dependence of government to maintain the base of Black America without providing any substance in return. Even today, the driving force behind policies like affirmative action is the liberal belief that Black America can't make it in America without assistance from the government. Such government assistance and lowering of educational standards have only weakened Black America. These lower educational standards, such as Ebonics, where English is mixed with slang, only places black American youth at a disadvantage.

The Republican Party believes in standards of high aspiration, provided by education, hard work, and a strong family to teach inner-values to their children. The Republican Party is the party of Abraham Lincoln, the first Republican president. Under President Lincoln, the Republican Party was formed as the anti-slavery party, which believed in a color-blind society where "all people are created equal."

The Democrats? They supported slavery and were the ones turning water hoses and dogs on black protesters in the 1960s. Remember Governor George Wallace? Democrat. Bull Connor? Democrat. United States Attorney General Robert Kennedy, Democrat, used wiretapping to spy on Martin Luther King. The former president of the Senate and United States Senator, Robert Byrd (Democrat of West Virginia) had commonly used the term "nigger." He was not only a former member of the Ku Klux Klan, he was a "Grand Kleagle"—an official recruiter who signed up members for $10 a head. He joined because it "offered excitement," and because the Klan was an effective force in "promoting American values."

Although prior to his death in 2010, he no longer claimed to be a Klan member, this one-time Democrat leader filibustered the 1964 Civil Rights Act for more than 14 hours. He also opposed the nomination of the United States Supreme Court's only two black justices, liberal Thurgood Marshall and conservative Clarence Thomas. During the vote of the 1964 Civil Rights Act, 82% of Republicans in the Senate voted for it, while only 64% of Democrats supported it.

As recently as the 1980s, Senator Ernest Hollings, Democrat of South Carolina, publicly referred to blacks as "darkies" and Hispanics as "wetbacks" without suffering any punishment from his party.

In 1983, Republican President Ronald Reagan signed into law Martin Luther King Day as a national holiday. However, in 1985, then-

Arkansas Governor Bill Clinton, Democrat, signed Act 985 into law, making the birthdates of Martin Luther King and Robert E. Lee, the general who led the Civil War Confederate Army, state holidays on the same day in Arkansas.

For 12 years, Governor Clinton did nothing to remove the Confederate symbol in the state flag, nor did he make any attempt to repeal a law that designated Confederate Flag Day as the Saturday immediately proceeding Easter each year. President Clinton has been hailed as "America's first black president" and is seen favorably in Black America; but what has he done for Black America? On May 5, 1993, he praised ex-Arkansas Senator J. William Fulbright as "my mentor," as he gave the nation's highest civilian award—the Presidential Medal of Freedom—to a man who spent the vast majority of his public career and life as a proud segregationist, who voted against the 1964 and 1965 Civil Rights Acts.

Republican President George W. Bush appointed more black Americans to higher positions than any other American president. If President Bush were a Democrat, many, if not most in Black America, would find his record commendable. However, since he was a Republican, he received no credit for the positive initiatives he had undertaken that would benefit Black America, including a voucher program for disadvantaged students in predominately black areas who are mired in under-performing schools, allowing parents a choice as to where they can send their children to school. However, this program has been blocked by Democrats.

If anyone in Black America votes or runs for office as a Republican, that person is immediately characterized as a traitor by the Democrat Party, often being slandering and threatened in order for the Democrats to hold on to a base they have taken for granted.

In 2006, Ken Blackwell and Lynn Swann each ran for governor in Ohio and Pennsylvania, respectively, while Michael Steele ran for the U.S. Senate in Maryland. Each faced racism as Oreo cookies were thrown at them, portraying them as black on the outside but white on the inside.

While there are racist people on both the right and the left side politically, according to a study at Yale, white Republicans were more likely to vote for a Republican candidate who is black, while white Democrats were less likely to vote for a black Democrat candidate.

Does the Democrat Party take advantage of those in Black America? Is it good for Black America to be represented mainly by one political party? Black America cannot gain political leverage if the Democrat Party is not forced to compete. The traditional solutions of the Democrat Party have not truly served Black America. It is time for Black America to believe they can do better and achieve the dream envisioned by Martin Luther King.

Frank Aquila, January 2008

Several of my friends teased me about not liking Senator McCain and then agreeing to act as his San Joaquin County chairman. Although I would not say I personally did not like the Senator, I just did not agree with some of his policies. However, I was proud to be his campaign chairman for my county. I took my position very seriously; and I undertook to do whatever I could to get him elected.

I stayed in touch with Darren, Shannon, and Brian, although it was not yet clear what we were expected to do within the California McCain campaign. The Senator planned to come through the Central Valley of California in May. With a limited amount of resources, the McCain campaign planned to focus on other moderate states, referred to as battleground states, more so than California, as it appeared not to be a Republican-friendly state. As it turned out, I had been given a great title but not much responsibility. I wanted to contribute more, so I began to research as to which person would be the best choice for Senator McCain's vice-presidential running mate.

Searching Sarah

In recent years, California has become more liberal and hostile toward the Republican Party, especially in the highly-populated Los Angeles, San Francisco Bay Area, and coastal communities. However, most of the Central Valley of California was and remains conservative. There just was not enough of a conservative population base in the more rural areas of the state to enable it to be a battleground state for the McCain campaign. I felt like I was living in the Socialist Republic of the State of California, a state of one-party rule with the Democrats' socialist and wacky agenda. I still believed that, with Senator McCain's moderate voting record and "maverick" persona, he could be competitive in the state.

I wanted to personally contribute to the campaign and know that I had accomplished something. I wanted to recommend someone who could compliment and electrify the ticket which would assist the Senator in winning the presidency. I researched different candidates on various news sites. Newsmax, an online news source, for example, listed 24 potential vice-presidential candidates for Senator McCain; but none of them completely satisfied me.

As I often listen to political radio talk shows while driving to and from work, I heard a host state Governor Sarah Palin of Alaska was going to be a rising star in the Republican Party and that someone should take notice of her. Although I had previously heard her name, I knew nothing about her; and she was not among the 24 potential vice-presidential candidates listed by Newsmax. I recall that, after she was chosen by Senator McCain on August 29, 2008, people began to ask, "Who is Sarah Palin"? But I had asked that question myself and had begun researching, six months earlier, in March 2008.

So who is Governor Sarah Palin? In March, the only fact I knew about Sarah was that she was the governor of Alaska. As I began to research, I became intrigued by her story and how she rose to governor. Sarah was a self-made woman and not your normal politician. She was principled, did not care about party labels, personal persona, or rhetoric. She was a woman of action and morality. She exposed corruption, even within her own party, while serving on the Oil and Gas Conservation Commission, becoming a Democrat darling. (9) She won the Republican primary against Governor Frank Murkowski, who had a powerful political family name in Alaska. She then went on to defeat Tony Knowles, a former two-term Democrat governor, in Alaska's November 2006 general election. She became very popular with Alaskans for stopping the "business as usual politics" and being a person who led not by words but by her own actions. Her overall approval rating was above 80% in Alaska, while some polls showed an approval rating as high as 90%. (10) She clearly was the most popular governor in America.

The younger Sarah Louise Heath was a lady of exemplary character, led by her faith in God. While leading a Fellowship of Christian Athletes chapter in high school, she was given the nickname "Sarah Barracuda," after playing with a fractured ankle on the Wasilla Warriors basketball team, which went on to win the state championship. (11) She was the team captain and led by a hard-working, self-motivated and disciplined example. (12) She was not a natural athlete and was often underestimated by her opponents as an "underdog." However, she was a natural leader. She led by example to achieve her goal of success beyond the expectations of others. This would be the repeated theme and story of her life.

As I continued to research Sarah, I was struck by how she was simply an ordinary woman determined to be the best she could be at everything she did. She was considered a "tomboy" with glasses and a "lady jock" involved in school sports. (13) She was humble and never vain about her looks or demeaning to others who may have been considered less attractive. In 1984, she entered the Miss Wasilla Pageant for a college scholarship. Again, she was underestimated and won the title of Miss Wasilla. (14) She went on to compete for the Miss Alaska title against other women. Many, if not most of those women, lived their entire lives involved in the trials of beauty pageants. She was not supposed to be there. She was an amateur. Diane Osborne, one of the sponsors of the Miss Alaska Pageant, revealed her concern for Sarah when she said, "I kind of worried how she would do on the stage," and "You have to have a certain go-get-'em to get up there and stand up for yourself, and she came across as such a shy, sweet girl." (15)

Although she did not win the Miss Alaska Pageant, she again exceeded expectations by placing first runner-up to Maryline Blackburn, who became the first African-American to win the Miss Alaska title. Sarah was also named Miss Congeniality and received her needed college scholarship money. (16) In the spirit of humility, she wrote a warm note to Ms. Blackburn on the back of a group photograph, "I do love you. You're more admired than even you know. And please keep God Number One. He's got great things for you, baby. Love, Sarah Heath."

Sarah went on to receive a bachelor's of science degree from the University of Idaho, majoring in communication journalism with a minor in political science. She impressed her adviser as a "go-getter," one of Sarah's characteristics throughout her adult life. (17) She was a natural in front of the camera and landed a job as a sports broadcaster in Anchorage. (18)

In 1988, Sarah married her high school sweetheart, Todd Palin, a BP Oil union field production operating supervisor and commercial fisherman. Todd and Sarah have five children whose names are not common. Each of their names represents thought and meaning of someone, something, or somewhere significant. Track, their oldest son, an All-Alaskan state hockey player, enlisted in the United States Army and served in Iraq. He was named after the sport of track and field, which was a sport Sarah loved to participate in with her father as the coach. Bristol, their oldest daughter, was named after Bristol Bay, a beloved fishing spot of her father. Some reports claim Sarah loved sports, including her time as a sports reporter, so much that she named her daughter after the town of Bristol, Connecticut, the headquarters of the ESPN sports network. Sarah had a dream of working in Bristol as a sports broadcaster. Willow, their middle daughter, was named after the Alaska state bird, the willow ptarmigan. Piper Indy, their youngest daughter, was named in tribute to the Piper Cub that Todd flies and the Polaris Indy he drove to win his first of four victories in the Iron Dog Snow Machine Race, a 2000-mile snowmobile race. Trig, their youngest son, was named after a great-uncle, a Bristol Bay fisherman.

During my initial research of Sarah, I learned that she was pregnant with Trig and nearly eliminated as a possible running mate for Senator McCain. Trig was born one month prematurely, with Down syndrome, on April 18, 2008. I continued to think about what an extraordinary lady Sarah was and submitted my first letter to the McCain campaign lobbying for her to be placed on the ticket as the vice-presidential nominee.

Todd and Sarah live a private life. As a wife, she is loving and faithful, supporting Todd's activities in fishing and as a champion Iron Dog racer. Sarah also assists Todd with their commercial fishing business. Sarah is also a loving, supportive, and nurturing mother. She has been involved in her children's schools and activities, encouraging them to excel in their goals and dreams, just as her own parents had previously encouraged her. She was president of the Parent Teacher Association (PTA), the largest volunteer child advocacy and grassroots educational policy organization in the world. She was involved in the PTA for 10 years, even while she served in public office as a Wasilla city council member and, later, mayor. While other politicians talk about education, Sarah puts her words into action, volunteering at the school, while raising young children herself.

Sarah's parents had her baptized as a Catholic as a baby and later, when they moved to Alaska, the family attended weekly services at the Wasilla Assembly of God Church during her childhood and teenage years. At age 12, Sarah committed her life to Jesus, professing Him as her Savior, and made a public confession of her faith when she was baptized, along with her mother and sister. Sarah was active in her church, singing in the choir and becoming involved in its youth ministry. Sarah's faith in God is the center in her life and was even while she was growing up. Her faith played a significant role in shaping her political future. (19) Sarah believes in the importance of being a testimony for Christ, not only in the church, but also in the community.

Ted Boatsman, one of Sarah's youth pastors, remembered Sarah as being "grounded" in her faith through her words and actions. He stated, "She has taken her honesty and lack of arrogance and turned them into real strengths. She's the same person now as when she was Wasilla's mayor. She treats people just the same." Another youth pastor, Theren Horn, had the most dramatic impact on Sarah's future. While speaking to a group of teenagers, he etched words into Sarah's mind that became her spiritual turning point in life, steering her toward a political future. Pastor Horn stated, "You are called by God for a purpose....Some of you will be called to political leadership." His statement had an immediate impact on Sarah's mind, creating a desire and dream within her to make a political difference. Years later, when Sarah was mayor of Wasilla and Pastor Horn visited her, she reminded him of that lesson and how his words impacted her life. She said, "I was called to politics, and that was the direction I took." Prior to Sarah making her famous vice-presidential acceptance speech in Minneapolis, Minnesota, her mother, Sally Heath, called Pastor Horn to tell him, "Whatever they say this is about, whatever they attribute this success to, we know where it came from. It came from your ministry in her life." (20)

Sarah has attended several evangelical churches since 2002, in both Wasilla and Juneau when she became governor. She always finds time to study the Bible, pray, and develop her relationship with God as a Christian. David Pepper, a pastor of the Church on the Rock in Wasilla, stated Sarah attended his church before she ran for governor in 2005. Sarah was described as a "genuine" and "authentic" lady. Pastor Pepper and other church leaders believe Sarah is a modern-day Esther, a queen whose story is recounted in the Old Testament of the Bible and who was credited with saving her people, the Jews, from destruction. (21)

As Sarah was raised in Alaska, she was also familiar with the Eskimo culture. Todd's ancestry is part Yupik Eskimo. The Yupik Eskimo culture has a tradition of honoring women who are supernaturally gifted to provide wisdom to the tribe. Naturally, women were leaders. The Yupik culture may have also influenced her desire to enter the political arena.

Through faith, culture, and determination, Sarah was destined to become a political leader. Her political career began in 1992, when she ran for the city council of Wasilla, the fifth largest city in Alaska. Recruited as a young, sharp resident of Wasilla, she became involved in city politics, realizing the decisions the city council made would affect her family and community. Her platform was to lower property taxes and limit government's role on the people, believing the people of Wasilla were "do-it-yourselfers" with no need of a "community organizer." (22)

The Wasilla city council members who recruited Sarah expected her to vote their way. But that was contrary to Sarah's political philosophy. She did not believe in "I'll rub your back and you rub mine" or "go along to get along" politics. Sarah believed she was a servant of the people, took her position seriously, was honest, principled, and did not believe in returning favors or being pushed or lobbied into a vote. Her conscience and what she believed to be right or wrong determined her vote. These characteristics would follow her throughout her political career. (23)

Almost immediately, she caused council members to become annoyed, a regular reaction of those who crossed her path in politics. She voted against an increase in the mayor's salary and government regulations that she believed would trample on the freedoms of the people of Wasilla. She did support a 2% sales tax, as long as property taxes were not increased, in order to allow Wasilla to have its own town police force. The sales tax passed and, the following year, Wasilla had its own police force. She personally read and reviewed each item in the city budget, every proposed regulation, ordinance, and any concern her constituents had. She always made herself available, taking calls at home, including nights, weekends, and holidays. There were sharp principled differences between Sarah and Wasilla's mayor, who promoted more government control, while she believed in limited government allowing for more individual freedom. She easily won a second term on the city council before venturing to challenge the mayor for his position.

Sarah was "underestimated" when she decided to run against the three-term mayor. She campaigned the old-fashioned way, going door to door, meeting voters, and talking about the city's issues. She campaigned on cutting property taxes and government spending, including the elimination of the very same pay raise the mayor received earlier, which she voted against while she was on the city council. She wrote that, when people asked for help from City Hall, they encountered "complacency, inaction, and even total disregard." She described the city's finances as "current tax-and-spend mentality" with "stale leadership." She suggested that a "new administration finally allows new input, fresh ideas, and ENERGY to work with the public to shape this city"! The voters responded, wanting "no more politics as usual," by electing Sarah as the new mayor of Wasilla. (24)

As mayor of Wasilla, Sarah was the chief administrator and, unlike the same position in most American cities, she had more responsibilities. She supervised the police department formed three years earlier while she was on the city council. She ran the public works department, the parks and recreation department, the planning office, the library, and the history museum. She presided at the council meetings and acted as the ceremonial representative of the city. She signed documents on behalf of the city and appointed, suspended, or removed city employees and administrative officials. She supervised the enforcement of the city laws, carried out the directives of the city council, and prepared and submitted annual budgets, including any newly-adopted programs. She prepared monthly city financial and operations reports, exercised legal custody over all city real and personal property and performed all other duties required by the council or by law. (25)

While many politicians gain their popularity by making promises, appeasing special interest, or granting favors and personal deals, a true leader is someone who will make difficult and even unpopular decisions in the interest of serving the people. Sarah was a leader, fought for limited government, elimination of government waste, whether or not a surplus or deficit existed, and took away special political perks. As she took her mayoral oath, she was serious in bringing "more efficient government" to the people and focused on the business they elected her to conduct, believing she was ultimately responsible to them. My childhood friend, David Martinez, who served with the U.S. Marines for 20 years, explained to me that a Marine's attitude is that, if someone says he can't do something, a Marine will say, "Get out of the way...I'll do it." That was Sarah's attitude. Whenever someone says it can't be done, she says, "Get out of the way...I'll do it." Her belief is there are those in politics who either eat better or sleep better, based on promises and decisions made and actions taken, and she has always preferred to sleep better.

As Sarah began her service as mayor of Wasilla, she was met with hostility by those who supported her long-time predecessor. She worked to control government growth, cut taxes that hindered both the private sector and the people of Wasilla, eliminated small-business inventory taxes and business license renewal fees, and cut personal property taxes. She also kept her promise to eliminate the mayor's pay raise, reducing her own salary by 10%. However, her critics complained and twisted her intentions to lead by example, accusing her of cutting her own salary to place herself in a lower tax bracket.

Sarah expected department heads in Wasilla to propose appropriate cuts within their departments to limit government growth and balance the city budget. When the police chief refused to reduce his department's budget and attempted to undermine Sarah's authority as mayor, she was forced to let him go. The city's librarian was a friend of the police chief; and both of them had campaigned against Sarah. She initially let the city's librarian go, feeling she was not "loyal" to her administration. She later reconsidered her decision, allowing the librarian to keep her position. Sarah had asked a "rhetorical question" to the librarian regarding the process of banning a book that may not have been appropriate for the city library. The librarian balked, claiming censorship, although no book was ever banned from the library. (26)

The museum director position was eliminated by Sarah; and two other department heads quit, which caused those affected to complain to the local press. The Frontiersman, the local Wasilla newspaper, had also supported the previous mayor. Blistering editorials were published condemning their own perceived thoughts of Sarah's leadership philosophy, opining that, "we are either with her or against her," in addition to articles claiming Sarah was on the verge of banning books from the library. (27)

There was some talk of recalls, but Sarah kept her mind focused on conducting the city's business. She secured funds needed to improve the city's infrastructure, paved roads, extended water and sewer lines, repaved the Wasilla Municipal Airport runway, put in many bike paths, and protected the region's many lakes by securing funding for storm-water treatment. She kept a jar including the names of all of Wasilla's residents, picking one name to call weekly in order to discuss the state of the city and how it was progressing.

Sarah won re-election in 1999 for her second mayoral term by over 75% of the vote. She introduced a temporary half-cent sales tax that built a multi-use sports center in the city, allowing sports to be played indoors throughout the year. Due to her transformation of the city, with the growth of small business and national chains opening for business in Wasilla, it became the fastest growing city in Alaska, growing by 26% in population during her term as mayor. Sarah was also elected president of the Alaska Conference of Mayors, leading several other mayors in dealing with issues, including municipal revenue sharing and advocating for local government control. (28)

As Sarah completed her second term as mayor, she again proved her critics wrong in their "underestimation" of her, exceeding her accomplishments beyond all expectations. She then set her eyes on seeking the position of Alaska's lieutenant governor in 2002. She campaigned as a hard-core fiscal conservative. Despite being outspent four-to-one by other well-known state officials, she finished second place in a five-way Republican primary and went on to assist other candidates in the 2002 general election.

Alaska U.S. Senator Frank Murkowski won the governorship in November 2002, which opened his former Senate seat for appointment by the Governor himself. There was speculation that Sarah would be chosen as his successor to the U.S. Senate. Sarah expressed interest, met with the Governor and, when asked what issue would be her key one as a senator from Alaska, she indicated it would be "energy." Governor Murkowski, instead, appointed his daughter, Lisa Murkowski, an Alaska state representative, as his successor. However, he did not forget about Sarah's interest in energy. In 2003, he did appoint Sarah to the Alaska Oil and Gas Conservation Commission as the Ethics Supervisor, for which she earned an annual salary of $124,400. Sarah accepted this appointment, knowing it would prove to be a great opportunity to learn more about Alaska's energy industry. (29)

The Alaska Oil and Gas Conservation Commission is an independent, quasi-judicial regulatory body that has a direct impact on people, companies, America, and the world. The Commission provides oversight of oil and gas development and production, oil and gas drilling, reservoir depletion, and metering operations in Alaska. It administers the Underground Injection Control Program for enhanced oil recovery and underground disposal of oil field waste. It also acts to protect underground freshwater and to resolve certain oil and gas disputes between owners. (30)

There were three governor-appointed commissioners to oversee the Commission. Sarah was appointed to represent the public sector, became chairwoman of the Commission, and oversaw ethical complaints or violations. She was expected to accept her six-figure salary and allow business to continue as usual. However, as she had proven, this was not part of her political philosophy. She had been appointed to a position, was going to take it seriously, and again, was "underestimated." Sarah had a strong personal belief the Commission had a duty to be fair, impartial, and keep the best interests of the country in mind, while she dedicated herself to verify no wrongdoing was taking place.

As Sarah began to undertake her duties, attempting to hold the oil and gas industry accountable to their contracts, she soon discovered ethics violations within the Commission itself. One of Sarah's fellow commissioners, Randy Ruedrich, was the Commission's Petroleum Engineer. Ruedrick was a contractor for an oil company (ARCO), while also serving as the State Republican Chairman and member of the Republican National Committee. He had used his position on the Commission to solicit money from the very oil and gas companies the Commission was charged with regulating. The U.S. Senate Energy and Natural Resource Committee was chaired by then-Senator Frank Murkowski in 1995. In 1995, Ruedrich, a former general manager of Doyon Drilling, testified to that Committee that disposing waste into the oil wells would improve environmental safety. It was later exposed that Doyon Drilling had also added hazardous material into the wells in an effort to save money. (31)

While serving on the Commission with Ruedrich, Sarah discovered he was sharing confidential Commission information with an energy lobbyist of a coal bed methane company that Ruedrich was supposed to be regulating. The credibility of the Commission itself, as well as Sarah's own as chairwoman and the ethics supervisor would be questioned. Governor Murkowski and state Attorney General Gregg Renkes refused to be involved in an investigation of Ruedrich, who himself had been appointed by the Governor. Sarah believed her commissioner position required her to tell the truth about unethical violations; however, this became difficult, since one of the other commissioners was involved in unethical activity. As she was prohibited by law from publicly discussing her concerns, she resigned, forfeiting her six-figure salary after less than one year on the Commission, due to a "lack of ethics" within the Commission itself. (32)

After her resignation from the Commission, Sarah exposed the unethical relationship between the Alaska Republican Party and the big oil industry. She filed a formal complaint against Oil and Gas Conservation Commissioner Randy Ruedrich, accusing him of benefiting from the very companies he was supposed to be regulating and exposing his unethical violations. Sarah also joined Democrat legislator Eric Croft in filing a complaint against Gregg Renkes. Renkes had close ties to Governor Murkowski and was accused of having financial conflicts of interest in negotiating a coal exporting trade agreement with Taiwan while having ownership interest in the company. Both Ruedrich and Renkes subsequently resigned, paying hefty fines. However, Ruedrich was reconfirmed as the state GOP chairman. (33)

As Sarah had given up a secure, high-paying position and exposed a leader within her own party, she seemed to have committed political suicide. There was no guarantee she would work again in the public sector, or even if she would be able to procure a private sector position. The Democrats would say she took that action to cause herself to look good and was "covering up for the GOP," while Republicans would never trust her as one who turned on a fellow Republican and "jumping on board with the Democrats." She now had gained several political enemies but proved, again, she was very much "underestimated," exceeding her duties beyond expectations. (34)

Sarah then spent time at home with her children and reflecting on her faith in God. She felt her political career had been cut short. From a Bible passage, Jeremiah 29:11-13, she read, "For I know the plans that I have for you, declares the Lord. Plans for peace and not for calamity, to give you a future and a hope. When you call upon Me, I will hear you; when you search for Me, you will find Me, if you seek Me with all your heart." Sarah prayed to God daily and asked Him for guidance and wisdom to assist her in making the right decisions. Sarah was soon provided her answer. The Alaskan people began to call upon her to run for governor. Juneau was full of corruption, and Alaska was in financial trouble. The growth of government bureaucracy was out of control. Oil companies held the reins of control. At the same time, the people became more and more disgusted with the same politics as usual. Sarah had become the trusted and independent voice of the people; and she proceeded to announce she would run for governor with a mission to change politics in Alaska.

Governor Murkowski had suffered politically after appointing his daughter to his former Senate seat and using state funds to purchase a jet for his travel. He was also facing criticism for negotiating a sweetheart deal with the oil producers on a natural gas pipeline.

Sarah was on a roll and connecting with the voters of Alaska. The Anchorage Press described Sarah as "a small-town, angel-faced mother of four, an avid hunter, and a fisher with a killer smile, who wears designer glasses and heels and hair like modern sculpture, who's taking it to the boys ever so softly." (35) Sarah ran her campaign on a clean-government platform, declaring that education, public safety, and transportation would be the three cornerstones of her administration. She won the three-way Republican gubernatorial primary with 51% of the vote and went on to defeat the former Democrat Governor Tony Knowles in the November 2006 general election, despite a third-party candidate, Andrew Halcro, who was backed by the GOP state chairman and Sarah's old nemesis, Randy Ruedrich.

In December 2006, Sarah Palin became Alaska's first female governor and, at age 42, she was the youngest governor in the state's history. (36) She was now the chief executive of the largest state in the United States, covering 20% of the total land mass of the entire country, holding 20% of the nation's crude oil reserves, and whose land and waters bordered both Canada and Russia. She wasted no time getting down to the business of her people with her amazing ability to multitask on several issues at the same time.

The first issue of business Sarah chose to address as governor was to push through a bipartisan ethics reform bill. Prior to her winning the governorship, many Alaskan lawmakers were under criminal corruption investigation, led by the U.S. Department of Justice, the

Federal Bureau of Investigation, and the Internal Revenue Service, for illegally receiving large campaign contributions from oil executives. Those lawmakers were known as the Corrupt Bastards Club (CBC) and were ultimately charged with bribery, conspiracy, and extortion for their involvement in illegal activities with Veco Corporation. Several of them went to prison. Sarah assisted the FBI in the investigation, and she signed the ethics legislation in July 2007, calling it the "first step" in cleaning up Alaska politics. (37)

The next issue Sarah took on as governor was energy and negotiating with big oil, the main players being Exxon Mobil, Alaska BP PLC, and Conoco Phillips. The Democrats have always tried to tie the Republican Party and big oil together as having a "cozy relationship" with each other. However, this cannot be said about Sarah. Even though her husband was employed by British Petroleum, she held all the oil and gas companies accountable for the actions they had previously promised. The large oil companies had political power and controlled many legislators but, with the Corrupt Bastard Club dissembled, along with the defeat of Governor Murkowski, they had to deal directly with Sarah. As governor, Sarah dealt with the big oil executives in the likeness of President Ronald Reagan when he was dealing with the Soviet Union. Sarah would "trust, but verify." She respected the industry and the contributions they made to Alaska as its main industry; however, she expected them to fulfill the obligations of their leases. She had campaigned against business-as-usual for the oil companies and business for the people.

Sarah was ready for the battle, using her experience as chairwoman of Alaska's Oil and Gas Conservation Commission, where she also supervised ethical complaints and violations from the oil industry. She also became chairwoman of the Interstate Oil and Gas Compact Commission during her time as governor, a position she used to acquire much of her expertise of the oil and gas industry. She wanted an open policy process that was friendlier to Alaskans and quickly rescinded 35 appointments made by former Governor Murkowski, including his former chief of staff, James Clark, to the Alaska Natural

Gas Development Authority. Sarah then appointed Tom Irwin as the natural resources commissioner. Irwin had been fired in 2005 for writing a memo stating that Governor Murkowski was going too easy on the oil companies in earlier pipeline negotiations. Irwin would go on to say, "Governor Palin didn't submit to the force and control of the large companies. She forced [them] into a fair and competitive process." Sarah also created Alaska's Petroleum Systems Integrity Office (PSIO) to oversee energy development and ensure oilfield equipment was safe to operate.

Governor Murkowski had worked a back-room deal with the oil companies, which held long-term leases to finance and build a natural gas pipeline under the North Slope of Alaska. The deal would have guaranteed a tax cut for the oil companies and would have assured that the rates would remain the same for decades; but the deal was rejected by the Alaska legislators. As the oil companies prepared to negotiate a new deal with Governor Palin, they soon learned that Sarah did not intend to allow them to call the shots any longer. Sarah respected the industry but would hold her ground and require the oil industry to negotiate on her terms. Her high school nickname, "Sarah Barracuda," would be resurrected by the press. She insisted the oil companies had an obligation to deliver gas through whatever pipeline Alaska built. The oil companies had been sitting on their leases with little action over the previous thirty years. Sarah believed in a market-driven plan for the oil companies to compete against each other on the pipeline to get the process moving. She pushed for public negotiations, proposed the Alaska Gasoline Inducement Act to allocate $500 million to begin the process of constructing a natural gas pipeline, and proposed a freeze in production taxes for ten years for those producers who agreed to transport their gas through the pipeline. (38)

Sarah clashed with the three oil companies who refused to negotiate with her on her terms. They refused to bid against each other on the project and would not commit their gas to the pipeline if another company was selected to build it. Sarah did not flinch or fall prey to their refusal or intimidation, even if it meant cutting off the company who employed her husband. She cut through the government regulations and got the process moving. She brought another company to the table to take action on the pipeline, leaving the other oil companies as spectators. Sarah signed legislation making Canadian-based TransCanada Corporation, which was the sole AGIA-compliant applicant, the licensee to build and operate the $26 billion pipeline. BP and Conoco Phillips both agreed to form a partnership with North Shore Oil to develop a competing pipeline called Denali. Together, the Trans-Canada pipelines were being built to transport natural gas from Alaska's North Slope, through Canada, to the lower 48 states, projected to be completed by 2018, while the Denali plan was being built and scheduled to be completed in 2013. Many in the industry believe both plans will ultimately come together. (39)

Exxon continued to balk at Sarah's proposals, so she attempted to revoke its license at the Point Thomson oil and gas fields, which is one of the largest undeveloped oil fields in America. Exxon had been sitting on its lease like an investment property, making excuses to each administration as to why it couldn't start drilling. Exxon had attempted a "plan of development" with the previous administration in 2005, but it was rejected due to a lack of firm commitment to produce oil and gas. According to Mark Myers, Alaska's oil and gas director, Exxon's "30-year record of non-development and delay...makes a mockery" of lease obligations. Sarah held Exxon on the grounds of its failing to develop on its lease since it had not drilled a well there since 1982. Exxon threatened with a lawsuit. Sarah responded that Exxon knew the way to the court house. Exxon buckled and brought in equipment to begin drilling on the oil and gas fields at Point Thomson. (40)

Former Democrat Governor Steve Cowper believed Sarah was the main reason the pipeline moved forward. He said, "The gas pipeline was such a muddle when she arrived that I thought to myself this will never be built." (41) Ultimately, her perseverance and determination caused the process to move, ending decades of gridlock on the pipeline.

Sarah then adopted a plan through the legislature to raise taxes on the oil companies' profits from 22.5% to 25%, which became known as Alaska's Clear and Equitable Shares (ACES). The oil companies again balked that the tax would affect their project investments. Conservatives in the legislature also disagreed with the increase in taxes. Sarah believed the resources belonged to the people of Alaska and, with the high energy cost; she used the revenue generated from the tax to give a special one-time payment of $1,200 to the people. The rebate was separate from the annual dividend check of $2,069 in 2008 that Alaskans received as part of their share of the state's oil wealth. Again, Sarah was "underestimated" as she has been her entire life—this time by the oil companies. However, again, she achieved her goals beyond the expectations of others.

Sarah was serious about reducing government spending and stated her opposition to excessive pork-spending projects, cutting Alaska's dependence on government funding. While various sources argue exactly how much was spent by Alaska during Sarah's governorship, all sources show that Alaska made substantial cuts in spending as well as reductions in federal earmark requests by as much as 80%, placing many requests in the "when hell freezes over stack." Sarah also refused to accept much of the 2009 controversial federal stimulus money, accepting only 55%. However, the legislature overruled her veto. She also used her line-item veto to cut millions more from the Alaskan state budget. Sarah also placed the state checkbook online, allowing the people of Alaska to see how the state money was being spent. (42)

While she was once open to the idea of the Granina Island Bridge, better known as the Bridge to Nowhere, she withdrew her support, as well as the state funding portion of the project, which ended the controversial project. She also kept a campaign promise to forward fund education, granting school districts greater flexibility in educational planning. Sarah would later make a statement regarding her veto of many state projects, stating, "Vetoes included within the decision-making process are not a reflection on the project itself but upon the state's responsibility to pay for the proposed projects." Sarah recognized the importance of changing the system and her obligation to responsibly govern.

Sarah continued to lead by example. She promised to sell the Westwind Two jet that was purchased by the Murkowski administration. Sarah placed it on eBay and sold it. She also opted to save Alaska money by dismissing the governor's personal cook as well as the driver for her state-issued Chevy Suburban. Sarah was perfectly fine with cooking her own meals as well as driving herself. She also accepted less state per diem for herself and her family than the former administration, even though she had a larger family. She was entitled to both a travel allowance and reimbursements to hotels but chose to drive home instead. All together, Sarah cut her gubernatorial expenses 80% below those of former Governor Frank Murkowski.

Sarah came under her own investigation after she fired Public Safety Commissioner Walter Monegan, whose services were in control of the governor. It was alleged that Monegan was fired for failing to fire a state trooper, Mike Wooten, who was Sarah's former brother-in-law. Sarah claimed the firing was due to differences in budgeting. The investigation became known as "Troopergate," and Monegan later stated that he was never specifically told by Sarah to fire Wooten. (43)

The Democrats hired an investigator, Representative Hollis "Gunny" French, who was a biased, staunch liberal and who lied about being in the U.S. Marine Corps while running for the legislature. The McCain campaign found a photograph showing French and others who called for the investigation at the Obama headquarters in Anchorage, Alaska during the investigation. The whole investigation was tainted, politically motivated, and lacked fairness and neutrality. The investigation concluded there was no evidence to support Monegan's refusal to fire Wooten as the reason for his dismissal, but it was likely a contributing factor. The McCain-Palin campaign then issued a statement that Sarah "acted within her proper and lawful authority in the reassignment of Walt Monegan."

Sarah, with the assistance of Senators Murkowski and Begich, fought for retirement benefits from the federal government for Alaska Territorial Guard members who fought during World War II, which was ultimately awarded by the federal government for these veterans. Sarah also signed legislation that authorized Alaska "to enroll in the Interstate Compact on Education Opportunity for Military Children."

Sarah was also a mother of a combat soldier. Her son, Track, had enlisted in the U.S. Army and is serving in Iraq. Sarah understands the anguish of knowing her child is serving in a hostile environment overseas and dealt with it while receiving her own media shots during the 2008 presidential campaign. Sarah acknowledges that she is proud of Track but, naturally, worries about him.

Then there is Trig. In March 2008, just as I began to do my own research on Sarah as Senator McCain's chairman from my county, there was a surprise announcement. Sarah was pregnant and would ultimately delivery Trig the following month, on April 18, 2008, just two days before I sent my first letter to Senator McCain's campaign recommending Sarah to be on the presidential ticket. Trig was born one month premature with Down syndrome. Sarah has always been one to respect God's gift of life and, instead of asking "Why us?," Todd stated, "Well, why not us?" They both had been vocal about being pro-life and understood that every innocent life has wonderful potential. Sarah acknowledged there was a double standard of men and women serving in public office, stating, "I can think of so many male candidates who watched a family while they were in office," and continued, "There is no reason to believe a woman can't do it with a growing family."

So who is Sarah Palin? Sarah spent ten years working as an executive in municipal government, as a mayor and governor of the largest state in America, un-intimidated by corrupt politicians while unwilling to compromise her values as to what is right and wrong. She served on numerous boards and commissions throughout Alaska. Sarah was a member of the working class of America, a union member working as a journalist, and married to a union worker in the oil fields. Sarah was Commander-in-Chief of the Alaska Army National Guard. She was a volunteer with her church and the Parent-Teacher Association (PTA). She is a life-time member of the National Rifle Association (NRA) and enjoys fishing and hunting. Sarah stays active running in marathons and caring for her children, including one with special needs. She is a pro-life advocate and a mother of a combat soldier. Sarah was also named one of Alaska's Top 40 under 40, Alaska's Public Works "Person of the Year," and was inducted into the Sigma Beta Delta Honor Society at Alaska Pacific University. Sarah Palin is the American story of an American girl living the American dream. Always "underestimated." Always "exceeding expectations."

Sarah on the Issues

As a social and fiscal conservative, it is vital for me to know the character of a candidate. Sarah Palin has established herself as one who is led by high morals, honesty, and integrity established by the values instilled in her by her family and her sincere faith in God. Also, as I continued to research Sarah as a potential vice-presidential candidate, it was important for me to learn her positions on various issues. I believed we needed a candidate who represented conservative thought, with whom we could agree on most of the issues.

Too many people choose or eliminate a candidate based upon a single issue. These people, one-issue voters, are not prudent. We should not have tunnel-vision but, rather, look at the entire picture of the candidate, including all opinions on various issues, and find one with whom we can agree on most of them. As it is impossible to even get our own family members to agree on every issue, how can we expect a hundred million people to agree on them? In addition, it is important to find a candidate who can relate to the people and has the ability to communicate well in explaining to the people why particular issues are important. This is where Sarah would compliment Senator McCain on the ticket. She was an executive and a conservative. Being younger, she could relate to younger generations and, being a woman, she could relate better to women. She could add strength in areas of the Senator's weakness. So what are Sarah's positions on the major issues concerning America?

Abortion, Marriage, and Gay Rights

Nothing exemplifies Sarah's true, unique character and conviction than her position on abortion. She is pro-life and believes that life begins at conception. Again, Sarah has proven herself to be an example of living by her actions, not by words or rhetoric.

In the midst of fulfilling the duties of a challenging career, Sarah found herself unexpectedly pregnant with a child who was to be born with Down syndrome. She could have found it convenient to abort a normal child in order to carry on her career. Knowing she was carrying a child with special needs, Sarah could have easily justified that fact in her own mind as an excuse to abort her baby. No one would have even known or suspected the pregnancy, as she had kept it private from the public almost her entire pregnancy. In fact, Sarah did not reveal her pregnancy until March 2008, just one month before she delivered Trig prematurely. However, she never considered abortion to be an option and rejects any sympathy for raising a child with special needs. Instead, she and Todd consider themselves uniquely suited to raise Trig. Liberals have great difficulty understanding Sarah's special appreciation for those who struggle, but she considers Trig her gift from God and understands that every innocent life has wonderful potential.

As a gubernatorial candidate in 2006, Sarah answered a questionnaire supporting funding of abstinence-before-marriage programs in schools. She also supports contraceptive education in schools, aware that some parents may not discuss certain topics with their children and agreeing children should be able to receive information from other resources.

Sarah disagrees with the Supreme Court decision in *Roe v Wade* and, instead, believes each state should determine its own laws without a federal mandate or public funds supporting abortion. While Sarah disagrees with the law, she also respects the U.S. Constitution and believes in the duty of an oath to uphold it and the law. Sarah is naturally against partial-birth abortion—abortion in the last trimester of a pregnancy. While she believes in the sanctity of life, that every baby is created with a future and potential, she does support the exception for abortion if a mother's life is endangered. As governor, Sarah also signed legislation granting birth certificates for stillborn babies.

During the presidential campaign, it was quickly revealed that her daughter, Bristol, was pregnant. Risking an adverse response from the public and media, Sarah was forthright and announced her love for her family and appreciation for her daughter's decision to choose life. Since the birth of her own son, Bristol has promoted abstinence as the alternative choice for teenagers.

When President Obama placed his hand on the Bible and took his oath of office, he swore to uphold the U.S. Constitution. While campaigning for president, he stated he supported traditional marriage but, as president, he has violated his oath by directing the Justice Department to no longer defend the Defense of Marriage Act, a federal law enacted by Congress. In essence, the President made himself a judge determining which laws he believed were right. He, therefore, over-stepped and violated his duties and oath to the U.S. Constitution. One wonders that, if Sarah Palin were president and ordered the Justice Department to no longer defend *Roe v Wade*, there would be an outcry by both liberal groups and the media of abuse of power and violation of the U.S. Constitution. Of course, Sarah's long-standing commitment to uphold the rule of law renders any such scenario extremely unlikely.

Sarah believes in traditional marriage as being between one man and one woman. She supports the public's right to settle the marriage issue, as between one man and one woman, by voting its will through a constitutional amendment. Although she personally opposes same-sex marriage, she is receptive to the concerns of discrimination. As governor, she complied with the Alaska State Supreme Court and signed same-sex benefits into law.

Sarah also supports the Safe Haven Bill she signed into law in 2008. That law allows a mother of an infant to give up her child into the physical custody of a peace officer, physician, hospital employee, fire station volunteer or employee, or emergency medical service without fear of prosecution. She believes adoption is the best plan for permanency for children in foster care.

Abortion is not just a choice—it has become a profitable business. I wrote the following letter to regarding the abortion business to a newspaper editor:

"The Abortion Business"

Abortion is a difficult, serious, and personal decision for many; but for others it is a profitable business. Each year, 42 million abortions occur worldwide, approximately 115,000 daily, with one in every five pregnancies ending in an abortion in America. (See www.abort73.com.) While the government should be doing more to prevent these abortions and encouraging life, Planned Parenthood enjoys a profitable billion-dollar business.

Often, women are forced into an abortion by a man, who does not want the baby, or teenaged girls, who have been subject to statutory rape by an older boyfriend. (See www.afterabortion.org/petition/Forced_Abortions.pdf. See also a 2008 ad, http://www.yeson4.net/.) A friend of mine, who performs ultrasounds, recently told me of a couple who went to determine the sex of their baby. When the couple found out "it's a girl," they left and returned approximately six months later. Again, "it's a girl" and, again, the cycle repeated itself two more times, until the fourth time, the couple was told, "it's a boy." Three times a child was aborted for being the wrong sex—a girl. This is wrong!

Abortion should never be a means of birth control or determining the make-up of your family. Often the emotional effects on the women can be mentally damaging with emotional trauma or even suicide. (*See* www.leaderu.com/orgs/tul/pap1.html.)

Another gruesome procedure is partial-birth abortion, which is an abortion in the last trimester (seven to nine months) of the pregnancy, where the half-born baby is forced to keep part of its body in the birth canal, preventing it from being completely born or the procedure would be considered murder. Scissors are then stabbed in the back of the baby's head to insert a tube to suck out the baby's brain and collapse the skull. As you can imagine, this causes excruciating pain to the baby before death. (*See* www.abortionfacts.com/literature/literature_9313pb.asp.) Michelle Obama called the procedure "a legitimate medical procedure." (*See* story by Illinois nurse Jill Stanek at www.wnd.com/news/article.asp?ARTICLE_ ID=51121.)

Occasionally, some babies are born alive before the abortion procedure is complete. Their live bodies are shelved in a utility room, without medical care, to die. When legislation was presented to force doctors to treat the children, then-Senator Barack Obama voted four times against a bill that provided aid to the baby who survived being killed. One survivor, Gianna Jessen, told her story. (*See* www.richleonardi.blogspot.com/2008/09/born-alive-truth.html.)

But why would Obama be against such a procedure? Follow the money given to Planned Parenthood. The Obama administration has given $1.5 billion to Planned Parenthood, including a 133% increase in funding for clinics in America. One billion in tax money has also been given for international abortion groups. Not surprisingly, all of the Planned Parenthood local action organizations and affiliates voted unanimously to recommend endorsing Obama for president, and he has rewarded their endorsement. Within minutes of Obama taking the presidential oath of office, the official Whitehouse.gov website was changed to add language supporting pro-abortion policies.

Planned Parenthood is an organization that profits from each abortion performed and accepted money in an undercover investigation from a man fronting as a racist donor who wanted his funds earmarked for aborting black babies. (*See* www.michellemalkin.com/.../planned-parenthoods-obscene-profits.) Planned Parenthood accepted the money. Does this mean Planned Parenthood is racist? Its founder, Margaret Sanger, has referred to blacks, immigrants, and indigents as "human weeds" and "reckless breeders." She cautioned, "We do not want word to go out that we want to exterminate the Negro population" but wrote that they were "spawning…human beings who never should have been born." She said, "the chief aim of birth control" is "more children from the fit, less from the unfit." (*See* www.dianedew.com/sanger.htm.)

The Democrats today are establishing many laws against the right to life. President Obama has appointed numerous liberals from pro-abortion organizations, such as National Abortion Rights Action League (NARAL), into critical positions within the government. Obama and the Democrats are pushing through a federal bill, called the "Freedom of Choice Act," that would end parental notification or consent for abortions on minors, mandate taxpayer-funding of abortions, allow abortions in military hospitals, end waiting periods before having an abortion, deny doctors the right to refuse to perform abortions, overturn many abortion clinic health regulations, and legalize partial-birth abortion. (*See* www.cc.org/olcampaign/stop_foca.)

On March 9, 2009, President Obama also signed Executive Order 13505 to force taxpayers to fund embryonic stem cell research, and removed funding for life-saving adult stem cells. Therefore, the government would fund the growing of embryonic stem cells of a human fetus up to eight weeks and then abort the fetus to use the stem cells for scientific purposes, even though scientists discovered in 2007 that adult stem cells were just as effective.

It is no wonder President Obama has appointed John Holdren as his science czar. Holdren has advocated the formation of a "planetary regime" that would use a "global police force" to enforce totalitarian measures of population control, including forced abortions and mass sterilization programs conducted via the food and water supply. According to Front Page Magazine and other sources, Holdren considers overpopulation as mankind's greatest threat, and he and his co-authors have advocated some of the following proposals in his book, "Ecoscience":

1. Forcibly and unknowingly sterilizing the entire population by adding infertility drugs to the nation's water and food supply.

2. Legalizing "ompulsory abortions," i.e., forced abortions carried out against the will of the pregnant women, as is commonplace in Communist China. Women in China, who have already had one child and refuse to abort their second child, are kidnapped off the street by the government authorities and forced to carry out the procedure to abort their baby.

3. Babies who are born out-of-wedlock or to teenage mothers to be forcibly taken away from their mothers by the government and put up for adoption. Another proposed measure would force single mothers to demonstrate to the government that they can care for their children, effectively introducing licensing to have children.

4. Implementing a system of "involuntary birth control," where both men and women would be mandated to have an infertility device implanted into their bodies at puberty and only have it removed temporarily if they receive permission from the government to have a baby.

5. Permanently sterilizing people whom the authorities deem have already had too many children or who have contributed to "general social deterioration."

6. Formally passing a law that criminalizes having more than two children, similar to the one-child policy in Communist China. (*See* www.informationliberation.com/?id=26965.)

Our Declaration of Independence reads, "We hold these Truths to be self-evident, that all Men are created equal, that they are endowed by their Creator with certain unalienable Rights, that among these are Life, Liberty and the pursuit of Happiness." While our Declaration of Independence refers to rights and life, the Democrats have clearly become the party of death.

Frank Aquila, July 2010

Civil Rights

Sarah considers herself a feminist who believes in equal rights for all and equal pay for equal work. She believes no one should be discriminated against based on race or gender and, in August 2006, she told the Anchorage Daily News, "No woman should have to choose between her career, education, and her child." However, she experienced the same double standards she is against from those demanding equal rights and protection. The National Organization of Women (NOW) and other feminist organizations were silent when Sarah faced sexist and discriminatory attacks just one week after being nominated as Senator McCain's running mate only because these liberal organizations, which claim to stand for equal protection and rights of all women, disagreed with Sarah on her political positions, including abortion. Sarah even acknowledged the determination of Hillary Clinton, who also took a lesser degree of the same sexism and discrimination based upon her being a female.

During the campaign, Sarah was criticized and judged as a mother. The media's repulsive attack was that she could not hold the position of vice president, as it would take away too much time from her responsibilities as a mother. Sarah responded back in an interview with Katie Couric on September 30, 2008, stating, "I'm a feminist who believes in equal rights, and I believe that women certainly today have every opportunity that a man has to succeed and to try to do it all, anyway. And I'm very, very thankful that I've been brought up in a family where gender hasn't been an issue." No one in the media questioned Barack Obama about being a father while he campaigned for president for 18 months or how he would balance his family life while serving as president. No one questioned what kind of father he is or how much time he spent with his daughters.

Sarah extended benefits to Americans with disabilities. As a mother of a child with special needs, she has shown her ability to understand the difficulties experienced by families or individuals who have special needs and issues. Sarah has worked to ensure that each individual with disabilities is respected as an equal citizen with equal opportunities, including education, employment, recreation, leisure, and social activities within the community. She declared July 26, the anniversary of the American Disabilities Act, a day for the people of Alaska to celebrate the expanded freedoms and equal opportunities of those with disabilities.

Sarah also recognized Juneteenth Day, a holiday commemorating the end of slavery in America. She proclaimed Juneteenth Day in Alaska, a day for the people of Alaska to reflect upon the importance of freedom and to encourage people to organize and participate in events in their communities.

She also recognized the birthday of Martin Luther King as a great man and American hero who encouraged Americans to look past their differences where all, regardless of color, were treated equal, receiving liberty and justice.

Governor Palin made March 20 Native HIV/AIDS Awareness Day in recognition of American Indians and Alaskan Natives who had a significant risk of the HIV/AIDS virus. She recognized the importance of focusing on the national effort, as well as tribal efforts, to bring education and prevention to those who needed it.

Sarah believes in providing equal rights to same-sex couples, is against any discrimination based upon sexual orientation, but recognizes marriage as between one man and one woman. Sarah vetoed a bill for same-sex benefits, which she later signed to comply with the Alaska State Supreme Court decision allowing same-sex couples to be eligible for equal benefits.

Crime, Drugs and Capital Punishment

Sarah supports adequate funding for public safety and stated as governor, "Feeling safe in our communities is not something which we can compromise on. There is the need for policing in all its forms, the court system, prosecutors, and corrections." Sarah established FBI Day in Alaska to support the FBI in its fight on global crime. She signed the Omnibus Crime Bill which strengthened laws for dealing with sexual predators and violent offenders as well as allowing police to collect DNA samples from adults arrested for any felony. She signed legislation requiring violent gang members to wear electronic monitoring devices as a condition of their probation. She believes we should not be "warehousing" those convicted of crimes; and those in prison should be rehabilitated and required to work. She also recognizes victims' rights, ensuring that victims of crime are treated with dignity and respect.

Sarah believes in capital punishment and stated during a debate for governor that she was in favor of capital punishment, especially in heinous cases where a child was murdered. Although capital punishment was abolished in the Alaska in 1957, Sarah stated she would support and sign any law passed by the legislature reinstating it.

Sarah stands firmly for enforcement of drug laws. Although she admits to trying marijuana when younger and cannot say, as President Bill Clinton did, that she never inhaled it, she did not like it. She pointed out it was legal under Alaska state law, although illegal under federal law. She does not agree with the legalization of marijuana, as she feels it sends the wrong message to children. However, she is not opposed to allowing doctors to prescribe something, such as marijuana, if it is believed that prescription will assist a suffering cancer patient.

Education and Labor

Sarah was raised in a home where a great deal of emphasis was placed on education. Her father, Chuck Heath, was a middle school science teacher, and some rooms in their home were like an amateur museum of nature, filled with wildlife exhibits. Her father taught Sarah and her siblings to respect science and school, expecting them to achieve good grades, and encouraged college attendance after high school. Sarah maintained that respect for her education, earning her bachelor's of science degree from the University of Idaho, majoring in communication journalism and minoring in political science.

In her gubernatorial campaign, Sarah emphasized education as one of her most important issues. She believed every Alaskan should have an opportunity to obtain an education, to work, and to achieve success. In 2008, in her State of the State Address, she emphasized the obligation to "open education doors to allow our youth to achieve their education." She believes every child should be cherished, loved, and taught as the future hope for our world. Sarah promised reform to education and brought forth a three-year plan to fund all school districts, focusing on early learning, providing opportunities for college, support for vocational-technological training, and workforce development, including parental rights to assist in choosing what is best for their children, whether that be vocational training, public education, private education, charter schooling, or home schooling.

Governor Palin fully funded kindergarten through 12th grade, including transportation and municipal school debt reimbursement, funding toward the increased retirement costs for local school districts, as well as "early funding of education" to allow school districts advanced notice of the funding they could expect from the state to properly plan their school budgets. She believes that teachers need to be paid a professional salary, that America needs to place more emphasis on our schools, and that the schools' focus should be on accountability and achievement. Sarah recommended revamping "no child left behind" by placing more flexibility in it, with a greater emphasis on teaching.

As a Christian, Sarah believes both evolution and creationism, or "intelligent design," should be available for all students to understand, providing students the opportunity to be exposed to both viewpoints. She feels a healthy debate among the students would be good for them but, as governor, never advocated or forced the state Board of Education to add creationism to the state-required curriculum.

Governor Palin believed in other alternative methods of education, including charter schools, home schooling, tutoring programs, and many other successful programs in Alaska. She supported equal treatment of home-schoolers across the state and respected the rights of those parents who used faith-based material. She believed that responsible government should assist any existing educational program that proves itself successful to provide each child the opportunity for an appropriate education. She was also interested in assisting students who were at-risk, providing both parents and children the educational material needed in their early years and approving after-school programs and centers to develop activities and assist children with their homework.

Governor Palin believed in a curriculum that teaches both ethics and character. The ABC method is a local educational program that involved core principles of trustworthiness, respect, responsibility, fairness, caring, and good citizenship. The program is centered around these principles with nightly homework focused on patriotism, ethics, and citizenship training. Sarah also believes "under God" should remain in our Pledge of Allegiance.

Governor Palin believed the University of Alaska should be available to Alaska's own students in order for them to not go without an education. She sought additional funding for specialty degrees in engineering and health care. She placed a great deal of emphasis on vocational and technological training as well as workforce development. She believed there should be a focus on foundational skills that students would need for the "real world." She sought additional funding for apprenticeship and construction programs. She coordinated with the Alaska Department of Labor and Workforce Development to start the Alaska Construction Academy to train both adults and students in the skilled careers of carpentry, electricity, plumbing, and welding.

Sarah also believes in vocational work requirements for those incarcerated to provide them an easier re-entry transition into society. She believes a society of skilled workers will benefit the local, state, and national economy. Sarah and her husband, Todd, were both union members; but she believe unions should be required to obtain the permission of the union members before using union dues to support political donations. She believes a union's responsibility is for the worker, not political interests.

Despite attacks alleging the contrary, Sarah believes in equal pay for equal work regardless of race or gender.

Economy and Taxes

Sarah is a fiscal conservative, believing in limited government, low taxes, and fiscal and individual responsibility. She is a firm believer in free-market capitalism and opening opportunities for all to compete, through reduction of taxes, to encourage the growth of small business. She believes people should be allowed to make their own choices and decisions in life, with government oversight but not government intervention at every level. With ten years of executive experience as mayor of Wasilla, the fifth-largest city in Alaska, and governor of Alaska, the largest state in America, Sarah cut people's taxes, reduced government spending, and even reduced her own individual entitlements available to her as mayor and governor.

Alaska stands out from other states, includes 20% of the land mass of America and is responsible for a large portion of the oil production in America. With its sparse population of approximately 700,000 people, there are less people in the state than in most metropolitan cities. As the tax base for Alaska's citizens is low, in order to supply the needs of the state, Alaska is dependent on its oil revenue and federal assistance to fund infrastructure. Therefore, it is difficult to provide a traditional financial assessment of Alaska. As a result, through my research, I noticed how many of Sarah's critics manipulated and twisted facts to distort her record as though she were a tax-and-spend liberal and not fiscally conservative. This conglomeration of half-truths and half-lies merely exposes the fact that Sarah Palin is truly a fiscal conservative.

While Sarah was governor, she did oversee the highest tax increase in Alaskan history; however, the increase was not imposed upon the people. It was on the powerful oil companies which had received preferential treatment, over many years, from the previous administrations. Sarah wanted to ensure Alaskans received their fair share of the income from the oil companies, which used publicly-owned land to produce their oil. Sarah's tax increase on the oil companies was a modest 10%, increasing their share of taxes on publicly-owned land from 22.5% to 25%. She then returned much of the money back to the people through a "rebate," separate from the yearly dividend Alaskans receive from the state's oil savings account. (44)

As governor, Sarah oversaw the largest state budget in Alaska history, as she required the oil companies to pay more into the state's coffers. Billions of dollars from the oil industry fueled the larger budget. Sarah did not spend the excess money but, rather, budgeted $2 billion for the state to place in savings and suspended the state's $.08 per gallon tax on gasoline. (45)

During her time as governor, Sarah substantially reduced federal earmark spending requests from the previous administrations, cutting a half-billion dollars from her first two state budgets. She cut $230 million the first year and $268 million the second year using the line-item veto, causing both Republicans and Democrats to cry foul over the denied federal funding requests, known as earmarks or pork. (46)

As mayor of Wasilla, her record took a similar road. She also reduced government spending while cutting property taxes. Her critics quickly point to the voter-approved half-cent sales tax that Sarah supported as mayor for an indoor recreation sports arena as their proof that she supports raising taxes. In actuality, what she did was cut property taxes, eliminate business taxes and fees, transformed the city into a larger commercial center, which ultimately expanded the city revenue in the budget by 50% from $6 million in 1996, when she was first elected mayor, to $9 million in 2002, her last year as mayor of Wasilla.

Sarah has a proven record as a fiscal conservative, delivering high levels of government services to the people, while reducing taxes and reckless government spending. Sarah supports extending the Bush tax cuts to all Americans and supports a plan to extend tax relief to business owners, in order to create jobs and expand businesses in America, just as she accomplished as mayor of Wasilla and as governor of Alaska.

Energy, Global Warming, and the Environment

There are arguably few people with greater knowledge regarding energy than Sarah. Energy is of great importance in the state of Alaska, where oil and gas are the primary resources, accounting for many jobs and state revenue. Energy has always been her key issue; and she gained her expertise in this area after serving as commissioner and chairwoman on the Alaska Oil and Gas Conservation Commission, in 2003 and 2004, and chairwoman of the Interstate Oil and Gas Compact Commission, in 2007 and 2008.

Energy is what drives every economy in the world, and energy is part of our everyday living in America. There is no greater resource and power. We need gasoline for our vehicles and electricity for our homes.

Electric vehicles need electricity, windmills need petroleum to manufacture their parts and blades, and solar panels are made using fossil fuels. Organic food purchased in stores require fossil fuel to harvest the product, trucks to deliver the product, and electricity to power the market where the product is sold and used to cook or refrigerate the product at home. Yet, the energy industry is regulated and controlled by the federal government, including bans on offshore drilling, laws blocking development in the Arctic National Wildlife Refuge (ANWR) in Alaska, restrictions on both clean coal projects, and nuclear power development. Essentially, the environmentalists and federal government have controlled the entire energy industry, restricting America from energy independence and causing dependence on foreign oil, which has not only hampered the growth of our economy but affects our national security.

Sarah has stated her motto, "Drill, Baby, Drill," loudly and clearly, stating now is the time to use our natural resources and remove government bans and restrictions that have been a detriment to America becoming energy independent. Democrats have tried to tie Republicans together with the oil companies as having "cozy relationships" in the past. However, they cannot do that with Sarah, who quit her $124,400-a-year job on the Oil and Gas Conservation Commission and blew the whistle on the unethical relationships between individuals in the Republican Party and the oil industry. Sarah took on the oil companies as governor, in the interest of the people, providing the people "rebates" through an increased tax on the oil companies. She set the rules with the oil companies on her terms, forcing them to start production that had not been seen for over 30 years. She also created Alaska's Petroleum Systems Integrity Office (PSIO) to oversee energy development, ensure oilfield equipment was safe to operate and, in particular, its expertise in preventing oil spills as a commitment to protect the water of Alaska.

Sarah strongly believes we should have several alternative means of energy, through both a comprehensive short-term and long-term energy plan, as 70% of the oil used in America is imported from foreign countries. Sarah also believes the states should have the ability to consider nuclear energy as an energy source, such as the newer, smaller, nuclear reactors that were developed and are now used in Alaska.

Although Sarah's preferred method of extracting oil is through land, she does support safe exploration of offshore drilling and embraced offshore drilling in 2008, after being previously opposed to it. She believes the federal government has implemented too many regulations and restrictions on the oil companies and should, instead, be overseeing the drilling process and holding those companies responsible for unsafe practices or use of improper equipment.

Currently, the Outer Continental Shelf (OCS) is off limits to offshore drilling but, in fact, recent studies indicate that oil is actually oozing out of the ground, both on shore and under the ocean floor, especially at Coal Oil Point in Santa Barbara County, California. Large amounts of natural gas and 11 to 160 barrels, or 450 to 6700 gallons, of oil seep into the water each day. It is estimated that the OCS has 112 billion barrels of oil and another 656 trillion cubic feet of natural gas. Therefore, if we drill in the OCS, we can reduce the pressure of oil on the ocean floor while reducing large amounts of oil seepage into the ocean, which should satisfy environmentalists. (47)

During the Gulf of Mexico oil spill, Sarah pointed out that environmentalists locked up safer areas on dry land. While she has a history of fighting against big oil and attempting to introduce fairer contracts, very few people are aware of President Obama's own "cozy relationship" with British Petroleum, the oil company responsible for the Gulf or Mexico oil spill. I wrote about this in the following letter to a newspaper editor:

"Obama's Oil Buddy"

In the 2008 election cycle, the top recipient of political donations from British Petroleum (BP) was Senator Barack Obama, as BP also spent a massive $16 million to influence legislation in 2009. No wonder it took the Obama administration nearly two weeks to respond to the Gulf oil spill. Nor did the federal government take control of preventing the oil from contaminating the Gulf shores, creating the largest environmental disaster in history.

What if President Bush were still in office and he done the same thing? When Hurricane Katrina hit New Orleans, the media blasted President Bush for a lack of federal response, which ultimately resulted in FEMA Director Michael Brown being replaced. Bush received much criticism for taking four days to go to New Orleans; and even critics like Louis Farrakhan accused Bush of blowing up the levees to cause New Orleans to flood. Yet, Barack Obama took 12 days to go to the Gulf Coast. Conspirators remain relatively silent after a poor federal government response in the federal-protected waters off the Louisiana coast, where the BP oil platform blew up, causing 5,000 barrels (210,000 gallons) to 100,000 barrels (4,200,000 gallons) of oil to flow into the ocean each day, based on various websites.

The media rarely mentions the mistakes caused by the Obama administration. They did not criticize Obama's Interior Secretary Ken Salazar when he went whitewater rafting during the disaster and "categorically excluded" a detailed environmental review of the drilling plans submitted by British Petroleum, as required by the National Environmental Policy Act, because it posed virtually no chance of harming the environment. We hear nothing about how the Obama administration gave a safety award last year on the very BP drilling platform that is leaking in the Gulf, or that the Interior Department claimed it inspected the drilling platform just 10 days before the accident, even though the rig's emergency shutoff valve purportedly had a dead battery. Environmentalists and the media would have gone wild if this happened under President Bush. The media would have accused Bush of being slow to respond and unconcerned about the environment, while conspirators would have accused Bush of doing this to raise oil prices for his oil buddies. Yet it took Obama eight days to fully deploy cabinet-level federal officials.

Many Democrats have already tried to somehow blame Bush but, according to a Washington Times editorial on May 25, 2010, "the Blame Bush game became increasingly worn and unconvincing." Louisiana Governor Bobby Jindal has tried to get the federal government to be proactive in controlling the spill and preventing this environmental disaster from reaching wildlife off the Louisiana coast by building sand berms along the coastal waters; but the federal government again was slow to respond to the request, which resulted in much wild life being killed.

As a result of this disaster, Obama has sought to cast blame on whomever he can and, according to the Washington Times editorial, "everything is somebody else's fault in Obamaworld." However, the Obama administration has oversight over the federally-protected water and the drilling industry. Therefore, Obama cannot escape some blame.

Representative Mike Pence stated, "The oil spill in the Gulf of Mexico is an ongoing tragedy, the American people deserve action to protect our Gulf, and they deserve answers. The American people deserve to know what happened on April 20th, and Congress should investigate it thoroughly. The American people deserve to know why the administration was slow to respond, why necessary equipment was not immediately on hand in the area, and why President Obama did not fully deploy cabinet-level federal officials until he spoke at the White House on April 28th."

After two months of oil continuing to flow into the Gulf and, according to Zogby polling, only 16% of the public approved of the federal government's handling of BP's Gulf oil spill. Obama was feeling the pressure to get something done. He was demanding that BP fix the problem and blamed it for its "slow and frugal efforts." Obama further stated that he sought an "ass to kick" for the oil disaster. Perhaps he should look for a "community organizer" who also deserves the same repercussion for his lack of organizing and failure to prevent the greatest environmental disaster in history. Sounds like Obama and BP make perfect mates as oil buddies.

Frank Aquila, June 2010

On May 24, 2010, Sarah pointed out in a letter, titled "Big Oil: Learning from Alaska's Experience," that U.S. Coast Guard Commander Thad Allen described the Obama Administration's approach to the oil spill crisis as "keeping a close watch," while BP was tackling the problem, at the company's own pace. She summed up in that letter, "Taking a tough stand to protect our environment, while domestically drilling for much-needed energy sources, is the only way the public can trust government and industry to safely work toward energy independence. We need to 'drill, baby, drill' responsibly, safely, and ethically. That's the way Alaska's Department of Natural Resources (DNR) accomplishes its mission in America's 49th state."

Governor Palin believes strongly in "drill, baby, drill" and argues that we should utilize our natural resources toward energy independence, which would also lower gasoline prices for consumers. She disagrees "with any candidate who would say we can't drill our way out of our problem or that more supply won't ultimately affect prices. Of course it will affect prices." She has been a proponent of natural gas, believes the lower 48 states will benefit from the natural gas pipeline now being developed in Alaska, and supports the distribution of natural gas. She worked tirelessly to cut government regulation through the Alaska Gas Inducement Act (AGIA), as oil companies have now teamed up to move natural gas through the $30-$40 billion 1,715-mile pipeline currently being built from Alaska through Canada into the lower 48 states. Sarah is ultimately responsible for spearheading the action on this project, which is the largest private-sector infrastructure project in North American history.

Governor Palin is also a strong proponent of opening up a small area of the Alaska National Wildlife Reserve (ANWR) for drilling, after a large pool of oil was discovered in that region. ANWR is about

19,286,722 acres; and Sarah has proposed opening a small area of approximately 2,000 acres, the size of the Los Angeles Airport, for drilling. She explains that drilling there is essential in reducing America's dependence on foreign oil. That area of ANWR is considered a wasteland with very little life. Environmental organizations have stated opening up the field to oil drilling would destroy the habitat and calving of the porcupine caribou in the region. However, studies have shown the heat generated from the oil pipelines actually assist the porcupine caribou in their reproductive state and would cause their population to grow. Studies of the porcupine caribou have further shown that ANWR is also not their only calving and habitat ground. This issue frustrated Sarah, as governor, and she stated, "I get frustrated with folks from outside Alaska who come up and say, 'You shouldn't develop your resources'."

And Governor Palin is absolutely correct on the issue. According to a recent study, according to the Denver Post, there are more oil reserves within the borders of America than all the other proven reserves on the earth. With reference to the 16,000-square mile area of the Colorado Rocky Mountain Region, named the Green River Formation, a barren stretch of land covering portions of Colorado, Utah, and Wyoming, James Bartis, a lead researcher stated, "We've got more oil in this very compact area than the entire Middle East." Utah Republican U.S. Senator Orin Hatch said, "The amount of oil is staggering. Who would have guessed that in just Colorado and Utah there is more recoverable oil than in the Middle East"? Geologist Walter Youngquist called the oil beneath the Green River Formation "a national treasure."

So how much oil is there? According to this particular study, there are approximately two trillion barrels of untapped oil. By comparison to other countries, the report's official estimates are: 8 times as much oil as in Saudi Arabia; 18 times as much oil as in Iraq; 21 times as much oil as in Kuwait; 22 times as much oil as in Iran; and 500 times as much oil as in Yemen—and this is just in the Colorado Rocky Mountain Region of the Western United States!

In other areas of America, there are 200 billion barrels of oil located in North Dakota, South Dakota, and Montana, while it is estimated that this oil discovery may even produce up to 500 billion barrels of oil. By comparison, there are only 260 billion barrels of oil in Saudi Arabia. It is estimated that, in Alaska alone, there is enough oil and natural gas to keep America independent from any other source for the next 200 years!

America has become so advanced in our technology and, with our environmental controls in place; we can absolutely extract all of this available oil without endangering the environment. The human race has a responsibility to protect the environment while, at the same time, supplying the resources to help us live. Without oil exploration, we will continue to depend on foreign oil while skyrocketing prices on oil will affect our everyday living. Prices on all items we purchase, including food, will continue to increase as the price of oil climbs. It is estimated that, if we explored and extracted our own oil, gasoline prices at the pump could drop to as low as $.60 to $1.20 per gallon (excluding the amount of taxes per gallon applied by each individual state), vastly assisting our economy, relieving hardships on struggling families, and all areas of our lives in America.

Could rising gasoline prices be really what the Democrats and President Obama want? According to an ABC News article, Obama's Department of Energy Secretary Steven Chu told the Wall Street Journal in September 2008, "Somehow we have to figure out how to boost the price of gasoline to levels in Europe." So what is the price of gasoline in Europe? According to the article, current gasoline prices in Europe are $7-$9 per gallon. Chu claims he favors gradually increasing taxes over 15 years so people will be persuaded to buy more fuel-efficient vehicles and live closer to their places of employment.

During a CNBC interview in 2008, Obama implied that he had no problem raising the cost of gasoline but would prefer a "gradual adjustment." This explains Obama's desire for his proposed multi-billion high-speed rail project, awarding the Democrat-desired alternative-energy contracts, and shunning anyone in the way as anti-environmentalist.

In addition, America is also rich in coal, with more reserves than just about anywhere else in the world. We have approximately 275 billion tons of coal, which is enough coal for America for the next 250 years!

According to various liberal sites, Governor Palin has been accused of being an anti-environmentalist. As governor, she was forced to deal with many false claims that she was not a friend of the environment or wildlife and, again, only half the truth was reported about her. Liberal sites have accused Sarah of supporting the killing of wolves in Alaska as part of a predator-control policy by the Alaska Department of Fish and Game. Hunters were required to show proof of the killed wolves by showing the left foreleg in order to receive their $150 bounty. While this is true, the fact reporters omit is that Governor Palin implemented this policy to increase the moose and caribou populations.

Governor Palin also opposed strengthening protections for the beluga whales in the Alaskan Cook Inlet. She pointed out that Alaskan scientists claimed hunting was the only factor causing the whales' decline, and the hunting of the whales had been controlled through co-operative agreements with the Alaskan native organizations. Recent studies have shown that the decline of the beluga whale has been halted through putting hunting controls into place. However, the beluga whale still remains an endangered species. Federal scientists do not attribute their decline in the Alaskan Cook Inlet to human population in the region.

As governor, Sarah had to deal directly with another environmental issue. Polar bears were listed as an endangered species, since their habitat was supposedly threatened by global warming. Sarah disagreed, stating the polar bears were well-managed while, in fact, their population had actually increased over 30 years as a result of conservation. Sarah actually sued the federal government's EPA department for misusing the Endangered Species Act, claiming, "the decision was not based on the best scientific and commercial data available," and argued that listing polar bears as an endangered species would actually cripple the energy development in the prime polar bears' habitat of Alaska's northern and northwestern coasts. Sarah claimed there was not enough evidence to support the listing, debunking the claim of global warming effects on polar bears. The Alaskan scientists and environmental groups also responded. This occurred before global warming, which is now referred to as "Climategate," was proven to be false, a worldwide hoax of lies and fraud, and a worldwide scam.

Many in America and the rest of the world had believed that global warming was truth and fact; and any who disagreed were labeled by the Democrat Party as anti-environment or against "Saving the Earth." However, through the discovery of leaked emails and documents from Hadley Climate Change Unit, it has been revealed that the information was intentionally falsified to show the climate of the earth was warming when, in reality, it has actually been cooling. (*See* http://whatreallyhappened.com/WRHARTICLES/globalwarming.html.) The environmentalists duped the American and world citizens with the documentary film promoted by Al Gore, "Inconvenient Truth," for which he received the Nobel Peace Prize for this convenient lie to advance the Democrat agenda and deceiving world citizens with false data alleging the earth was warming.

News corporations, like NBC, gave favorable coverage to the Democrat agenda, including the advancement of global warming in its news coverage. NBC is owned by General Electric, which has supported the Democrat Party and would benefit from any advancement of alternative-energy contracts.

The Green Earth movement became so powerful that international treaties were signed; and corporations and legislators throughout the world became "environmentally friendly" to combat global warming. Now, each of our own personal lives have been affected by this hoax—what type of vehicle we drive, our inability to extract our own oil in America, and the "eco-friendly" light bulbs we must use (which contain mercury) but have been mandated by Congress. (*See* www.businessandmedia.org/articles/2008/20080326103035.aspx.)

Now, President Obama and the Democrat Party are still aligned to push America toward globalization by attacking capitalism as the cause of destroying the earth. "Cap and Trade" promotes the communist ideals and government controls to save the people by saving the planet through a global tax and redistribution of wealth by trading carbon pollutions on a world market. The cost of this would be $3 trillion to reduce fossil fuel by 80% by 2050 in a scam for Americans to pay our ecological debt. (*See* www.storyofstuff.com/capandtrade.)

BP, which I explained earlier was a large contributor to the Obama campaign, actually helped write impending "Cap and Trade" legislation and would have benefited from its passage. Stanley Greenberg, a BP advisor, owned a Washington, D.C. apartment and, ironically, allowed Obama's former chief of staff, Rahm Emanuel, to live there rent-free for five years. Greenberg's consulting firm re-branded "British Petroleum" to the slogan "Beyond Petroleum," in an effort to make BP known as a "green petroleum company," as BP is not just an oil company but, also, an energy company. BP is ready to reap the rewards offered through "Cap and Trade" that it and the Democrats put together in their legislation. (*See* http://newsflavor.com/world/usa-canada/bp-wrote-cap-and-trade-plot-thickens/#ixzz0ssEw8D00.) Again, anyone who attacks the environmental movement or questions its philosophy are branded anti-green, anti-eco-friendly and non-lovers of the planet.

Unfortunately, we have seen politicians who have become more interested in environmental issues stifling the interest in energy development. Prior to the global warming hoax being corrected, Governor Palin was skeptical about the misleading information that greenhouse emissions from man had caused, conducted, or engaged in the effects of climate change or global warming. She still believes that we should be capping carbon emission and doing what we can to keep the planet clean. She has pointed out that few countries care about the environment and air as much as America does. Our equipment is very environmentally-friendly compared to the rest of the world. Yet, since we have limited our own natural resource production, we have placed ourselves in a position to rely on foreign oil from countries which pollute more emissions into the atmosphere than America would ever allow. Therefore, in 2007, Governor Palin created a Climate Change Sub-Cabinet charged with preparing a climate change strategy for Alaska, recommending guiding Alaska's mitigation and adaptation efforts, and exploring ways to promote the development of renewable energy.

Sarah believes we are stewards of the earth and, while we should utilize the resources available, we should also protect the natural environment. She also believes we should encourage other nations to protect the environment as well as tap into alternative energy. Sarah also believes we should be using alternative energy while conserving fuel, our petroleum products, and our hydrocarbons to keep the planet clean, while we continue to explore our own oil resources. In May 2008, Governor Palin signed a bill to spend $250 million on renewable energy power plants that will run on solar, wind, hydroelectric, and natural gas. Governor Palin proposed a statewide energy plan in January 2009 that set a goal of 50% of Alaska's power to be generated by renewable resources by 2025. This is twice the amount of 25% promised by then-candidate Senator Obama during his presidential campaign. According to the Alaska Energy authority, Alaska is already generating 25% of renewable resources.

Sarah has a short- and long-term comprehensive energy plan that goes beyond "drill, baby, drill." She promotes easing restrictions and regulations that hamper production but promotes oversight on the energy industry to protect the workers, as well as the environment, while alternative energy is developed for our future. The Democrats have no immediate energy plan, except limiting production and raising taxes, in order to force Americans to stop using our natural resources. I pointed this out in the following letter to a newspaper editor:

"Democrats' Energy Plan Equals High Gas Prices"

During the 2006 election, the Democrats tried to link the Republican Party as the cause of high gas prices. In 2006, the national average for gasoline was $2.18 per gallon, and Nancy Pelosi stated on April 24, 2006, "Democrats have a commonsense plan to help bring down skyrocketing gas prices," and "Democrats have a plan to lower gas prices." However, since the Democrat Party took control of Congress in January 2007, gasoline has doubled to $4.49 per gallon. Why? The reason is as simple as supply and demand, not smoke and mirrors, as the Democrats so often try to portray to the people.

Every country runs on oil, and because the United States uses more oil than it produces, we must pay the world market price for oil. We now import 65% of the oil we use from other countries. Even though we have the resources in America to be energy independent, the Democrats have blocked every effort to make this a reality.

Alaska sits on a pool of oil, which could be explored without disrupting the Arctic National Wildlife Refuge. The people of Alaska overwhelmingly support this proposal. Now, the Russians have begun exploration for oil in the Arctic Circle. Oil is also known to be in Utah, Colorado, and off the coast of California and Florida. Florida recently declined exploration of oil off its coast. As a result, Cuba has made a deal with China to tap into the same pool of oil 60 miles off the coast of Florida. Because China and Cuba lack the superior technology we have in America, they would benefit from our resources. However, if an oil spill did occur, they will take the oil, leaving America with the potential oil spills to clean up.

In 1995, the Republican-controlled Congress passed a bill to open a small region (ANWR) in Alaska to tap into the available oil. The Democrats protested, claiming there would be no results "for 10 years." Ultimately, the Congressional bill was vetoed by President Clinton. Even by the Democrats' own timetable, America could have been energy independent of foreign oil in 2005!

As usual, the Democrats have attempted to stop our own exploration of oil in America. This has put our environment and our economy at risk because we are forced to rely upon the world for oil. Compared to other nations in the world, America has superior, environmentally-friendly technology guided with environmental laws to gather the resources while protecting the environment.

In 1990, the Democrat Party led Congress to mandate the use of cleaner-burning gasoline, which forced oil companies to use the additive MTBE for the purpose of cleaning up the air. However, this additive contaminated drinking water.

The Democrats have also stopped all progress on any oil or gasoline refinery being built in America since the 1970s.

Frank Aquila, November 2007

Foreign Policy and National Security

Foreign policy is tied to national security, and there are many issues directly related to both, including free trade, military, war, homeland security, and immigration.

Many have tried to distort Sarah Palin's record by taking her comments out of context in an attempt to make her seem inexperienced in matters of foreign policies, especially when she stated, "you can actually see Russia from land here in Alaska." Sarah was correct in the statement that Russia can be seen from Alaska. However, her statement was not made as a comment to portray that was the extent of her foreign policy knowledge but, rather, just stated a fact. Instead, the statement was ridiculed and distorted by "Saturday Night Live" to make people believe she even said she can see Russia from her backyard!

Sarah Palin gained considerable experience in foreign policy in her time as governor. Governor Palin had to work directly with two neighboring countries—Canada by land and the Russian territory within a couple miles off the coast of Alaska. It was necessary for Governor Palin to negotiate sensitive agreements, including agreements regarding fishing rights with both countries, in order to keep peace. She also worked to expand partnerships overseas with Alaskan companies, negotiating several free trade agreements. Under her leadership, Alaska exported to over 100 foreign countries, generating $3.9 billion in exports, which was the second-highest level in Alaskan history. (48)

Governor Palin also hosted many delegations from around the world, two of which were a delegation from China, to observe the delivery of rural health care throughout Alaska, and a delegation from Canada, to discuss the economy and trade issues. Sarah stated, "We live in an increasingly interconnected world, and improving global literacy among our citizens contributes significantly to our nation's foreign policy, economic competitiveness, and national security."

Sarah is critical of President Obama's foreign policy. She views his decisions as misguided as she watches the President reach out to hostile countries and dangerous dictators, while apologizing for past American policies or stating to the world that America "has shown arrogance." Sarah believes our foreign policy should distinguish America's friends from those who are our enemies, and that we should seriously recognize the threats we face as a nation.

As Commander of the Alaska Army National Guard, Governor Palin supported the ground-based missile defense system at Fort Greeley and other Alaskan bases that were vital for the protection of America's mainland against foreign enemies. Governor Palin requested the Missile Defense Agency funding to be fully restored "to guarantee our protective measures remain the best in the world." However, the Defense Department refused to comply, cutting funding for the program. Sarah disagreed, stating, "Fort Greeley plays a crucial role in the nation's security." Sarah was critical of the Obama administration's cuts to the national defense system, including the missile defense programs when North Korea conducted rocket tests on April 5, 2009.

Besides traveling to Canada and Mexico, Sarah has visited other countries. Governor Palin was active in visiting military troops and those serving from Alaska. She traveled to Kuwait, near the Iraq border, and into Kosovo, to learn about the mission of those serving, and visited injured soldiers in Germany. She continued her international journeys after she left the governor's office, visiting both India and Israel to share her vision of America. Sarah is interested in building our relations with countries who are our allies. She stated that India and America should continue cooperation and praised the free-market principles and urban economic resurgence through free trade practices that India has employed. Sarah also recognizes Israel as a key ally and spent time in discussions with the Prime Minister of Israel regarding "the key issues facing his country," as she wishes to see the relationship between America and Israel grow and strengthen.

Sarah has always been a supporter of Israel and wants to affirm "strong bonds of friendship" between America and Israel. Governor Palin signed a resolution confirming Alaska's support for Israel. On September 2, 2008, Governor Palin met with the American Israel Public Affairs Committee (AIPAC), a pro-Israel lobby, where she stated she would "work to expand and deepen the strategic partnership between the U.S. and Israel." After the meeting, a spokesman from AIPAC stated Governor Palin "expressed her deep, personal, and lifelong commitment to the safety and well-being of Israel."

During the 2008 vice-presidential debate, Sarah stated, "Israel is our strongest and best ally in the Middle East. We have got to assure them that we will never allow a second Holocaust, despite, again warning from Iran and any other country that would seek to destroy Israel that that is what they would like to see. We support Israel. A two-state solution, building our embassy, also in Jerusalem, those things we look forward to being able to accomplish, with this peace-seeking nation, and they have a track record of being able to forge these peace agreements."

In an interview with Barbara Walters, Sarah expressed her support for the expansion of Israeli settlements in Palestinian territories stating, "I believe that the Jewish settlements should be allowed to be expanded upon, because the population of Israel is going to grow. More and more Jewish people will be flocking to Israel in the days and weeks and months ahead. And I don't think that the Obama administration has any right to tell Israel that the Jewish settlements cannot expand." Sarah believes a two-state solution is best to resolve the Israel and Palestinian conflict but does not second guess Israel's right to defend itself. If Israel does not hold its ground in negotiations with the Palestinians, it will not be able to hold on to its land. The Arab nations' goal is to take back all the land of Israel, piece by piece, until Israel no longer exists.

However, the Obama administration has not been as friendly to Israel. According to The Washington Times, on February 17, 2011, "Obama is siding with Israel's enemies. He is slowly fracturing America's longstanding alliance with the Jewish state and leaving it isolated on the world stage." The article continues, stating Israel is "our best friend in the Middle East and the region's only genuine Western-style democracy," resulting in a "wedge between Washington and Jerusalem. Israelis rightly will conclude that Mr. Obama is willing to betray a pivotal pro-American ally in order to appease the 'Arab Street'." The article goes on to state, "During his presidency, Mr. Obama has appeased and emboldened radical Islamists."

According to USATaxpayer.org, the Obama administration's 2009 budget gave $7.5 billion to Pakistan, $400 million to Palestine, $23 million to Kenya for abortions, $150 million in stimulus grants to the Muslim Brotherhood, and $900 million to the Palestinian Liberation Organization (PLO), as well as "hundreds of millions" of our tax dollars to "refurbish mosques" as part of a "community relations" effort, according to a news report. At the same time, Obama was attempting to rewrite American history when he announced to the world, while visiting Turkey, that we are not a Christian nation. Are we a Christian nation?

"Is America a Christian Nation?"

Is America a Christian nation? From the writings of Columbus to the Mayflower Compact to the Declaration of Independence to the structure of the U.S. Constitution, America's founders clearly applied Christian principles in the foundation of America.

James Madison, the architect of the U.S. Constitution, stated, "Religion [is] the basis and Foundation of Government." Madison was inspired by the Holy Bible in the formation of our three equal branches of government. He used Isaiah 33:22, "For the Lord is our Judge. The Lord is our Lawgiver. The Lord is our King. He will save us." Through this verse, Madison formed the judicial, legislative, and executive branches of our government.

The Declaration of Independence is the document that makes the U.S. Constitution legal. Of the 55 signers of the Declaration of Independence, 52 were deeply-committed Christians, some of whom were ministers. It was the same Congress that formed the American Bible Society, immediately after creating the Declaration of Independence. This document says that our rights come from "our Creator" (God) and the U.S. Constitution was signed "in the year of our Lord" 1787, after the Treaty of Paris was signed in 1783, ending the Revolutionary War, with the documented writing, "in the name of the Holy and undivided Trinity" (God, Jesus, and the Holy Spirit).

The very first act of the first congress was to bring in a minister and have congress led in prayer. The Continental Congress then voted to purchase and import 20,000 copies of scripture for the people of this nation. Afterward, four chapters of the Holy Bible were read.

In 1892, the United States Supreme Court declared, "This is a Christian nation," and "Our laws and our institutions must necessarily be based upon the teachings of the Redeemer of Mankind. It is impossible that it should be otherwise; and in this sense, and to this extent, our civilization and our institutions are emphatically Christian."

After World War II, congress declared, "In God We Trust" on our currency. Christian holidays, Christmas and Thanksgiving, have been declared national holidays, and "one nation under God" is in our Pledge of Allegiance. The preamble to the state constitutions of every one of the 50 states in the United States makes an unapologetic declaration of God.

References to God are engraved on numerous national monuments. On the Washington Monument, it is engraved on the aluminum capstone, the Latin phrase Laus Deo, which means "Praise be to God." Lining the walls of the stairwell are carved tribute blocks that declare such Biblical phrases as "Holiness to the Lord" and "Search the Scriptures." On the U.S. Capitol, in the House chamber is the inscription, "In God We Trust." On the Supreme Court Building, in a number of places, are images of Moses with the Ten Commandments. When you enter the Jefferson Memorial, you will find many references to God. A quote that runs around the interior dome says, "I have sworn upon the altar of God, eternal hostility against every form of tyranny over the minds of man."

While liberals have tried to remove references to God and confuse people with misinterpretations, such as "separation of church and state," this phase is not even in the U.S. Constitution. The phase "separation of church and state" was first written by President Thomas Jefferson in a letter to the Baptist Association of Danbury in Connecticut. The founding fathers did not want a government run by a particular religion, as in the "Church of England," where people could not worship freely. Therefore, a separation was intended to protect government from control by a religion and to protect religion from control by government, not to build a confrontational wall to keep government and religion separated.

History shows that George Washington, Thomas Jefferson, James Madison, Benjamin Franklin, John Adams, and many of our other founding fathers established America as a Christian nation. Here are some of the recorded references of what they actually said:

"God who gave us life gave us liberty. And can the liberties of a nation be thought secure when we have removed their only firm basis, a conviction in the minds of the people that these liberties are a gift of God? That they are not to be violated but with His wrath? Indeed, I tremble for my country when I reflect that God is just; that His justice cannot sleep forever." Thomas Jefferson, 1781

"Suppose a nation in some distant region should take the Bible for their only Law Book, and every member should regulate his conduct by the precepts there exhibited…What a paradise would this region be." John Adams, 1756

"We have been assured, sir, in the sacred writings, that 'except the Lord build the House, they labor in vain that build it' I firmly believe this; and I also believe that without His concurring aid we shall succeed in this political building no better than the builders of Babel." Benjamin Franklin, June 28, 1787

"It is the duty of all nations to acknowledge the Providence of Almighty God, to obey His will, to be grateful for His benefits, and to humbly implore His protection and favor." George Washington, October 3, 1789, who not only started the tradition of being sworn in as president with a Bible, but who knelt down and kissed the Bible. President George Washington later said, "It is impossible to rightly govern a nation without God and the Bible."

"Providence has given to our people the choice of their rulers, and it is the duty as well as the privilege and interest of our Christian nation to select and prefer Christians for their rulers." Chief Justice John Jay, October 12, 1816

With all this, President John Adams stated, "The Bible is the best book in the world," and President Thomas Jefferson stated, "The Bible is the source of Liberty."

These are just a few of the several hundred documented quotes and writings of our founding fathers. If a president or politician made any of these statements today, the liberal media would viciously attack them as intolerant religious extremists, and liberal judges would accuse them of violating the very Constitution that they created. As President Dwight Eisenhower and, later, President Gerald Ford stated, "Without God there can be no American form of government nor an American way of life. Recognition of a Supreme Being is the first impression of Americanism. Thus, the founding fathers saw it, and thus, with God's help, it will continue to be."

The historical record is clear. America is a Christian nation. As President Ronald Reagan once said, "If we ever forget that we're one nation under God, then we will be a nation gone under."

Frank Aquila, December 2009

Understanding America as a Christian nation is relevant to understanding why the Islamic terrorists are interested in destroying America. There is only one of two sides from which to choose. Either you support Israel's right to exist as a Jewish state, or you choose the right of the Islamic nations that wish to "wipe Israel off the map," in the words of Iranian President Mahoud Ahmadinehad. Sarah has clearly supported the effort of Israel, while President Obama, according to an article in The Washington Times, has "appeased and emboldened radical Islamists" with his foreign policies.

To understand the relevance of Israel and why there is so much conflict between Israel and many other nations in the Middle East, I wrote about it in a letter to a newspaper editor explaining why America was attacked on September 11, 2001:

"Why was America attacked on September 11, 2001?"

It is amazing that many people still do not understand why America was attacked on September 11, 2001. Why do these terrorists want to kill us? Liberals, peace activists, and the uninformed believe if we "appease" the terrorists, they will leave us alone and there will be peace. It is not that simple. Due to "political correctness" and a fear to discuss religion, most people do not understand why America was attacked on September 11, 2001.

The root of the terrorist hatred can be traced to the first book of the Bible, Genesis, Chapters 12-22. God had promised Abraham a son and through him would be a "great nation." Years later, Abraham had two sons, Ishmael and Isaac. Isaac had been chosen by God to receive His promise of a great nation, which is Israel. Ishmael became a "wild man" and the father of many nations.

Each day, the media reports on much turmoil in the Middle East. The descendants of Ishmael claim Israel to be their land. These nations that hate Israel are governed by Muslim extremists, such as Iranian President Mahoud Ahmadinehad, who has gained authority in government vowing to destroy Israel, while supporting terrorist networks like al-Qaeda, Islamic Jihad, Hamas, Fatah, and Hezbollah. They use the Qur'an (Surah 8:60-65) to justify themselves as "militant Muslims," approving murder to force their faith upon the world and reclaim Israel as "their land."

The hatred of Israel is extended to America because America has become the "Great Satan" as Israel's main ally, causing the main barrier for these terrorist networks to occupy Israel. Their hatred has yearned for "jihad," which is a "holy war" against America.

During the Clinton administration, Osama bin Laden made a declaration of war against America. The Clinton administration ignored the threat and essentially did nothing as Islamic terrorists launched several terrorist attacks on American interests, including:

1993: Bombing of World Trade Center (6 Americans killed, 1000 injured).
1993: Attack in Mogadishu (18 American soldiers killed, 73 injured).

1995: Bombing of Khobar Towers (19 American soldiers/airmen killed, hundreds wounded).

1998: Bombings of U.S. embassies in Tanzania and Kenya (225 people killed, 5,000 injured).

2000: Bombing of the USS Cole (17 American sailors killed, 39 injured).

As al-Qaeda continued to attack America with no American response, Osama bin Laden stated in 1998, "Clinton appeared in front of the whole world threatening and promising revenge, but these threats were merely a preparation for withdrawal. You have been disgraced by Allah and you withdrew; the extent of your impotence and weakness became very clear."

With the signal of American weakness, al-Qaeda planned and executed the attack on September 11, 2001, which was an attack to take down our economy (World Trade Center), our national defense intelligence (Pentagon) and our function of government (the White House or the U.S. Capitol, depending on whom you ask).

These terrorist networks will continue to fight until they achieve their goal of death to the infidels and occupation of Israel. In the Bible, the prophet Ezekiel (Chapter 38) and Zachariah (Chapter 14) state that, in the last days, these countries will line up against Israel, including Persia, which is today's Iran.

The terrorists' goal is to destroy America. Appeasement to enemies who are unafraid to die for what they believe will only embolden them and cause them to perceive America as weak. We often try to stay "politically correct" or not discuss religion to avoid offending others; but it is the only way to understand why America was attacked on September 11, 2001.

Frank Aquila, March 2008

Sarah Palin believes we should be supporting democracy throughout the Arab world, and we should align ourselves with those who are our friends "to spread democracy for those who desire freedom, independence, tolerance, and respect for equality." She understands there are those "who hate America and hate what we stand for, with our freedoms, our democracy, our tolerance, our respect for women's rights." Sarah has stated that we should not be negotiating with dictators who would try to destroy what we stand for as a nation. She has pointed out this would be "beyond bad judgment" and "dangerous."

Sarah has also disagreed with the Obama administration's approach to war and its referring to an "overseas contingency operation." On February 6, 2010, Sarah stated, "It's not politicizing our security to discuss our concerns, because Americans deserve to know the truth about the threats that we face and what the administration is or isn't doing about them." She continued that "replacing 'war' with an 'overseas contingency operation' reflects a world view that is out of touch with the enemy we face. We need to call it what it is. A terrorist is a terrorist and not a 'man-made disaster'."

Through intelligence from President George Bush's administration, another attack on America was avoided. However, how many attacks have been avoided, and why have we weakened our intelligence in fighting the war on terror? In one of my letters to a newspaper editor, I compiled several different lists of those attacks America has avoided, as well as a list of those attacks that have occurred throughout the world through the end of the Bush presidency:

"Have We Forgotten September 11, 2001?"

Al-Qaeda declared war against America in 1998, and they are still at war against America. Sadly, the Obama administration has directed the removal of any use of the term "war of terror." Homeland Security Secretary Janet Napolitano also avoids any mention of "terrorism" and "vulnerability" in any discussion. A terrorist act is now being called a "man-made disaster," and the "global war on terror" will now be called an "oversees contingency operation."

We are dangerously returning to the same mentality and policy that allowed America to be attacked on September 11, 2001. President Obama's policies have made America once again vulnerable against those who support jihad against America. For all who criticized President Bush, he kept America safe from a terrorist attack 2,866 days since September 11, 2001. During that time, the terrorists have made several attempts to attack America or American interests:

December 2001: Richard Reid, a self-professed follower of Osama bin Laden, attempted to blow up a plane with explosives hidden inside his shoe.

May 2002: Jose Padilla, charged with being "enemy combatant" and attempting to plant "dirty bomb" in attack in America.

September 2002: FBI arrested "Lackawanna Six," also known as "Buffalo Six," an al-Qaeda cell that attended "jihad" camp in Pakistan to conspire with terrorist groups.

May 2003: Iyman Faris, American citizen charged with plotting to use blowtorches to collapse Brooklyn Bridge.

June 2003: Virginia Jihad Network, 11 men from Alexandria, Va., trained for jihad against American soldiers, convicted of violating Neutrality Act, conspiracy.

August 2004: Dhiren Barot, Indian-born leader of terror cell, plotted bombings on financial centers.

August 2004: James Elshafay and Shahawar Matin Siraj sought to plant bomb at New York's Penn Station during Republican National Convention.

August 2004: Yassin Aref and Mohammed Hossain plotted to assassinate Pakistani diplomat on American soil.

May 2005: Thwarted attack, called "Second Wave," planned to use East Asian operatives to crash hijacked airliner into building in Los Angeles.

June 2005: Father and son Umer Hayat and Hamid Hayat; son convicted of attending terrorist training camp in Pakistan; father convicted of customs violation.

August 2005: Kevin James, Levar Haley Washington, Gregory Vernon Patterson, and Hammad Riaz Samana, Los Angeles homegrown terrorists, plotted to attack National Guard, Los Angeles International Airport (LAX), 2 synagogues, and Israeli consulate.

December 2005: Michael Reynolds plotted to blow up natural gas refinery in Wyoming, Transcontinental Pipeline, and refinery in New Jersey; Reynolds was sentenced to 30 years in prison.

February 2006: Mohammad Zaki Amawi, Marwan Othman El-Hindi, and Zand Wassim Mazloum accused of providing material support to terrorists, making bombs for use in Iraq.

April 2006: Syed Haris Ahmed and Ehsanul Islam Sadequee cased and videotaped Capitol and World Bank for terrorist organization.

June 2006: Narseal Batiste, Patrick Abraham, Stanley Grant Phanor, Naudimar Herrera, Burson Augustin, Lyglenson Lemorin, and Rotschild Augstine accused of plotting to blow up Sears Tower.

July 2006: Assem Hammoud accused of plotting to bomb New York City train tunnels.

August 2006: Liquid-explosives plot to explode 10 airliners over United States thwarted.

March 2007: Khalid Sheikh Mohammed, mastermind of September 11, 2001 and author of numerous plots, confessed in court in March 2007 to planning to destroy skyscrapers in New York, Los Angeles, and Chicago; Mohammed also plotted to assassinate Pope John Paul II and former President Bill Clinton.

May 2007: Fort Dix plot, 6 men accused of plotting to attack Fort Dix Army Base in New Jersey; plan included attacking and killing soldiers using assault rifles and grenades.

June 2007: JFK plot, 4 men accused of plotting to blow up fuel arteries that run through residential neighborhoods at JFK Airport in New York.

September 2007: German authorities disrupt terrorist cell planning attacks on military installations and facilities used by Americans in Germany; Germans arrested 3 suspected members of Islamic Jihad Union, group having links to al-Qaeda and supports al-Qaeda's global jihadist agenda.

Terrorists have also made several attacks outside America, including:

April 2002: Explosion at historic synagogue in Tunisia, killing 21, including 11 German tourists.

May 2002: Car exploded outside hotel in Karachi, Pakistan, killing 14, including 11 French citizens.

June 2002: Bomb exploded outside American consulate in Karachi, Pakistan, killing 12.

October 2002: Boat crashed into oil tanker off Yemen coast, killing 1.

October 2002: Nightclub bombings in Bali, Indonesia, killing 202, mostly Australian citizens.

November 2002: Suicide attack on hotel in Mombasa, Kenya, killing 16.

May 2003: Suicide bomber killed 34, including 8 Americans, at housing compound for Westerners in Riyadh, Saudi Arabia.

May 2003: 4 bombs killed 33 people, targeting Jewish, Spanish, and Belgian sites in Casablanca, Morocco.

August 2003: Suicide car bomb killed 12, injured 150, at Marriott Hotel in Jakarta, Indonesia.

November 2003: Explosions rocked Riyadh, Saudi Arabia, housing compound, killing 17.

November 2003: Suicide car bombers simultaneously attacked 2 synagogues in Istanbul, Turkey, killing 25 and injuring hundreds.

November 2003: Truck bombs detonated at London bank and British consulate in Istanbul, Turkey, killing 26.

March 2004: 10 bombs on 4 trains exploded almost simultaneously during morning rush hour in Madrid, Spain, killing 191, injuring more than 1,500.

May 2004: Terrorists attacked offices of a Saudi oil company in Khobar, Saudi Arabia, took foreign oil workers hostage in nearby residential compound, leaving 22 people dead, including 1 American.

June 2004: Terrorists kidnapped and executed Paul Johnson Jr., an American in Riyadh, Saudi Arabia; 2 other Americans and BBC cameraman killed by gun attacks.

September 2004: Car bomb outside Australian embassy in Jakarta, Indonesia, killing 9.

December 2004: Terrorists stormed U.S. Consulate in Jeddah, Saudi Arabia, killing 5 consulate employees.

July 2005: Bombs exploded on 3 trains and bus in London, England, killing 52.

October 2005: 22 killed by 3 suicide bombs in Bali, Indonesia.

November 2005: 57 killed at 3 American hotels in Amman, Jordan.

January 2006: 2 suicide bombers carrying police badges blew themselves up near celebration at Police Academy in Baghdad, killing nearly 20 police officers; al-Qaeda in Iraq took responsibility.

August 2006: Police arrested 24 British-born Muslims, most of whom had ties to Pakistan, who allegedly plotted to blow up as many as 10 planes, using liquid explosives.

September 2006: Attack by 4 gunmen on American embassy in Damascus, Syria, foiled.

January 2007: U.S. Embassy, Athens, Greece, was fired on by anti-tank missile causing damage but no injuries.

April 2007: Suicide bombers attacked government building in Algeria's capital, Algiers, killing 35 and wounding hundreds more; al-Qaeda in Islamic Maghreb claimed responsibility.

April 2007: 8 people, including 2 Iraqi legislators, died when suicide bomber struck inside Parliament building in Baghdad; organization that included al-Qaeda in Mesopotamia claimed responsibility.

In another attack, Sarafiya Bridge that spanned Tigris River was destroyed.

June 2007: British police found car bombs in 2 vehicles in London; attackers reportedly tried to detonate bombs using cell phones but failed; government officials said al-Qaeda linked to attempted attack. The following day, an SUV carrying bombs burst into flames after it slammed into an entrance to Glasgow Airport; officials said attacks were connected.

December 2007: More than 60 people killed, including 11 United Nations staff members, when al-Qaeda terrorists detonated 2 car bombs near Algeria's Constitutional Council and United Nations offices.

January 2008: In worst attack in Iraq in months, suicide bomber killed 30 people at home where mourners were paying respects to family of man killed in car bomb.

February 2008: Nearly 100 people died when 2 women suicide bombers, believed to be mentally impaired, attacked crowded pet markets in eastern Baghdad; U.S. military said al-Qaeda in Iraq had been recruiting female patients at psychiatric hospitals to become suicide bombers.

April 2008: Suicide bomber attacked funeral for 2 nephews of prominent Sunni tribal leader, Sheik Kareem Kamil al-Azawi, killing 30 people in Iraq's Diyala Province.

April 2008: Suicide car bomber killed 40 people in Baquba, capital of Diyala Province, Iraq.

April 2008: 35 people died, 62 injured, when woman detonated explosives she was carrying under her dress in busy shopping district in Iraq's Diyala Province.

May 2008: At least 12 worshipers killed, 44 injured, when bomb exploded in Bin Salman Mosque near Sana, Yemen.

May 2008: Suicide bomber on motorcycle killed 6 U.S. soldiers, wounded 18 others, in Tarmiya, Iraq.

June 2008: Female suicide bomber killed 15, wounded 40, including 7 Iraqi policemen, near courthouse in Baquba, Iraq.

June 2008: Suicide bomber killed at least 20 people, including 3 U.S. Marines, at meeting between sheiks and Americans in Karmah, town west of Baghdad.

June 2008: 4 American servicemen killed when roadside bomb exploded near U.S. military vehicle in Farah Province.

July 2008: 9 U.S. soldiers, at least 15 NATO troops, died when Taliban militants boldly attacked American base in Kunar Province, which borders Pakistan.

August 2008: About 24 worshippers killed in 3 separate attacks as they made their way toward Karbala to celebrate birthday of 9th-century imam Muhammad al-Mahdi.

August 2008: Bomb left on street exploded and tore through bus carrying Lebanese troops, killing 15 people, 9 of them soldiers.

August 2008: At least 43 people killed when suicide bomber drove explosives-laden car into police academy in Issers, town in northern Algeria.

August 2008: 2 car bombs exploded at military command and hotel in Bouira, killing 12.

August 2008: As many as 15 suicide bombers, backed by about 30 militants, attacked U.S. military base, Camp Salerno, Bamiyan.

September 2008: Car bomb and rocket struck U.S. embassy in Yemen as staff arrived to work, killing 16 people, including 4 civilians; at least 25 suspected al-Qaeda militants were arrested for attack.

November 2008: At least 28 people died, over 60 more injured, when 3 bombs exploded minutes apart in Baghdad, Iraq; officials suspected explosions were linked to al-Qaeda.

November 2008: In series of attacks on several Mumbai landmarks and commercial hubs in India, popular with Americans and other foreign tourists, including at least 2 five-star hotels, hospital, train station, and cinema, about 300 people wounded, nearly 190 people died, including at least 5 Americans.

Imagine what we don't know and how many American lives have been saved. The terrorists only have to be successful once to claim success and achieve their goal.

Now, the Obama Administration and the Democrats want to take us back to a pre-9/11 mentality. President Obama's first official presidential act was to begin proceedings to close Guantanamo Bay, a prison island used to house 245 hardened terrorists. He reduced our government's methods of interrogating these terrorists, including waterboarding, which saved thousands of lives in the May 2005 plot to hijack airliners into buildings in Los Angeles. He granted the terrorists further legal rights, and even U.S. Constitutional rights, in spite of their vow to destroy America. Other terrorists have been released to return to the battlefield to wage war on our military once again or plan their next attack against American interests.

President Obama and the Democrats have made America less safe, as they have reduced our intelligence and interrogation ability to prevent a future terrorist attack. They have crippled our intelligence of surveillance by weakening the Patriot Act and allowing the Foreign Intelligence Surveillance Act to expire, which prevented our government's listening in on suspected terrorists.

On February 15, 2008, Michael McConnell, then-Director of National Intelligence, warned that, because of the expiration of the Protect America Act, "some critical operations...would probably become impossible." He added, "Under the Protect America Act, we obtained valuable insight and understanding, leading to the disruption of planned terrorist attacks."

While the Democrats have turned their heads away from the real enemy, they have no problem labeling conservatives who oppose abortion, favor strict immigration enforcement, support the Second Amendment, protest big government, or represent veterans, as potential "domestic terrorists" whom our government should watch.

If the Obama Administration cannot recognize who the real terrorists are, or that we are in a global war on terror, how can we expect it to protect America?

Frank Aquila, December 2008

Sarah agrees in the terrorism plan which was summed up by the words of President Ronald Reagan, "We win, they lose." She believes terrorists who hate and conspire against America with well-coordinated events should be treated as wartime enemies, not as criminal suspects, and should continue to be housed at Guantanamo Bay. Closing Guantanamo Bay is not an option. She believes terrorists who have massacred hundreds of innocent lives should not be accorded the same constitutional and legal privileges that suspected criminal suspects are allowed as Americans and should not be allowed trials in the American courts system. She warns that granting such rights and privileges to foreign-born terrorists could jeopardize our national security and risk further American lives by granting terrorists the right to remain silent.

Governor Palin views the greatest measures America can contribute to counterterrorism is to promote democracy and democratic ideals, stating, "It's not just to keep the people safe, but to be able to usher in democratic values and ideals [around] the world." She agrees with President Reagan that America is the "beacon of light" for those who seek democratic values, tolerance, and freedom in the world.

As the training ground for al-Qaeda was based in Afghanistan, Sarah was disturbed by comments made by then-Senator Obama that troops in Afghanistan were "air raiding villages and killing civilians," prior to his becoming president. She supports the war effort in Afghanistan and urges Obama to "devote the resources necessary in Afghanistan." Sarah believes "we can win in Afghanistan," and "we must do what it takes to prevail."

While governor, Sarah stated in Iraq, "I respect our military personnel and understand the importance of Alaska's National Guard. As I watched our military men and women being deployed, I recognized how important it is for their families to know how much Alaska and America supports them." Sarah generally supported the American presence, but recognizes, "mistakes were made." She believes we must stay in the country until victory is achieved rather than risking "waving the white flag of surrender." Her son, Track, has served time in Iraq with the U.S. Army. She did agree with an exit strategy to keep our troops safe, but has never expressed a "timeline for withdrawal."

While some troops are still in Iraq, victory was eventually achieved with no credit being given to President George W. Bush. Instead, Vice President Joe Biden referred to the victory as one of Obama's "great achievements," even though Obama stated in 2007 that the surge in Iraq would fail. Obama gave no credit to Bush during his 2011 State of the Union address for the victory in Iraq. Sarah Palin's response to the Iraqi victory is that "change happened, that's a great thing for America."

Now Obama has involved America in a third war in Libya. However, unlike previous wars, Obama has violated the U.S. Constitution by attacking a country without consulting Congress, instead seeking authority from the United Nations. Sarah stated she would have handled things differently with "less dithering." Obama should have immediately notified Congress and sought congressional approval. It was Obama himself who stated America did not have the power to attack a country (Iraq) that was not a threat to America. Bush not only sought congressional approval, he offered a time table and immediately explained the plan of war to the American people. Obama took nine days to explain to the America people what the objective of the attack in Libya was, although it was in direct conflict with his earlier statements. However, Obama justified going to the United Nations, claiming it was not a war but a humanitarian issue. He first stated we were not going after Gadhafi, and then he stated we are.

Sarah stated she would have been more decisive from the beginning with a plan to support the "freedom fighters" through military action approved by Congress. She believes we cannot be involved in every war, such as Rwanda, Sudan, Darfur, Yemen, or other countries in similar conditions. She stated we should be "in it to win it" or use "economic sanctions" against the government. She stated many are wondering what we are actually doing in Libya and has criticized Obama regarding confusion as to whether we are at war.

Sarah has criticized the "Obama Doctrine" as "full of chaos and questions," stating there is no game plan as well as a lot of confusion of inconsistencies that could worsen the conflicts in the Middle East. She also criticized Obama on the confusion as to whether we are at war. Even Obama seems confused by his own policies. He claimed in an interview, on December 20, 2007, with the Boston Globe, speaking of the Iraq War, "The president does not have power under the Constitution to unilaterally authorize a military attack in a situation that does not involve stopping an actual or imminent threat to the nation." Sarah questioned, quite rightly, are we employing intervention, war, or skirmish? She pointed out that America's interests are not met if Gadhafi stays in power, and there are even further dangers we may have opened up. Who would take over for Gadhafi if he is removed? Would it be the Muslim Brotherhood that apparently has taken over in Egypt and has ties to al-Qaeda? We may be making things worse no matter what happens in Libya.

Obama's statement that he would negotiate with Iran and North Korea has repeatedly been criticized by Sarah, as she believes both dictators are dangerous, and it is naive to meet without preconditions. She has stated personally that Iranian President Ahmadinejad is not one with whom to negotiate, and that nuclear weapons in the hands of the Iranian government are extremely dangerous to everyone on the globe. Sarah would also not second guess Israel if she were to attack Iran if provoked, as Ahmadinejad has stated he would wipe Israel off the face of the earth, and it is obvious who are the "good guys" and the "bad guys." She firmly believes it is time for tough actions and sanctions against Iran and other countries where people are struggling, oppressed, and fighting for their freedom. When the brave Iranian people tried to stand up to their dictator, no actions or sanctions were taken by the Obama administration.

Governor Palin believes a strong military and sound energy policies are key to America and our national security. She believes that an energy-independent nation is a matter of national security. While she is a firm believer in free-market capitalism, she also believes in trade conducted fairly where all parties are allowed to compete in a fair, democratic process, and doesn't feel that process is being managed fairly in America as it relates to energy. In a 2008 interview on Fox News, Sarah pointed out there is an imbalance of trade with 70% of America's oil being imported. Sarah stated, "those dollars should be circulating within our own economy," continuing that is part of our "national security and of our future prosperity, being able to quit relying on foreign sources of energy."

Sarah pointed out again, in the October 2, 2008 vice-presidential debate, that, "We're circulating $700 billion a year into foreign countries, some who do not like America, instead of those dollars circulating here, creating thousands of jobs and allowing domestic supplies of energy to be tapped into and start flowing into these very, very hungry markets. Energy independence is the key to this nation's future, to our economic future, and to our national security."

As governor, Sarah was uncomfortable with a bid from a Chinese company to build Alaska's 1,715-mile natural gas pipeline. Sarah felt there was a fine line between free markets and national security with the energy-thirsty Communist Chinese controlling the manpower, technology, and funding of the pipeline. Sarah felt it was not in the best interest of our national security and rejected the application, based on it being incomplete, before rewarding the job to TransCanada for the Alaska Pipeline Project.

Sarah has hope for a stable and peaceful relationship with China and would like to see further Chinese investment with America, as long as the interest of national security is not threatened. Although China is a superpower with a nuclear and military build up, the relationship between America and China is based on economic independence. She would urge the Chinese to be more open about its political policies to settle the imposed threat it has on other nations. Sarah has also stated that the food and safety record of the Chinese has raised concern throughout the world, as well as the lack of human rights of those living in China.

Trade was always important to Governor Palin. However, she wanted to keep Alaska first as well as protect the interests of America. Alaska exported to over 100 foreign countries, with its trade exports growing more than 12% in 2006, topping $4 billion, in Sarah's first year as governor. Alaska's relationship with international communities was stable and transparent while the international markets and companies trusted Alaska.

Part of our national security is overseen by the Department of Homeland Security, which was established after September 11, 2001, to allow government enforcement agencies to properly share intelligence information. Sarah believes it is a duty and an obligation of the President to defend our country. She supports efforts to do away with the extremist Islamic terrorists whose main goal and purpose is to attack and destroy America. After September 11, 2001, President

Bush missed a perfect opportunity to secure our borders as an issue of national security. As our borders are not secured and any person can enter our country through any passage, we now have an estimated 12 million illegal immigrants living in America, posing a possible threat to America.

Sarah believes securing the borders should be our top priority before dealing with illegal immigration. She does not feel deporting illegal immigrants are an economical or humane way to deal with the issue. Although she rejects amnesty, she believes a pathway to citizenship should be available to illegal immigrants already here who have not violated federal law. However, she believes those who have followed the legal process for citizenship should most definitely receive first preference and available opportunities.

As governor, Sarah supported and signed legislation requiring only those who can prove their legal identification to procure a driver's license. She does support providing assistance to illegal immigrants who have legitimate needs, including vocational training, gang prevention, assistance to the elderly, as well as communication and outreach into their communities. She has stated, "I understand why people would want to be in America. To seek the safety and prosperity, the opportunities, the health that is here. It is so important that, yes, people follow the rules so that people can be treated equally and fairly in this country."

Sarah has endorsed Arizona Governor Jan Brewer's immigration plan, the "Secure The Border—Support Arizona Campaign." She believes we should learn from history, and those protecting our borders should be provided resources to effectively perform their duties. Sarah also supports Arizona's "Support Our Law Enforcement and Safe Neighborhood Act," which charges any alien in Arizona not carrying registration documents, required by federal law, with a misdemeanor when stopped by police for committing a violation of the law.

Guns and Hunting

Sarah has always been a strong supporter of an individual's right to keep and bear arms as provided for in the Second Amendment to the U.S. Constitution. She was raised to live off the land near the Talkeetna Mountains of Alaska, and her father taught her and her siblings to hunt and fish. Sarah is a long-time member of the National Rifle Association (NRA) and often hunted with her father, even occasionally joining her father to hunt moose before school.

Sarah praised the U.S. Supreme Court's decision to overturn Washington, D.C.'s ban on handguns and believes any restriction placed on the possession of firearms violates our U.S. Constitutional right to bear arms.

While serving as governor of Alaska, Sarah was criticized and pressured by liberal organizations and Hollywood celebrities who wished to have Alaska ban guns, hunting, and end the state's wildlife practice of predator control, such as wolves feeding off moose and caribou herds. Sarah resisted all pressures and preserved for Alaskans their right granted by the Second Amendment.

Sarah has also been in favor of firearm safety and education programs for Alaskan youth and joined Texas in a multi-state *amicus* brief in support of the *MacDonald* case involving the Second Amendment. In June 2008, she signed a law granting free hunting, trapping, and fishing licenses to all members of the Alaska National Guard and Reserve.

Sarah has stated, "I am a lifetime member of the NRA; I support our Constitutional right to bear arms and am a proponent of gun safety programs for Alaskan youth. I grew up hunting and fishing in Alaska, and I am proud to raise my children with this same uniquely Alaskan heritage. Anti-hunting groups who oppose hunting and fishing rights will be the winners, if we allow them to pit us against ourselves. As an

Alaskan with strong beliefs on this issue, I am confident in my ability to build consensus among diverse user groups and reconcile the many competing interests...."

Health Care

As governor, Sarah committed herself to serious health care reform. However, she has been outspoken against a plan to mandate health care coverage, a publicly-funded health care program under which the government controls the health care industry. She believes the solutions for health care should not come from Washington; but rather, the solution is flexibility and relief from government regulations via free-market competition in health care. She believes that less litigation will create greater competition and more private-sector choices to drive down the costs of health care, reduce the need for government subsidies, and allow patients access to medical pricing information.

Sarah believes it is the government's responsibility to provide free-market solutions, enact tort reform and deregulate the health care industry, allowing more competition in health care between the states. She would like to see artificial lines between the states erased so we can seek better health care plans across state lines, creating further competition and reducing the cost of health care and prescription drugs. Sarah has proposed "providing Medicare recipients with vouchers that allow them to purchase their own coverage" and a $5,000 tax credit for families to purchase their own health care coverage based on their needs.

President Obama's legacy was to be centered on his health care overhaul. Sarah was very critical of the overhaul and, in a September 23, 2010 article entitled, "Lies, Damned Lies—Obamacare 6 Months Later; It's Time to Take Back the 20!," Sarah pointed out Obama took control of one-sixth of the private sector economy. She emphasized a large number of doctors are leaving the Medicare system due to cuts in reimbursements forced on them by Obamacare. She pointed out insurance premiums are expected to rise as much as 25% and that Obamacare funds abortions. Also, she stated small businesses will face higher health care costs, new Medicare taxes and higher regulation compliance costs, while larger businesses will find it less expensive to pay the $2,000 per employee fine than to insure their employees.

Sarah had previously warned, in August 2009, that she was concerned about "death panels" in the health care legislation. She was widely criticized by the media that the information was not true. However, she now points out the legislation of "death panels" is, in fact, true. She reinforces the fact that Obamacare rations health care, with the power of an independent board having statutory power to decide which categories of treatment are worthy of funding, to deny a patient's request for treatment. Sarah refers to this as "a panel of faceless bureaucrats making life and death decisions."

However, on January 31, 2011, U.S. District Judge Roger Vinson, Senior Federal Judge for the Northern District of Florida, ruled on the health care law, siding with the 26-plaintiff states, opining, "The individual mandate is unconstitutional and not severable; the entire act must be declared void." The case is being appealed by the Obama administration and will likely work its way up to the United States Supreme Court.

Religious Principles

Sarah has strong faith and is deeply rooted in her religious beliefs as a Christian. She stated on October 25, 2006, during the 2006 Alaska gubernatorial debate, "Faith is very important to so many of us here in America, and I would never support any government effort to stifle our freedom of religion or freedom of expression or freedom of speech." However, she has never allowed her personal religious beliefs and core values to dictate her public policies. She has set aside her personal objections to abortion, homosexuality, and other issues, stating in a 2006 interview with the Associated Press that she was "not one to be out there preaching and forcing my views on anyone else."

As governor, Sarah vetoed a bill for public funding of private Christian schools in Alaska, citing that she recognized it as unconstitutional, since it is illegal to use public funding to finance any religious institution. She was accused of not being a real conservative or Republican due to her veto of the bill.

Sarah did declare a National Day of Prayer in Alaska. The Continental Congress, in 1775, called for a National Day of Prayer. President Lincoln, in 1863, established a proclamation for a day of "humiliation, fasting, and prayer." President Reagan, in 1988, established the first Thursday in May every year as the National Day of Prayer. Sarah encouraged Alaskans to keep the faith, prosperity and peace of their state, nation and world in mind on that day.

Sarah also supported and signed the Christian Heritage Week Proclamation in October 2007, reminding Alaskans of the influence Christianity has played in the rich heritage of America. She remembered Christians who have made America great and did not hesitate to express their faith. She also declared a week in November as Bible Week in Alaska, citing that early Americans used the Bible for divine guidance, comfort, and encouragement; and that the Bible has influenced art, literature, music, and codes of law, including James Madison, the father of the U.S. Constitution.

During the 2008 presidential campaign, then-Senator Obama stated in San Francisco that people in Pennsylvania were bitter Americans, clinging to their guns and religion. Sarah took the comment personally, stating she was one of those Americans and felt it was inappropriate for Senator Obama to make inappropriate comments about one group of Americans while speaking to another group of Americans.

On June 10, 2010, Sarah expressed her displeasure on another issue, via Twitter, that the floodlights of the Empire State Building would honor the Communist Mao on September 9, 2009 with red and yellow lights to celebrate the 60th anniversary of the founding of the People's Republic of China, but the floodlights would not be changed to blue and white in honor of Mother Teresa's 100th birthday.

Sarah is also opposed to the construction of the Ground Zero Mosque, known as Park 51, a 13-story mega mosque with an Islamic cultural center overlooking the site where the World Trade Center once stood before the terrorist attack on September 11, 2001. Through Twitter, Sarah pointed out, "the Ground Zero mosque is UNNECESSARY" and "it stabs hearts," expressing her sympathy for those who lost loved ones in the attack on innocent lives in America. Those arguing for the mosque cited freedom of religion. One mosque is already in the vicinity of the proposed Ground Zero Mosque, and offers to allow a mosque in another location were rejected. Why is this site so important for those who wish to build the Ground Zero Mosque? It is because it is two blocks away from Ground Zero and offers a symbolic victory center for those who support the mosque. The City of New York's Landmarks Commission did have the right to reject its location, yet it chose to be "tolerant."

Is the location appropriate? Should a museum for the Japanese military be placed at Pearl Harbor, or should the KKK be allowed to build a "Shrine of Reconciliation" on a site near a black church? Tolerance is what allowed America to be attacked on September 11, 2001. America is again putting forth a blind eye and allowing those that hate us to use our own laws against us. We should be able to recognize what this mosque really is—a victory center and sign of conquest for the radical Muslim terrorists who used their faith to justify the murder of nearly 3,000 Americans in the name of Islam. The site is insensitive and disrespectful to those family members who will now see the shadows of the in-your-face mosque fall over them as they visit the sacred site where their loved ones' lives were lost.

It is a tradition of Islam to build a mosque on historical sites as a sign of victory and conquest. Other mosque locations include Hagia Sophia in Turkey, the Temple Mount in Jerusalem, the Great Mosque of Cordoba in Spain, the Qutub Minar in Afghanistan, the Ummayed Mosque in Damascus, and a Bari Mosque at the site of the destroyed Hindu God Ram's temple in India, to name a few. Every mosque sends a message, "We conquered you, took your holy site, and now you belong to us," which is the message these Islamists want to send naming the Ground Zero Mosque "Cordoba House," their Grand Mosque. Stunningly, the name "Cordoba" comes from the North African Muslim army which, in the year 711, conquered Spain and established an Emirate in Cordoba, demolishing a cathedral there and constructing a mosque on its site. Osama bin Laden's successors and other radical Muslim terrorists would love nothing more than to plant the flag of Islam as a victory symbol in the capital center of the world and site of the attack on America on September 11, 2001.

What is even further troubling about this mosque is those who seek the funding and from where the funding is coming. Feisal Abdul Rauf, the Imam of the Ground Zero Mosque and head of the American Society of Muslim American Advancement, refuses to acknowledge Hamas as a terrorist organization, even though the U.S. government has declared it as one. He has also stated U.S. foreign policy was responsible for the attack on September 11, 2001. In his own book, "The Call from the WTC Rubble: Islamic Da'wah from the Heart of America Post-9/11," Rauf's "Islamic Da'wah" is a "call" he intends to use for the 9/11 Mosque as his springboard for proselytizing Islam into America. Rauf has sought $100 million from the homelands of the 9/11 terrorists, including Saudi Arabia; and, to the dismay of some, the U.S. government funded with American tax dollars his trip to those Arab nations to seek that funding. Rauf also has the endorsement for the Ground Zero Mosque of President Obama, who stated, "Muslims have the right to practice their religion." No one is suggesting any Muslim be denied the right to practice their religion. However, Sarah stated, "it stabs hearts" by placing a mosque near the memorial site for those families and the rest of America.

Social Security

On October 6, 2010, Sarah expressed that America needs to make some tough decisions, in our generation, to assure that future generations can have the same opportunities as we do. She believes that the private sector needs to thrive to create jobs to ensure that finances continue to go into the system. She believes those currently relying on Social Security must not be adversely affected; but she is realistic that some changes in the system may be necessary, including future year eligibility. Sarah has always used every opportunity to express her love for senior citizens and has publicly pledged to never let them down.

It is a shame that our previous political leaders have not taken the initiative as a nation to provide the security of Social Security, which has created an enormous problem for those who will be relying on it for future generations. In a letter to a newspaper editor, I wrote about the coming collapse of Social Security, and how we, as a nation, have failed the system:

"The Collapse of Social Security"

The Trustees of the Social Security program stated on May 12, 2009 that Social Security will begin paying more in benefits than it is receiving in 2016, and Social Security will be completely depleted by 2037, hurting our elderly who would depend on the money for their retirement.

The Republican Party has attempted bold moves to save Social Security from going bankrupt, while the Democrats turn a blind eye to the problem, stopping the reform to save Social Security.

In 2005, President Bush warned, "If we do not act now to avert that outcome, the only solutions would be dramatically higher taxes, massive new borrowing, or sudden and severe cuts in Social Security benefits or other government programs," offering a solution to privatize part of Social Security for younger participants.

The Republican plan would allow people the option to manage 18% (one of six dollars) of their Social Security as an Individual Retirement Account (IRA), providing individuals the option of their investments, including stocks, bonds, mutual funds, gold, or any other commodity to gain a higher percentage of return than the 2% annual return they would receive from the government. This would historically increase the amount of revenue into the program, which needs to hold funds separate from other government funds.

The Democrat Party blocked the reform and offered no solutions of its own. Others won't even admit that a problem exists. During the 2004 presidential campaign, the Democrats made allegations that the Republicans were going to stop sending retirees their Social Security checks, attempting to use scare tactics to gain votes from the elderly.

In March 2000, Democrat Senator Al Gore, Tennessee, stated in reference to Social Security, "If it ain't broke, don't fix it. Shore it up the way we always have." Democrat Senator Charles Schumer, New York, said Social Security should get "fine-tuning" rather than a replacement "with something completely different," as the Democrats killed all reform.

But why would the Democrats block Social Security reform, including privatization of accounts for individuals? It is about control. Democrats have always thought of the people's money as being their party's money. People may believe they have irrevocable rights to these benefits. But Social Security decisions are up to the politicians, who can decide to delay the retirement age so older Americans would actually die before they would be eligible to collect what they contributed into the system or their time collecting Social Security would be shortened. This would allow the government to keep more of the money contributed into the system.

Why does it hurt the Democrats so badly that they stand against allowing people to actually manage part of their Social Security? Because Democrats do not like people to become financially independent, since the Democrats' political power is built upon the foundation of government dependence. The Democrats must, therefore, prevent the people who depend on Social Security from ever enjoying a sense of independence, thus requiring them to depend on a Democrat-controlled government to supply their needs.

In the meantime, Social Security has amassed $4,000,000,000,000 ($4 trillion) of unfunded liability and, if major changes are not made quickly, the government will be only able to pay 70 cents on each dollar of promised benefits. But how has Social Security amassed so much debt at a time when so many are expecting it to be there for their retirement?

In 1935, President Franklin Roosevelt established Social Security as a retirement savings program for Americans. The Social Security program was introduced as a voluntary program, and the Social Security Act of 1935 set the wage threshold at $3,000 to each participant. Income earned above this amount was not subject to Social Security taxes. The money was to be set aside in an independent "trust fund" to fund the Social Security Retirement Program, separate from the federal government's general operations fund and other government programs. However, by law, the Democrats forced all Social Security surpluses to be loaned out to the federal government, with the government required to pay the money back into the Social Security program with interest. The Democrat-controlled Congress should have required this money to remain separate.

As the new-age liberal Democrats came into power, the blueprint of this successful program began to be chipped away at the foundation, engendering future potential problems for millions of Americans who would rely on their Social Security checks. The $3,000 wage threshold has been increased 20 times since the program's introduction, requiring people to pay more Social Security taxes. Then, the Democrats eliminated the income tax deduction for Social Security (FICA) withholdings, as then-Vice President Al Gore, Democrat, cast the tie-breaking vote, which raised the taxation of Social Security annuities up to 85%, and President Bill Clinton, Democrat, signed the bill into law.

In 2000, Social Security taxes accounted for about 25% of all federal tax collections, which is equivalent to 6 weeks of salary in Social Security taxes each year. In 2001 President Bush's budget proposal stated, "Social Security payroll taxes must not be increased as they have been 20 times since the program began in 1937."

It is clear the Democrats and their ideology cannot be trusted. They believe our tax money and Social Security contributions belong to them. Now, with the problem about to surface in a couple years with the retirement of the baby boomers, they would like to blame the Republican Party. However, the Republican Party has been on the record trying to save Social Security through reforms similar to IRAs where the return is much more significant. However, the Democrats have lied to the American people with scare tactics, claiming Republicans want to take away their Social Security. Retirees have not lost their Social Security, but soon the money will not be there.

Now, with Medi-Cal and Medi-Care joining Social Security on the verge of bankruptcy, this has not stopped the Democrats from pandering or making further promises to persuade voters to vote for them. The Democrats have promised baby bonds, government-run health care, free college, and even free daycare. All of this sounds great if you do not have to pay for it, but where does it stop? Should everyone be entitled to a free government-supplied car? Who is going to pay for this? Add these programs together, and these promises add up to another $1 trillion of new spending, while our national debt is already approaching $12 trillion beyond the additional debt of Social Security and Medicare programs.

The Democrats have forgotten the founding principles of "limited government" and "individual accountability." They are attempting to lead us more and more toward Socialism, where more and more people become dependent and controlled by the government.

The Democrat Party has changed over the years. President John F. Kennedy once stated, "My fellow Americans, ask not what your country can do for you—ask what you can do for your country." The Democrats today ask a different question, and America tomorrow will face further consequences as we still have not fixed Social Security.

Unfortunately, the Social Security problem is still there, and without reform to a broken system, all Americans who rely on Social Security will suffer, regardless if they are Republican or Democrat.

Frank Aquila, May 2009

Stem Cell Research

As Sarah is pro-life, she disagrees with embryonic stem cell research, where a fetus is allowed to grow solely for its embryonic stem cells. Recent technology allows for the removal of stem cells from both umbilical cords and bone marrow. Therefore, as science can utilize adult stem cells, Sarah supports this method of research which is not destructive to life.

Welfare and Poverty

As governor, Sarah encouraged benefits to low-income families through the Earned Income Tax Credit (EITC), a federal refundable income tax credit available to people who work but earn low wages. Although many Alaskans were eligible, they were unaware of the EITC, which provided them a financial incentive to work by allowing them to keep more of the money they earned. She proclaimed February 1st as EITC Awareness Day, urging those who were eligible to apply for the financial benefits from the EITC program. EITC has assisted hundreds of thousands of welfare recipients to enter the workforce, with approximately $60 million being designated to various families or individuals in Alaska, lifting many out of the poverty level.

Sarah is a firm supporter of the Salvation Army's charity work, recognizing its rich history and deep roots as a Christian organization, serving and assisting people throughout Alaska and around the world. As governor, she proclaimed November 15th as Red Kettle Day in Alaska, encouraging all citizens to donate to local charities. She is also a supporter of funding faith-based initiatives to benefit those in need of assistance.

After reflecting over all of the major issues concerning America, many politicians say or do whatever they can to get elected without taking a stand on any particular controversial issue. That is why so many Americans now distrust our politicians and government. So many of our politicians are, in fact, out of touch with middle-America, enticed by their own personal entitlements or power, having forgotten the working class and the real values that made America great!

Sarah is the anti-politician who comes from middle-America and holds her moral values close to her heart. She understands what it means to be a public servant, has never explored or exploited politics for her own personal entitlement, and honestly desires to serve people. She became mayor out of concern for the future of her children. She became governor out of concern for the people of Alaska. And, however she positions herself in the future; it will surely be out of her concern for the people of America.

Chapter 4
Lamestream Media Mafia

"America will never be destroyed from the outside. If we falter and lose our freedoms, it will be because we destroyed ourselves." ~ Abraham Lincoln

Journalism is Dead in America

Sean Hannity has often stated on his radio program, "2008 is the year journalism died in America," and he has been proven to be absolutely correct. Immediately upon Senator McCain's selection of Governor Palin as his vice-presidential running mate, the media outlets collectively took upon themselves a frenzy of relentless investigations of her, reporting anything and everything they came upon, regardless of whether the information was factual or pure fiction, thereby performing a great disservice to not only Governor Palin, but the American people. More information was reported on Governor Palin, in less than one week, than was reported about Senator Obama in the year-and-a-half he had been campaigning for president. The media went "dumpster diving" in a blatant effort to find any trash they could about Governor Palin, struggling to find any "dirt." Unfortunately for the media, no affairs, no shady business dealings, and no credible individuals to speak out negatively regarding her personal character or integrity came to light. Instead, what the media did find was that Governor Palin held the then-highest approval rating of any governor in the United States, one who had earned her approval ratings through solid accomplishments, fighting corruption, and making government work for the people of Alaska. The media learned that Governor Palin had always been and continued to be an authentic, rare politician who has integrity, principles, and whose words and actions follow each other.

In spite of this, Governor Palin faced more outrageous, ridiculous questions and false accusations than any other presidential or vice-presidential candidate in American political history. As in previous presidential campaigns, in the 2008 campaign, the media respected the privacy of each of the families of Senators Obama, Biden, and Mc-Cain, instead focusing on their personal political histories. "Journalists" did not afford Governor Palin the same courtesy! Rather than professionally "reporting" on her achievements or accomplishments in the offices to which she had been elected and re-elected, the media made it perfectly clear its chosen focus would be on demeaning Governor Palin and her family.

The media's investigative reporters immediately set up camp in Alaska to locate any possible critics or enemies of Governor Palin, especially in Wasilla, to provide them a microphone to America. All opinions and accusations were reported as facts, with the media injecting their own opinions, also disguised as facts, in order to discredit Governor Palin. Obviously, the media despised her charisma and integrity, fully intent on making her appear as an incompetent female office-holder incapable of performing the duties of vice president. They entertained convoluted "birth conspiracy" stories regarding her pregnancy with Trig, including accusations that she hadn't "looked pregnant" and must have "faked" her pregnancy to cover for her daughter, Bristol, who must have been "the real mother." When those accusations were proven untrue, they opined that Governor Palin did, in fact, give birth to Trig but unfairly alleged she was not a responsible mother, as she had returned to work too soon after Trig's birth and that, during her pregnancy, she had been "irresponsible by traveling in an airplane"! Next, attacks were made against Governor Palin's 17-year-old daughter, Bristol, with no hesitation in reporting of Bristol's then-pregnancy. It was also reported that Governor Palin's husband, Todd, had one arrest for driving under the influence of alcohol in his early-20s, 22 years prior to the campaign. The media reported the same allegations made by the Obama campaign that Governor Palin was "too inexperienced as a former mayor of a small city." Disgustingly, among others, there were even photo shots of her legs and, in a new all-time low for cable news, CNN posted a doctored photograph of Governor Palin, which had been altered to portray the Governor in a bikini holding an AK-47.

The television industry and its celebrities have also focused much of their attention on a negative or false portrayal of Governor Palin. Among others, Saturday Night Live has and continues to portray a negative public perception of Governor Palin. HBO plans a documentary, "Game Changers," scheduled to air prior to the 2012 election, which portrays Sarah Palin as ignorant and unqualified for the presidency, again, intending to negatively influence public opinion of her.

So who exactly are the media, and are they, in fact, biased against conservative candidates? We must follow the money. General Electric owns NBC, while Disney owns ABC, and CBS owns Viacom. Lists of contributions to political candidates are provided on opensecrets.org. The vast majority of the entire music, movie, and television industry donated $8.6 million to Senator Obama. Members of the motion picture industry gave $12.7 million to Democrats, while donating only $1.3 million to Republicans. Commercial television donated $3.3 million to Democrats but only $2.2 million to Republicans. It is also interesting to note that Rupert Murdock and News Corporation, which is the parent company of FOX News, contributed $1.02 million to Democrats and less than $500,000 to Republicans in 2008. It is common for various companies or industries to make contributions to both political parties and individuals within those political parties in order to secure their positions no matter who prevails.

Jeffery Immelt, CEO of General Electric (GE), and his Political Action Committee (PAC) have contributed millions of dollars to the Democrat National Committee and to the Obama presidential campaign. GE's sister company, GE Financials, also gave its full contribution limits to the Democrats. MSNBC, which is owned by GE and Microsoft, donated an additional $1.2 million to Senator Obama. In addition, other PACs and organizations with ties to GE and Microsoft contributed to Senator Obama. Immelt and NBC's new chief, Jeff Zucker, have instructed CNBC to stop criticizing President Obama's economic policies. MS-

NBC continually referred to the TEA Party movement as racist. (49) GE, NBC, and the Obama agenda are all tied together. GE, as a corporation owning a major media outlet, is using its power to influence politics in order to make money for itself from government contracts.

Now, GE appears to have received its payback from the Obama White House. According to the Washington Examiner, GE is the beneficiary of billions of dollars in government contracts through the cap and trade legislation. GE also received billions of tax-funded dollars in the financial bailouts. Further, ABC News reported GE paid "not a penny in taxes in 2010." In fact, GE received a $3.2 billion tax benefit. This was while the top corporate tax bracket is at 35%, and President Obama has spoken for two years regarding the necessity to reform corporate taxes to "simplify, eliminate loopholes, treat everybody fairly"! GE earned $14.2 billion in profits in 2010, but $9 billion was from offshore profits. This was the second consecutive year GE recorded profits of billions of dollars without paying any taxes. During that same period, between 2007 and 2009, Immelt was a close adviser to President Obama, even serving as chairman of Obama's Council on Jobs and Competitiveness. Ironically, under Immelt's leadership, 21,000 American workers lost their jobs at GE, and 20 American factories were closed. Today, more than half of GE's workforce is located outside of America.

No wonder many Democrats have stated over the years, "I didn't leave the Democratic Party, it left me."

The ultimate power player of media influence on the American people is George Soros, one of the wealthiest men in the world, with a personal fortune of approximately $13 billion. Soros is considered by many as "the most dangerous man in America." He is the high-powered fuel of the Democrat machine, whose tangled web finances all aspects of liberal causes through his Open Society Institute (OSI).

The following organizations are known to be directly funded by Soros and OSI: (*See* http://www.discoverthenetworks.org/view-SubCategory.asp?id=1237.)

1. Arab American Institute and Bill of Rights Defense Committee, which "accuse America of violating the civil rights and liberties of many of its residents."

2. Mexican American Legal Defense and Educational Fundcalls, Lawyers Committee for Civil Rights Under Law, NAACP, and National Council of La Raza, which "depict America as a nation whose enduring racism must be counterbalanced by racial and ethnic preferences in favor of non-whites."

3. Sentencing Project, Critical Resistance, and Leadership Conference on Civil and Human Rights, which "portray the American criminal-justice system as racist and inequitable."

4. Center for Community Change, Gamaliel Foundation, Ruckus Society, American Institute for Social Justice, Institute for America's Future, People for the American Way, Democracy for America, and Midwest Academy, each of which calls for "massive social change and for the recruitment and training of activist leaders to foment that change."

5. Center for Economic and Policy Research, Center on Budget and Policy Priorities, Ella Baker Center for Human Rights, and Ella Lazarus Fund, which "disparage capitalism while promoting a dramatic expansion of social-welfare programs funded by ever-escalating taxes."

6. Health Care for America Now, "a vast network of organizations," which support socialized medicine in America.

7. Project Vote, Catalist, Brennan Center for Justice, Progressive States Network, and Progressive Change Campaign Committee, each of which strives "to move American politics to the left by promoting the election of progressive political candidates."

8. The American Prospect, Inc. magazine, the "media reform" organization called Free Press, Independent Media Institute, The Nation Institute, Pacifica Foundation, Media Matters for America, and Sundance Institute, each of which promotes "leftist ideals and worldviews in the media and the arts."

9. Alliance for Justice and American Constitution Society for Law and Policy, which "seek to inject the American judicial system with leftist values."

10. Center for Constitutional Rights, National Security Archive Fund, American Civil Liberties Union (ACLU), and Human Rights Watch, which "oppose virtually all post-9/11 national security measures enacted by the U.S. government."

11. Constitutional Project and Lynne Stewart Defense Committee, which "defend suspected anti-American terrorists and their abettors."

12. Amnesty International and Global Exchange, which "depict virtually all American military actions as unwarranted and immoral."

13. American Friends Service Committee and Justice at Stake, which "advocate America's unilateral disarmament and/or a steep reduction in its military spending."

14. Catholics in Alliance for the Common Good, Sojourners, People Improving Communities through Organizing, and Catholics for Choice, which "advance a leftist agenda by infiltrating churches and religious congregations."

15. Institute for Policy Studies, New America Foundation, and Urban Institute, each of which are "think tanks that promote leftist policies."

16. American Immigration Council, Casa de Maryland, Immigrant Legal Resource Center, Migration Policy Institute, LatinoJustice PRLDF, Immigration Policy Center, National Immigration Forum, and National Immigration Law Center, all of which promote "open borders, mass immigration, a watering down of current immigration laws, increased rights and benefits for illegal aliens and, ultimately, amnesty."

17. Earthjustice, Green for All, Natural Resources Defense Council, Alliance for Climate Protection, Friends of the Earth, and Earth Island Institute, all of which "promote radical environmentalism."

18. New Yorkers Against the Death Penalty, Witness to Innocence, Equal Justice USA, Death Penalty Information Center, People of Faith Against the Death Penalty, and Fair Trial Initiative, each of which opposes "the death penalty in all circumstances."

19. Feminist Majority, Ms. Foundation for Women, and National Partnership for Women and Families, all of which "promote modern-day feminism's core tenet—that America is fundamentally a sexist society where discrimination and violence against women have reached epidemic proportions."

20. Center for Reproductive Rights, NARAL Pro-Choice America, National Abortion Federation, Planned Parenthood, and Choice USA, which all promote "not only women's rights to taxpayer-funded abortion on demand, but also political candidates who take the same position."

21. United Nations Foundation and Coalition for an International Criminal Court, both of which "favor global government which would bring American foreign policy under the control of the United Nations or other international bodies."

22. Drug Policy Alliance, Andean Council of Coca Leaf Producers, and Banco de Columbia, each of which supports the legalization of drugs. Soros has also contributed millions of dollars to other groups

for the legalization of drugs, as well as $1 million to the California ballot measure to legalize marijuana for personal use in that state.

23. Project of Death in America, Death with Dignity National Center, and Compassion in Dying Federation of America, each of which supports "euthanasia for the terminally ill."

24. Greenlining Institute and Center for Responsible Lending, each of which "have pressured mortgage lenders to make loans to undercapitalized borrowers, a practice that helped spark the sub-prime mortgage crisis and housing-market collapse of 2008."

25. In 2003, Soros founded and coordinated the "Shadow Democratic Party," or "Shadow Party," created to network unions, non-profit activist groups, and think tanks of organizations that identified themselves with the liberal agenda. Hillary Clinton and Harold McEwan Ickes were also principle organizers. Ickes coordinated the administrative core of the Shadow Party through America Coming Together, America Votes, Center for American Progress, Joint Victory Campaign 2004, Media Fund, MoveOn.org, and Thunder Road Group, which are all leftist organizations. These organizations set the agenda for Soros and assisted him in advancing his own personal political and social agendas. The Shadow organizations also raise enormous amounts of money, ultimately controlling which Democrat candidate they will support, forcing their agendas to move in the liberal directions they desire. As Eli Pariser, the director of the MoveOn.org PAC, stated, "Now it's our party. We bought it, we own it…" (*See*, http://www.freerepublic.com/focus/f-news/2427193/posts.)

26. Citizens for Responsibility and Ethics in Washington, almost all of whose targets are Republican.

27. Faithful America, which promotes the redistribution of wealth, an end to enhanced interrogation procedures vis-a-vis prisoners-of-war, the enactment of policies to combat global warming, and the creation of a government-run health care system.

28. Gisha: Center for the Legal Protection of Freedom of Movement, an anti-Israel organization seeking to help Palestinians "exercise their right to freedom of movement"; I'lam, an anti-Israel NGO seeking the development and empowerment of the Arab media giving voice to Palestinian issues; Institute for Public Accuracy, anti-American, anti-capitalist and anti-Israel organization; and World Organization Against Torture, which works closely with groups condemning Israeli Security Measures against Palestinian terrorism.

29. Grantmakers Without Borders, which is supportive of leftist environmental, anti-war and civil rights groups, in addition to being generally hostile to capitalism, deeming it one of the chief "political, economic, and social systems," giving rise to a host of "social ills."

30. Human Rights First, which supports open borders, the rights of illegal aliens, filed *amicus curiae* briefs on behalf of terror suspect Jose Padilla, and is opposed to the Guantanamo Bay detention facilities.

31. Suozzi, English and Klein, PC, an influential defender of Big Labor, headed by Harold Ickes.

32. Tides Foundation and Tides Center, major radical left funders.

33. The following are the remaining Soros/OSI directly-funded organizations: Air America (now defunct), All of Us or None, American Bar Association Commission on Immigration Policy, American Family Voices, American Federation of Teachers, American Immigration Law Foundation, American Library Association, American Prospect, Inc., Association of Community Organizations for Reform Now, Black Alliance for Just Immigration, Brookings Institution, Campaign for America's Future, Campaign for Better Health Care, Campaign for Youth Justice, Campus Progress, Center on Wisconsin Strategy (COWS), Change America Now, Common Cause, Defenders of Wildlife, Democracy Alliance, Democracy 21, Democracy Now!, Democratic Justice Fund, Democratic Party, Economic Policy Institute, Electronic

Privacy Information Center, EMILY's List, Energy Action Coalition, Fair Immigration Reform Movement, Four Freedoms Fund, Free Exchange on Campus, Funding Exchange, Global Centre for the Responsibility to Protect, Human Rights Campaign, Immigration Defense Project, Immigration Workers Citizenship Project, Independent Media Center, Institute for New Economic Thinking, Institute for Women's Policy Research, International Crisis Group, J Street, Jewish Funds for Justice, League of United Latin American Citizens, League of Women Voters, MADRE, Malcolm X Grassroots Movement, Massachusetts Immigrant and Refugee Advocacy Coalition, Mercy Corps, Military Families Speak Out, National Coalition to Abolish the Death Penalty, National Committee for Responsive Philanthropy, National Committee for Voting Integrity, National Council for Research on Women, National Council of Women's Organizations, National Lawyers Guild, National Organization for Women (NOW), National Priorities Project, National Women's Law Center, Peace and Security Funders Group, Peace Development Fund, Physicians for Human Rights, Physicians for Social Responsibility, Ploughshares Fund, Presidential Climate Action Project, Prison Moratorium Project, Proteus Fund, Public Citizen Foundation, Rebuild and Renew America Now, Res Publica, Social Justice Leadership, Southern Poverty Law Center, Think Progress, U.S. Public Interest Research Group, Universal Healthcare Action Network, US Action, Working Families Party, and YWCA World Office in Switzerland.

In addition to the above-named organizations, which are directly funded by George Soros and OSI, the following are secondary affiliate organizations known to be funded indirectly through them: Center for Progressive Leadership, John Adams Project, Moving Ideas Network (MIN), New Organizing Institute, Think Progress, and Vote for Change.

In actuality, Soros has influenced his liberal opinion into the American culture as well as contributed approximately $5 billion invested in over 100 liberal organizations and causes, but that is not the full extent. Amazingly, some of these organizations also receive federal funding, including the ACLU. National Public Radio (NPR), funded through the federal government with taxpayer money, has become a major media source for liberal politics. As NPR is considered a non-profit organization, it is able to legally withhold the list of its donors. It is known that NPR has received millions in undisclosed donations. It was recently revealed that Soros made a single $1.8 million donation to NPR, the main purpose of which was to launch the "Impact the Government" project. This particular donation by Soros is specifically being used to hire 100 reporters in all 50 states to influence news and public opinion to become even more liberal than it already is. In short, ultimately the news will become campaign propaganda camouflaged as news.

However, as Soros is not satisfied only with elevating liberal news sources, he is also working to silence the opposition to the liberal philosophy. He is funding Media Matters, a leftist media watchdog information center, which monitors conservative news and opinions. This strategy is to abandon monitoring of most other media sources, by assembling a legal team to focus directly on FOX News to contain its reports and influence against the mainstream media's liberal agenda. This legal team's responsibility is to file lawsuits, including supposed defamation of character, invasion of privacy, or any other allegations it chooses, whether or not the allegation has any basis. (50)

Soros has also teamed up with billionaires Herb and Marion Sandler, who both profited from the savings and loan crisis, by founding an organization called Pro Publica, which is designed to provide investigative columns to news outlets, including newspapers and websites. (51)

Soros also has influence through his son, Alexander, who is noted to be the top donor to Democrats among college students.

Soros is also involved in influencing all election results and investigations through his "Secretary of State Project" (SOS Project). Through this project, Soros has been able to influence and continues to influence and assist Democrats running for the office of secretary of state across all 50 states. The primary duty of each secretary of state is to ensure the integrity of the voting process and certify elections. However, with Soros in control of the ultimate responsibility of the secretaries of state, he can be assured that suspected voter fraud will receive a minimal amount of investigation, if any at all.

George Soros has also been known to funnel money to ACORN, which has been responsible for immeasurable amounts of voter fraud across the United States. Early in his career, President Obama was an attorney for ACORN. Former NBC anchor, Tom Brokaw, sat on the board of the Robin Hood Foundation, a liberal foundation supported by Soros, which has also provided millions in funding to ACORN.

As if this were not enough, George Soros is also directly affecting campaigns with his billions of dollars circumventing campaign finance laws. Democrat Senator Al Franken, one of the current U.S. Senators from Minnesota, is a former talk-show host for Air America, a far-left media outlet, which was burdened by a tremendous amount of debt. However, The Democracy Alliance, funded by Soros, Peter Lewis, the CEO of Progressive Insurance, and Hollywood producer, Rob Reiner, together underwrote a debt payment up to $8 million to Air America. This allowed Franken to receive a large amount of up-front money toward his costs in running for the U.S. Senate. In effect, George Soros and friends ran completely around the campaign finance laws. Therefore, through this underwriting, instead of Franken receiving the campaign finance limit of $2,100 per individual donor, he was able to receive almost $22,000 per day. At the same time, Air America provided free airtime for Franken and promoted websites encouraging donations to other liberal candidates.

The Soros deception and web of entanglement is also tied to religion through funding to Sojourners. Soros attempts to use redistribution of wealth as a religious requirement to transform the worldview of the Marxist philosophy into the church as a brand of social justice. Using the religious left, revenue has tripled in less than ten years, assisting in the election of Obama and other leftist Democrats.

George Soros is a profoundly dangerous man to America, using billions of his personal dollars to promote his extreme left-wing philosophy and agenda. He is working tirelessly to infiltrate our entire political process, destroy America as she was founded, and destroy our moral fabric. I believe that it is apparent that Soros has an ultimate goal which is to lead America toward a disguised plan of a one world economic order, through one global government, global currency, global taxes, global climate change regulations, and a global army, all controlled by the United Nations. He vehemently opposes Israel, the war on terror, organized religion, and the U.S. Constitution, including the individual rights it grants Americans, especially the right to bear arms.

Unfortunately, the fact that George Soros controls such a vast amount of the major media outlets means that the media does not report on him whatsoever. Most Americans have absolutely no idea who George Soros is, the plan he has developed through his conferences, or the mandate he has placed on the media market to institute and perpetuate his deception. There is no doubt in my mind that liberals have fully infiltrated the entire media market and will work to keep silent anything over which they do not have control. Therefore, it is not surprising that federal records indicate journalist contributions favored Democrats by a 15:1 ratio over Republicans in 2008. The disparity was even greater among journalists, by a 20:1 ratio, who donated to the Obama campaign versus that of the McCain campaign. It has been evident for years that over 90% of journalists have supported and donated to Democrats, becoming an essential part of the American Democrat Party machine. No wonder Sean Hannity stated, "2008 is the year journalism died in America."

Sarah, Obama, and the Media

Respected professional journalism is considered fair and balanced coverage of the news, revealing only corroborated facts. All opinions should be balanced by alternative viewpoints. In the 2008 presidential election, the media was not only biased, it obviously acted as an agent for the Obama campaign, in large part delivering his presidential victory. The media glorified Senator Obama, reported on stories describing him by the word "messiah," while shielding him from many unanswered questions about his past. To this day, America continues to know very little about his past, his experience, or his relations with associates and individuals who have influenced his thinking or positions. The media praised and protected Senator Obama, using its power and influence to repeat and promote his campaign's talking points and to unleash a full frontal attack against Governor Palin's character. This unfair, unprofessional reporting influenced public perception that Governor Palin was unqualified, unintelligent, and unelectable since they could not, in fact, discredit her accomplishments and achievements. CNN even went so far as to report on its front-page bets from viewers that Governor Palin was going to withdraw from the race due to the heavy criticism made against her, in spite of the fact there were no valid reasons provided.

The mainstream media and Senator Obama had together aligned themselves against Governor Palin, continually stating she was simply an unqualified and inexperienced small-town mayor. But how would Governor Palin have actually compared to Senator Obama had the media reporting been professional, fair, balanced, and factual? Was Governor Palin qualified to hold the title of vice president of the United States?

Executive Experience

When executive experience is considered, none of the resumes of the other contenders, Senators McCain, Obama, or Biden, contained ANY executive experience. During the 2008 Republican National Convention, former New York Mayor Rudy Giuliani stated, "She [Sarah] has more executive experience than the entire Democratic ticket." (52) Governor Palin was, in fact, the only candidate on the two presidential tickets to have any executive experience. She served as mayor and manager of Wasilla, which is the fifth largest city in Alaska, after serving the previous four years on the city council. She served as commissioner on the Alaska Oil and Gas Commission. As governor of Alaska, which is approximately 20% of the entire land mass of America and shares its territorial borders with Canada and Russia; she managed a $10 billion budget and more than 24,000 state employees. By contrast, Senator Obama had absolutely no executive experience, although he did claim many times to have it, stating he had managed his campaign for 18 months. In January 2005, he became the junior U.S. Senator from Illinois and authored no significant legislation. Although it was never called into session, he was the chairman of the Senate Subcommittee on Europe. Previously, he was as an Illinois state senator from 1997-2004, where he voted "present" over 100 times without taking a stand on any significant issue. Prior to 1997, he was a "community organizer."

Military Affairs Experience

Governor Palin was the commander-in-chief of the Alaska National Guard and received United States national security briefings. In addition, her oldest son, Track, enlisted in the U.S. Army and served in combat in Iraq.

Senator Obama had absolutely no military affairs experience.

Entitlements and Earmarks

The media was quick to falsely report that Governor Palin was originally in support of the "Bridge to Nowhere," a $200 million federal earmark project, before she corrected them, stating she had consistently fought against the project. Yet, the media failed to reveal the fact that this project passed by a 91-4 vote, with Senators Obama and Biden voting for the legislation, Senator McCain voting against it, and five senators not voting at all. In total, federal earmark requests for Alaska were reduced by as much as 80% by Governor Palin. (53)

In an effort to save Alaska taxpayers unnecessary expenditures, Governor Palin sold the governor's plane and released both the governor's personal chef and driver, while reducing her own salary and state per diem reimbursements, as she had previously done as mayor of Wasilla.

There is no record of any eliminated entitlements requested by either Senators Obama or Biden. In fact, Senator Obama actually used his position to assist his wife, who was promoted by her hospital-employer several months following his election to the U.S. Senate. After Mrs. Obama's promotion, Senator Obama requested a $1 million federal earmark to the hospital. (54)

Banning Books vs. Banning Guns

The media sensationalized on the 12-year-old issue that Sarah Palin had "banned" library books while she served as mayor of Wasilla. Outlets reported Sarah had fired the Wasilla's librarian for her lack of support and loyalty, but failed to fully report that Sarah had retracted the dismissal and allowed the librarian to stay. In fact, the librarian never stated that Sarah fired her due to her "refusal to ban" books. In an effort to affect public opinion, the media failed to accurately report that Sarah never asked for any book to be banned but, rather, merely questioned the librarian regarding the process of banning books. Not surprisingly, the New York Times and Time Magazine falsely reported the story for other media outlets, elaborating their biased opinions as fact. Amazingly, an on-line list suddenly appeared of books that Sarah allegedly attempted to ban, including "Harry Potter," which had neither been written nor published at the time of Sarah's conversation with the librarian! For the record, both June Pinell-Stephens, chairwoman of the Alaska Library Association's Intellectual Freedom Committee, and the Frontiersman confirmed no books were banned from the library's shelves.

While the media focused on this inaccurate issue, it ignored Senator Obama's record on his attempt to ban the use of firearms. As a state senator, Obama worked to pass legislation in Illinois preventing law-abiding citizens from owning firearms. He carried his anti-firearms position on to his presidency, banning nearly one million American rifles, including the Carbine rifle and the M1 Garand, which General Patton once described as "the greatest battle implement ever devised." President Obama set the precedent that America can consider certain firearms as illegal, restricted, or banned altogether. Ultimately, this goal is to employ international law, rather than American law, as a means of circumventing the U.S. Constitution, thus removing altogether Americans' right to own and carry firearms. In addition, President Obama is appointing liberal judges who disagree with the second amendment. This is perpetuating the plan orchestrated by George Soros and his financed OSI to organize a global ban on guns, through the creation of international gun-control regulations, undermining and eliminating the second amendment of the U.S. Constitution.

College Education

Sarah Palin graduated from the University of Idaho in 1987, with a bachelor's of science degree in journalism communication and a minor in political science. All of Sarah Palin's education records are available and confirmable.

On the other hand, Barack Obama's academic records are sealed, from his kindergarten through law school years. Barack Obama attended Occidental College, a small liberal arts college in California, from 1979-1981, with no earned degree. It is assumed Barack Obama earned a bachelor's of science degree in international relations from New York's Columbia University in 1983. However, there is no record of him attending Columbia from September 1981 through September 1982, according to documentation of the National Student Clearinghouse. In fact, there is no record of Barack Obama residing anywhere or attending any other university in America during that time period. So where was Barack Obama from September 1981 to September 1982? Barack Obama has claimed he visited Pakistan for a month or two, but there is no documentation as to where he was the rest of that year. His Pakistan visit was not even revealed until his own admission of the fact in April 2008 at a San Francisco fundraiser.

In his second book, "Dreams from My Father: A Story of Race and Inheritance," Barack Obama revealed his move from Los Angeles to New York, where he arrived without money and became friends with Sohale Siddiqi, whom Obama refers to as "Sadik." Sadik happened to be a cocaine-using Pakistani residing illegally in America. Obama moved out of his apartment and in with Sadik in the fall of 1981. Both of his books, "Dreams of My Father: A Story of Race and Inheritance" and "Audacity of Hope: Thoughts on Reclaiming the American Dream," fail to mention any trip to Pakistan. Also unknown is how he could travel to Pakistan, as he didn't even have enough money for an apartment. It is also interesting to ponder that, at that time; American citizens were not allowed to legally travel to Pakistan. Who financed his trip? How was he able to travel to Pakistan if he was an American citizen? Did he use another passport from another country? What did he do in Pakistan? How long was he in Pakistan? These are absolutely valid questions demanding answers regarding any person running for the office of president of the United States. But questions and investigations by the media, once again, were, and continue to be, absent.

When Barack Obama was elected president, he appointed John Brennan, a former CIA operative, as a deputy national security adviser. CNN revealed that during the 2008 campaign, an employee of Brennan, who was a consultant to the Obama campaign, had illegally accessed Obama's passport on three occasions. As if this were not enough to raise eyebrows and red flags, Barack Obama has his passport sealed. Yet, the media continues to refuse to ask any questions.

In September 1982, Barack Obama returned to Columbia University and received his degree in September 1983. However, no one appears to have known him. Obama claimed to be involved in the Black Student Organization. FOX News contacted 400 of Obama's former classmates, none of whom were able to remember him. In September 2008, The New York Sun reported, "The Obama campaign has refused to release his college transcript, despite an academic career that led him to Harvard Law School and, later, to a lecturing position at the University of Chicago."

Also missing is Barack Obama's thesis paper from Columbia University. Michael Baron, a former Columbia professor who also donated $1,250 to the Obama campaign and wrote a letter of recommendation on behalf of Barack Obama for his admission into Harvard, stated the thesis paper may have been thrown away. Columbia has no copy available in its archives and, on July 24, 2008, the Obama administration advised NBC News they were unable to release copies of his thesis paper.

Jack Cashill, a World Net Daily reporter, reported that Barack Obama's grades at Columbia University were mediocre, stating, "We know enough about Obama's Columbia grades to know how far they fall below the Harvard norm, likely even below the affirmative action-adjusted black norm at Harvard."

So how did Barack Obama gain admission to Harvard? Who funded his education and residence there? After Barack Obama graduated from Columbia University, he worked as a community organizer in Chicago, before his acceptance into Harvard. One person who was influential in assisting Barack Obama was Khalid al-Mansour, who is a principal adviser to Saudi Prince al-Waleed bin Talal. It is unknown when or where al-Mansour met Obama. What is known is al-Mansour spoke on university campuses, including Columbia University, and was a well-known lawyer in the black community. He is an orthodox Muslim, Black Nationalist, educator, author, and outspoken enemy of the nation of Israel. According to a Newsmax article, al-Mansour has accused Jews of "stealing the land the same way Christians stole the land from the Indians in America." He was also reportedly a mentor of the Black Panther Party in the early 1960s with a professed hatred for white people. Al-Mansour used his personal connection with Percy Sutton, a former Manhattan Borough president, attorney for Malcolm X, and business partner of al-Mansour, to assist in Barack Obama's admission to Harvard.

Senator Obama claimed during his presidential campaign that he paid his way through Harvard with student loans. However, no evidence has been produced by anyone that Barack Obama received any student loans, despite a formal request by the Chicago Tribune to release his student loan details. Further, according to a Newsmax article, Percy Sutton revealed al-Mansour personally raised money to assist Barack Obama during his law school years. Barack Obama graduated from Harvard Law School in 1991.

Despite the fact that the media refuses to wade into the issue, there are an enormous number of questions and a dearth of non-answers on the personal life of Barack Obama.

Private Sector Employment

Prior to her entering the world of politics, Sarah Palin was a sports reporter, covering both high school and college sports. She then became a news anchor for the Anchorage NBC-affiliate. In addition, Sarah also assisted her husband with their commercial fishing business.

In 1985, prior to entering Harvard Law School, Barack Obama spent three years as a community organizer and teacher of the Saul Alinsky method, working for a group named The Developing Communities Project. What is a community organizer? Even Barack Obama can't answer that question. He wrote in "Dreams of My Father: A Story of Race and Inheritance," "When classmates in college asked me just what it was that a community organizer did, I couldn't answer them directly." It is not clear what role he played, what his accomplishments were, or even what qualifications community organizing provided him to become president. Alinsky, who was a left-wing radical Marxist and Socialist, wrote about the community organizer in his book, "Rules for Radicals," identifying a successful organizer as "an abrasive agent to rub raw the resentments of the people in the community, to fan latent hostilities of many people to the point of overt expression." Alinsky teaches organizers to steer groups toward confrontation in forms of picketing and demonstrating. He advises organizers to first tackle small issues and projects, such as demanding the repair of street lights and, as the group gains confidence, to take on larger projects encouraging groups of people to take action.

Barack Obama was also a civil rights attorney representing ACORN, an organization widely known and indicted in several states for its connections to voter fraud. Yet, his resume indicates no significant accomplishments in his law practice nor a well-known reputation within the legal community.

Barack Obama was a lecturer of constitutional law at the University of Chicago Law School from 1992-2004. Yet, in 2001, he expressed his own contempt for the U.S. Constitution on WBEZ-FM, a Chicago radio station, stating it limited the government's ability to "redistribute wealth." Later, as President, he referred to a cite from the U.S. Constitution in a State of the Union Address before Congress, when he actually was citing from the Declaration of Independence. In the same speech, he had the audacity to then lecture the U.S. Supreme Court Justices in attendance regarding a recent Supreme Court ruling. Did our mainstream media correct or report on Barack Obama's lack of knowledge on legal issues he should fully understand having gained a law degree from Harvard Law School?

Unions

While employed as a sports reporter during the late 1980s, Sarah Palin was a union member of Local 1547. During his tenure with British Petroleum, her husband was a member of the United Steelworkers Union.

Barack Obama has never belonged to a union; however, he is endorsed by unions.

Spouses' Occupations

Todd Palin is a self-employed salmon fisherman. He is a former North Slope production supervisor for British Petroleum (BP), which he left after 17 years, when BP became involved in negotiations with Governor Palin regarding natural gas lines.

Michelle Obama was an assistant to former Chicago Mayor Daley and a former associate at the Chicago Sidley Austin law firm.

Michelle is also a former vice president for community and external affairs at the University of Chicago Hospital, a former associate dean of student services at the University of Chicago, and a former executive director for the Chicago Office of Public Allies. As mentioned previously, Michelle received a pay raise (160%) within months of Barack Obama's election to the U.S. Senate, with the hospital receiving a $1 million federal earmark requested by Senator Obama after her promotion. (55)

Had Todd Palin continued his employment with BP and received a 160% pay raise, and had BP received money or special favors through the Alaska governor's office, would the mainstream media have reported it?

Corruption

Sarah Palin doesn't lead by talk, she leads by actions. She is an example of the rare elected official who says what she means and means what she says, never compromising the principles she believes are right. She has always been a woman of integrity, led by honesty and high morals, always recognizing her service to the people as being more important than a position's benefit to her.

Her most notable fight on corruption occurred during her tenure as chairwoman of the Alaskan Oil and Gas Conservation Commission as its ethics supervisor. She recognized corruption from the misuse of office by a fellow commissioner, who was also the chairman of the Alaskan Republican Party and a member of the National Republican Committee. She resigned, giving up an annual $124,400 position, reported the corruption, even if it would possibly mean alienating herself from the Republican Party or losing a position that guaranteed a comfortable salary.

Governor Palin assisted the FBI in an investigation that later led to six legislators, known as the "Corrupt Bastard's Club," being found guilty for their unethical service and corruption as Alaska legislators.

Barack Obama, on the other hand, has used his positions for his personal political power and expediency. When running for the office of Illinois state senator, Obama received financial support from Iraqi billionaire Nadhimi Auchi. Auchi was convicted of corruption in France and also personally profited from the food for oil program scandal— a program which was intended to assist the Iraqi people with food in exchange for oil delivered to France. Accuhi assisted Obama in the purchase of his million-dollar mansion in a suspicious real estate deal with political fund raiser, Syrian Antoin "Tony" Rezco, who was later convicted on 16 counts of corruption. Rezco was a major contributor to former Illinois Governor Rob Blagojevich, who was also found guilty of corruption after attempting to sell the U.S. Senate seat vacated by Obama when he became President. Rezco had assisted Obama with $250,000 in campaign funding and used Obama's senate office.

As mentioned, Rezco assisted Obama in the purchase of his up-scale Chicago Kenwood neighborhood million-dollar mansion. However, according to public records, there are three other individuals listed as the current owners of the Obama's home. In December 2008, World Net Daily reported one of those owners is William Miceli, the attorney for convicted Rezco, who was also an associate and contributor to the Obama campaign. The two other owners are Probate Judge Jane L. Stuart and Obama's accountant, Howard Wineberg.

In addition to campaign finances, both Obama and Blagojevich relied upon Rezco for personal and political advice. Rezco worked with Stuart Levine, who served on the Illinois Public School Teachers Pension Fund Board. Levine also was a member of the Illinois state board that decided which hospitals were built and a panel member of an organization that decided which investment firms received funds from the $40-billion pension fund of retired teachers. Rezco maintained a donor list for both Blagojevich and Obama, with large sums of money being distributed to both. One donor was John Rogers, head of Ariel Capital, who donated $12,500 to Blagojevich in 2004 and $25,000 to Obama, according to state and FEC records. Obama, as an Illinois state senator, appeared before the Illinois Pension Fund Board and lobbied it to invest in more business to black-owned investment houses through Ariel Capital. As a result, Ariel gained substantial wealth. However, in 2006, a federal investigation became public indicating that investment returns by Ariel were insufficient and were, in actuality, a slumlord scam with checks being written for Blagojevich and Obama by investors in an effort to ultimately use the political clout of Blagojevich and Obama to gain the investment through the retirement board.

Prosecutors discovered two donations, $10,000 each, made to Obama's U.S. Senate campaign, by Joseph Aramanda and Elie Maloof. Aramanda and Maloof received a kickback from Glencoe Capital, an investment firm, which secured a $50 million deal. Aramanda's son was provided an intern position during the summer of 2005 in Senator Obama's Washington office, which the Obama staff admits was a result of a request made by Rezco.

According to a Black Enterprise.com 2004 article, Obama's lure of pension funds to raise campaign money dates back to 1999 and states Obama "was instrumental in the formation of a coalition of black investment firm owners and legislators in Illinois to create an initiative that would award black-owned firms with the management of some of the state's retirement funds."

Again, the mainstream media failed to reveal Senator Obama's ties to corruption.

Religion

Sarah Palin is a born-again Christian and accepted Jesus Christ as her personal Savior at the age of twelve. She finds time to pray, study her Bible and develop her personal relationship with God. She believes each person has a purpose from God, which prompted her toward politics. When Palin's home church, Wasilla Bible Church, was destroyed by fire in December 2008 by arson, the media ignored the story.

On January 24, 2007, Barack Obama's campaign claimed he has never been a Muslim, was not raised in the Muslim religion, and is a committed Christian. Less than two months later, on March 14, 2007, the campaign released another statement, "Obama has never been a practicing Muslim," adding that Obama had spent time as a child in an Islamic center in his Indonesian neighborhood, underscoring the Islamic training he received as a student of the Muslim religion. In Hawaii, Obama attended an affluent Catholic school; however, he was registered as a Muslim. Obama was raised by his Muslim stepfather, Lolo Soetoro, and his family was Muslim, including his father, grandfather, grandmother, Sarah, and half-brothers and sisters.

While living in Indonesia, Obama was required to study Islam daily, read and recite from the Qur'an, pray, and study the laws of Islam. In his book, "Dreams From My Father: A Story of Race and Inheritance," Obama admits studying the Qur'an while attending a "Muslim school." According to his teacher and principal, Tine Hahiyary, Obama had also participated in "mengaji," which is an advanced study of the Qur'an, and only devoted Muslims are allowed to participate in this study.

On February 27, 2007, in an interview with Nicholas Kristof of the New York Times, Obama recited the Muslim call to prayer, the Adhan, "with a first-class [Arabic] accent." In the opening line of the Adhan is the Shahada, which states:

"Allah is Supreme! Allah is Supreme!
Allah is Supreme! Allah is Supreme!
I witness that there is no god but Allah.
I witness that there is no god but Allah.
I witness that Muhammad is his prophet...."

Obama must have known from his study of the Qur'an that reciting the Shahada is a Muslim declaration of faith and that this publication, through the New York Times, would send a message to all Muslims throughout the world. However, Obama still denies to the American people that he is a Muslim, despite all the evidence, including a statement by a former classmate, Emirsyah Satar, "He [Obama] was often in the prayer room," and "He was quite religious in Islam; but only after marrying Michelle, he changed his religion." It is unknown to what extent Obama, in fact, changed his religion or for what purpose.

When Obama arrived in Chicago in 1983, after graduating from Columbia University, he began his work as a "community organizer" and needed to connect with his community. He joined a huge Black Nationalist church, Reverend Jeremiah Wright's Trinity United Church of Christ. Reverend Wright is also a former Muslim, who preaches Black Liberation Theology from the ideology of Marxism with roots in the black religious experience. Joining Trinity provided Obama a strong political base, a well-connected mentor and opportunities to develop many relationships. According to his first book, "The Audacity of Hope: Thoughts on Reclaiming the American Dream," Obama's religion allowed him to find some spiritual "street creed." Trinity adopted the Marxist ideology in 1968, introduced through Reverend James Cone, who introduced the black value system with a commitment to the following concepts:

1. Commitment to God;
2. Commitment to the black community;
3. Commitment to the black family;
4. Dedication to the pursuit of education;
5. Dedication to the pursuit of excellence;
6. Adherence to the black work ethic;
7. Commitment to self-discipline and self-respect;
8. Disavowal of the pursuit of "middleclassness";
9. Pledge to make the fruits of all developing and acquired skills available to the black community;

10. Pledge to allocate regularly a portion of personal resources for strengthening and supporting black institutions;

11. Pledge allegiance to all black leadership who espouse and embrace the black value system; and

12. Personal commitment to embracement of the black value system.

What is even more concerning is that this was also the belief of Dr. Khalid al-Mansour, who assisted Obama in gaining admission to Harvard Law School. In a video entitled, "Christians Designed Discrimination", which was uploaded by You Tube user IslamStudios, al-Mansour states, "White people don't feel bad, whatever you do to them, they deserve it. God wants you to do it and that's when you cut out the nose, cut out the ears, take flesh out of their body; don't worry because God wants you to do it."

The Black Liberation Theology embraces a black god who is totally exclusive to the black community. Obama has admitted that one of the first things that attracted him to Trinity was the "black value system." Cone stated, "Black theology refuses to accept a god who is not identified totally with the goals of the black community. If God is not for us and against white people, then he is a murderer, and we had better kill him. The task of black theology is to kill gods who do not belong to the black community...Black theology will accept only the love of God which participates in the destruction of the white enemy." Both Black Liberation Theology and Islam share the common belief that America is an oppressor which must be destroyed by their god.

Trinity also has ties to Islam. Usama K. Dakdok, a Christian minister dedicated to reaching the Muslim community, contacted Trinity posing as an Egyptian Muslim interested in joining the church. The caller asked if he would have to give up his Muslim faith to join the church. The church employee responded, "No. We have many Muslim members in our church."

Obama has never professed an acceptance of Jesus Christ as the Son of God like Christianity acknowledges Jesus, but has referred to Jesus in the traditional Muslim manner that he was a "wonderful teacher." Obama's actions don't represent Christianity. Neither does his church. He attended and participated at Trinity for 20 years, listening to Reverend Wright preach racism, hatred, and the bashing of America. The god of Black Liberation Theology is not the loving, forgiving, wise, and powerful God that Christians know. Obama has also stated that Jesus Christ is not necessary for salvation. He doesn't believe in the sanctity of traditional marriage or the sanctity of life. He supports the homosexual lifestyle and recognized "Pride Month" for a lifestyle which is forbidden in the Bible in Leviticus 20:13 and Romans 1:24-27. He is strongly opposed to the Israeli policy of expanding settlements and doesn't believe their land is from God, as promised to the Jews in Genesis 12:1-3, Numbers 34:1-12, and Joshua 1:1-4. The White House Christmas tree was even adorned with an ornament of the Chinese revolutionary, Mao Tse-tung, who is believed to have caused the deaths of 40-70 million of his own people during his rule from 1949-1976. Despite these facts, the mainstream media continues to report that Obama is a Christian as if that is a closed issue and a fact.

Family

When Michelle Obama criticized America and unpatriotically commented, "For the first time in my adult life, I am proud of my country," Senator Obama suggested to the media that they should leave his wife alone. However, the media refused to leave Governor Palin's family alone, attacking anything and everything about her and her family, including her children!

The media reported that Todd Palin received a violation ticket for fishing without a license and, as mentioned earlier, that he had been arrested for a DUI charge in 1986, 22 years prior to the campaign. It also reported that Todd was a member of the American Independent Party (AIP), quickly pointing out the AIP had called for a vote on whether Alaska should remain a state or secede from the Union. This was an outright attempt to place doubt as to whether Sarah also believed his philosophy, even though Sarah has been a registered Republican since May 1982.

However, the media minimally reported on Senator Obama's addiction to cigarettes and refused to report his marijuana and cocaine usage during his college days, facts he admitted in his autobiography. In addition, the media barely reported the fact that Obama's running mate, Senator Biden, had been accused of plagiarism multiple times.

Most Americans do not even know the name, Jill Jacobs, wife of Vice President Biden. No media attention was ever reflected on her or their children. The media failed to report that Biden's son, Hunter, was a consultant to a major credit card company. Senator Biden voted in favor of regulatory legislation which benefited that credit card company after it paid a large amount of money to Hunter. The media also didn't report that Hunter was involved in an investigation and lawsuit for defrauding his former business partner out of millions of dollars.

The media produced conflicting reports in the very first week of Governor Palin's nomination as to whether she was really the mother of Trig or had faked her pregnancy to cover for her daughter, Bristol. Other reports announced that Bristol was also pregnant. Governor Palin quickly clarified the issue by announcing Bristol was, in fact, pregnant and made the following announcement on September 1, 2008, "Bristol and the young man she will marry are going to realize very quickly the difficulties of raising a child, which is why they will have the love and support of our entire family. We ask the media to respect our daughter's and Levi's privacy as has always been the tradition of children of candidates." The media denied Palin's request. The media also played on Governor Palin's recent pregnancy to question her ability to hold the office of vice president, while using her children as media-driven punching bags in their blatantly obvious cause. Attempts were made, using "sexism," to portray Governor Palin as a mother who needed to have time to be home to raise her children and implied she was "selfish" for agreeing to the vice-presidential run.

A rigorous "hands off" policy had been placed upon the media with regard to Chelsea Clinton when Governor Clinton ran for the presidency and continued during his 8-year presidency. During the Clinton campaign, when Senator Gore's son was arrested for narcotics and speeding, the coverage was muted as "a private teaching moment," and the media was advised to "move along." However, the media failed to show even a modicum of respect for Bristol Palin's privacy. The New York Times ran three stories on its web site about Bristol's pregnancy. CNN exploited her pregnancy as an opportunity for sex education. MSNBC and the Huffington Post each ran stories on the expectant father. Slate, which is owned by the Washington Post, initiated a "Name Bristol Palin's Baby Contest." US Weekly published the headline, "Babies, Lies, and Scandal" on the cover of its magazine featuring Governor Palin.

Mayor Rudy Giuliani jumped on the Palin "sexism" issue at the Republican National Convention stating, "How dare they question whether Sarah Palin has enough time to spend with her children and be vice president. How dare they do that? When do they ask a man that question?" The media never questioned Senator Obama about the time he would have to balance with his daughters if elected. No one questioned how much time Obama spent with his girls during his non-stop campaign appearances. Todd Palin clarified he would be a stay-at-home parent, while Michelle expressed she would not be a stay-at-home parent should Senator Obama be elected president—her mother would be their two daughters' caretaker. The media never flew with those statements. Although males and females are required to be treated equally in the workplace, the media showed open bias and hypocrisy on this issue. The media openly assumed that, as a female, Governor Sarah could not handle being a mother and her position as vice president, while assuming Senator Obama, as a male, could handle being a father and his position as president. This was an amazing example of the "sexism" double standard by the very people who proclaim superiority on their understanding of sexual equality.

In August 2006, Governor Palin told the Anchorage Daily News that, "no woman should have to choose between her career, education, and her child." Sarah Palin is an extraordinary woman who has proven she can handle balancing a career and raising her family. During her public school years, she awoke at sunrise to hunt with her father before heading off to school. After school, she participated in basketball practice and still had time to complete her chores and homework assignments. Sarah has never been one to make excuses or accept pain as a reason to not act. During her basketball days, as her team captain, she played in the championship game with a fractured ankle. She traveled to Dallas, Texas, one month prior to Trig's due date, where she delivered a speech, even though her amniotic fluid began to leak during that speech. Immediately following her speech, she contacted her obstetrician and returned to Alaska for Trig's delivery. Three days after giving birth, Governor Palin returned to work!

Most mothers multitask, whether or not they have a career, with the ability to be actively involved in their children's sports, activities, and school, while balancing the needs and responsibilities at home. Mothers who choose a career and children are quite able to balance their responsibilities throughout the day, setting priorities, but always loving their children and never making excuses. Sarah has a warrior spirit to love her children, be a good mother, and love her country, which attributes originally drove her into politics.

In an interview with Katie Couric, on September 30, 2008, Sarah stated, "I'm a feminist who believes in equal rights, and I believe that women certainly today have every opportunity that a man has to succeed, and to try to do it all, anyway. And I'm very, very thankful that I've been brought up in a family where gender hasn't been an issue." However, the feminist movement, which is supposedly for advancement and equal rights of women, was silent when the media and other outlets trashed Sarah and her family. Why? Because Sarah is a conservative and doesn't fit the feminists' political agenda, which is, in fact, not about advancement and equal rights of all women but advancement of their own liberal agenda, actually using women as their pawns. These "feminist" organizations, which choose the women they want to advance, never once came to Sarah's aid or offered assistance, since her views are conservative, including a pro-life stance on abortion. Lisa Bennett, the National Organization for Women (NOW) communications director, wrote, "You're trying to take up our time getting us to defend your friend, Sarah Palin. If you keep us busy defending her, we have less time to defend women's bodies from the onslaught of reproductive rights attacks and other threats to our freedom, safety, livelihood, etc.!" (56)

NOW has been in conflict with Sarah in the past. As recently as the 2011 Super Bowl, NOW attempted to prevent an advertisement featuring Heisman-winning college quarterback, Tim Tebow, with his mother, who discussed her decision to give birth to Tim, who grew up to be an all-star quarterback at the University of Florida, even though her doctors recommended an abortion during her pregnancy. Sarah stated on FOX News, "It certainly isn't an offensive message. For NOW to have chosen this, [they are] picking a wrong battle I think, to come across sounding quite offended by hearing that a pro-life commercial will air on the Superbowl, it's baffling."

On March 19, 2011, Bill Maher, on the Bill Maher Show, called Sarah a "dumb twat." After Maher's comment, NOW begrudgingly defended Sarah. However, Lisa Bennet stated in a warning to conservatives for being forced to defend Sarah against the tasteless slur, "We are on to you, right-wingers!" (57)

Given Names

The media had no problem making comments on the "amusing" names of Governor Palin's five children. Katie Couric, as she prepared for the CBS Evening News prior to the 2008 Republican National Convention, was caught making fun of the boys' names. However, when it came to Senator Barack Hussein Obama's name, the media, and even Senator McCain, scolded anyone for using or emphasizing the "Hussein" middle name. Senator Obama wanted "Hussein," which is a Muslim name, ignored throughout the presidential campaign. However, after he was elected, President Barack Hussein Obama traveled to Muslim countries, where he boasted about his Muslim heritage and middle name.

Birth Certificate

Governor Palin, after the media reported multiple and conflicting stories, was questioned as to whether or not Trig was her real son or if she had "faked" her pregnancy to cover for her daughter, Bristol. When asked by Rusty Humphries, in a December 3, 2009 interview, whether the question of President Obama's birth certificate was a legitimate one to ask, Sarah responded, "I think it's a fair question, just like I think past association and voting records—all of that is fair game." Sarah continued, stating, "The weird conspiracy theory freaky thing that people talk about that Trig isn't my real son—'You need to produce his birth certificate, you need to prove that he's your kid,' which we have done. Maybe we can reverse that."

On April 27, 2011, President Obama produced to the public a certificate of live birth, which places the issue at rest. Or does it? There are some important issues and suspicious details to consider. The released birth certificate is on totally different print stock than other birth certificates released during 1961. There is no embossed seal on it, since only an "uncertified copy" was released. Further, how was it actually finally discovered, in light of the fact that the Democratic governor of Hawaii stated, just three months previous to its release, that he couldn't find any record of any birth certificate?

Most Americans believe that the first so-called "birther" to question Obama's birth certificate and eligibility to be president had to be a Republican, but it wasn't. The theory of Obama's birth certificate first emerged in the spring of 2008, when Senator Hillary Clinton's supporters circulated an anonymous email that questioned the citizenship of Obama. In the email it stated, "Barack Obama's mother was living in Kenya with his Arab-African father late in her pregnancy. She was not allowed to travel by plane then, so Barack Obama was born there, and his mother then took him to Hawaii to register his birth." This email was verified by Snopes in April 2008.

Philip J Berg, a self-avowed Democrat supporter of Hillary Clinton and former Pennsylvania Deputy Attorney General, also raised the issue. Berg filed a complaint in federal court on August 21, 2008 that alleged, "Obama carries multiple citizenships and is ineligible to run for president of the United States" under the U. S. Constitution, Article II, Section 1. The lawsuit further claimed that, "All the efforts of supporters of legitimate citizens were for nothing, because Obama cheated his way into a fraudulent candidacy and cheated legitimately eligible natural born citizens from competing in a fair process and the supporters of their citizen choice for the nomination."

Former President Bill Clinton also made a comment in an interview on Good Morning America, on August 4, 2008, questioning Obama's eligibility to be president stating, "That everybody has a right to run for president as long as they're qualified under the Constitution." Was Clinton asserting that Obama was not qualified under the U.S. Constitution?

The U.S. Constitution, Article II, Section 1, Clause 5, states, "No person except a natural born Citizen,…shall be eligible to the Office of President…"

Senator McCain's eligibility to run for the presidency was also questioned, with lawsuits having been filed in California and New Hampshire, as he was born in the Panama Canal Zone. However, his parents were both United States citizens, and his father was serving in the United States Navy in Panama at the time of the Senator's birth. The issue was brought before the U.S. Senate and, in April 2008, a nonbinding resolution was approved declaring McCain's eligibility to serve as president.

Governor Palin has removed herself from the issue, has never suggested that President Obama was not born in the United States, and has never asked for him to produce his birth certificate. Rather, she has remained focused on Obama's policies, stating on February 2011, "The faith, the birth certificate, others can engage in that kind of conversation. It's distracting. It gets annoying. And let's just stick with what really matters." (58)

The issue of President Obama's birth certificate took on new interest in January 2011, when Neil Abercrombie, the newly-elected Democratic Governor of Hawaii and friend of Obama, announced he wanted to put the issue to rest as to whether Obama was born in Hawaii or Kenya. Governor Abercrombie announced he would produce the birth certificate and end the controversy. However, he later announced he couldn't locate any birth certificate or record of birth in any hospital in Hawaii, which actually included a signature by any doctor. Hawaii's health director, Dr. Neal Palafox, who was responsible for maintaining birth records, resigned under "mysterious circumstances." His immediate resignation was a mystery, as the Department of Commerce and Consumer Affairs reported there had been no complaints regarding Dr. Palafox over the previous five years.

President Barack Hussein Obama, Jr.'s grandmother revealed the story of his birth in Mombasa, Kenya, after his mother went into labor while swimming at an ocean beach in Mombasa. She stated, "On August 4, 1961, Obama's mother, father, and grandmother were attending a Muslim festival in Mombasa, Kenya. Mother had been refused entry to airplanes due to her nine-month pregnancy. It was a hot August day at the festival, so the Obamas went to the beach to cool off. While swimming in the ocean, his mother experienced labor pains so was rushed to the Coast Provincial General Hospital, Mombasa, Kenya, where Obama was born a few hours later, at 7:21 p.m., on August 4, 1961. Four days later, his mother flew to Hawaii and registered his birth in Honolulu as a certificate of live birth which omitted the place and hospital of birth." (*See* video of President Obama's grandmother stating she was present at his birth in Mombasa, Kenya, at http://www.

youtube.com/watch?v=-4FqVRWgrNw&eurl=http://blog.barofinteg-
rity.us/2008/11/01/barack-nate-dhalani.aspx?ref=rss.)

Adding further doubt, the Honolulu Advertiser published photo-
stats of the original long-form birth certificates of twin daughters born
to Eleanor Nordyke at Kapi'olani Maternity and Gynecological Hospital
in Hawaii on August 5, 1961, one day after Barack Obama was supposedly born at the same facility. A close examination of the birth certificates issued by Kapi'olani to the Nordyke twins clearly indicates the
registration numbers precede the number assigned to Barack Obama,
even though he was supposedly born there on the day prior to them.

Twin Susan Nordyke was born at 2:12 p.m., Hawaii time, and assigned Certificate No. 151-61-10637, filed with the Hawaii registrar on
August 11, 1961. Twin Gretchen Nordyke was born at 2:17 p.m. and
assigned Certificate No. 151-61-10638, also filed with the Hawaii registrar on August 11, 1961. According to a version of Barack Obama's
purported short-form birth certificate, available from FactCheck.org,
he was assigned a higher certificate number than the Nordyke twins.
The online image indicates his Certificate No. 151-1961-10641, in spite
of the fact he was supposedly born in the same hospital on August
4, 1961, one day prior to the twins. Also, his certificate was registered
with the Hawaii registrar on August 8, 1961, three days prior to the
Nordyke twins' certificates. The Hawaiian newspapers released birth
announcements of babies born within that period of time without any
mention of Barack Obama's birth.

Adding to the confusion and opinions on this subject is a 2009
report in the Nigerian Observer, obtained by World Net Daily, which
lists Barack Obama as Kenyan-born. (See http://www.nigerianob-
servernews.com/4112008/4112008/news/news1.html.) Tim Adams,
Honolulu's former senior elections clerk, has signed an affidavit declaring the "long-form and the hospital-generated document absent."
In addition, World Net Daily reported that documentation also mysteriously missing regarding Barack Obama are his kindergarten and
Punahou school records, which most likely would contain a copy of

his birth certificate. According to attorney Gary Kreep, "His Occidental College records are important, as they may show he attended there as a foreign exchange student," as Obama attended Occidental under his Indonesian name, "Barry Soetoro." Regarding this issue, it is important to note that the Indonesian government doesn't recognize dual citizenships. Kreep requested to view Obama's Occidental records, but Obama's team of attorneys prevented the college from honoring Kreep's request. Obama's Columbia University records, Columbia thesis, Harvard Law School records, Harvard Law Review articles, scholarly articles from the University of Chicago, passport, medical records, legislative and scheduling records from his years as an Illinois state senator, Illinois State Bar Association records, any baptism records, and his adoption records are all unavailable, mysteriously "lost," or sealed from the public. Furthermore, Barack Obama admittedly traveled to Pakistan in 1981 or 1982 when, during those years, U.S. citizens carrying U.S. passports were prohibited from entering Pakistan.

All of this covering up is quite curious considering that Senator Obama campaigned for a more "open government," "more transparency," and "full disclosure." So, why did it take three years for Barack Obama to release his birth certificate? Furthermore, how was it mysteriously discovered when Hawaii's Governor Neil Abercrombie stated it was not there just three months prior to its release? Therefore, speculation continues to remain that Obama's certificate of live birth is not authentic. Its likeness to other Hawaiian birth certificates during that same period of time differs, as those were printed on totally different paper stock. The one released also was not embossed by the official seal of the state of Hawaii. Why wasn't it certified? And why did the White House agree to only release a copy of the "uncertified copy," in a "full disclosure" effort to finally set the issue to rest? In doing so, it has caused continuing suspicion over the controversy!

On May 1, 2011, World Net Daily reported that Ivan Zatkovich, who has a resume as an expert witness for 10 years, and 28 years of experience in computer science and document management, studied the document released by the White House. Mr. Zatkovich stated that documents normally contain one layer of PDF, but Obama's copy had multiple layers of PDF, indicating it had been scanned multiple times. He explained documents that are usually scanned multiple times have been modified or edited in some fashion. He pointed out, with regard to this specific document, the various items containing a different layer include the main text, mother's occupation, date accepted, and the stamp, signature and "time stamp" of the state registrar. His investigation, according to World Net Daily, indicated that, once the additional layers were removed, leaving only the background layer, a white border could be seen where text appears on other layers. The report concluded that the overlays were of a higher resolution than the background layer. Mr. Zatkovich stated the only two plausible explanations were someone changing the content of both the text and stamp or enhancing the text for legibility. His report concludes, "There is no specific evidence of how or why that content would have been changed, but the evidence clearly indicates that the document was changed."

Complicating the issue of the authenticity of Barack Obama's certificate of live birth is the recently-revealed evidence that his Selective Service form has been doctored, according to blogger Debbie Schlussel. Ms. Schlussel discovered the Selective Service registration form was not completed and submitted when Obama was younger, but the form was completed in 2008 and then altered to look older. Ms. Schlussel realized the forgers neglected to alter the "Document Location Number," which clearly shows a 2008 Selective Service form. The forgers also made two other mistakes on the document, showing the transaction date as September 4, 1980, Barack Obama's 19th birthday, and the location of registration was in Hawaii. On that date, Barack Obama was thousands of miles away at Occidental College in Los Angeles, California. Stephen Coffman, a former high-ranking federal agent confirms the allegations by Ms. Schlussel that this fraudulent act alone is considered a felony.

On March 29, 1975, President Ford signed Proclamation 4360, eliminating the registration requirement for all 18- to 25-year-old male

U.S. citizens. However, on July 2, 1980, President Carter signed Proclamation 4771, retroactively re-establishing the Selective Service registration requirement for all 18- to 26-year-old male citizens born on or
after January 1, 1960. President Obama was born on August 4, 1961.
The first registrations after Proclamation 4771 took place on Monday,
July 21, 1980, for those men born in January, February, and March 1960
at U.S. Post Offices. Tuesdays, Wednesdays and Thursdays were re-
served for men born in the later quarters of the year, and registration
for men born in 1961 began the following week, beginning on July
28, 1980, the week Barack Obama was required to register. Note that
September 4, 1980 was a Thursday. Under current law, all male U.S.
citizens are required to register with Selective Service within 30 days
of their 18th birthday. In addition, foreign males between the ages of
18 and 25 living in the United States must register. In 1980, men who
knew they were required to register and did not do so could face up
to five years in jail or a fine up to $50,000 if convicted. The potential
fine was later increased to $250,000. (See http://en.wikipedia.org/wiki/
Selective_Service_System.)

Another extremely disturbing discovery is Barack Obama's many
Social Security numbers. Attorney Orly Taitz appears to be the first to
have made this discovery. She hired Neil Sankey, a private investigator,
who used Intelius, LexisNexis, ChoicePoint, and other public records
to conduct a search on Obama's prior addresses and Social Security
numbers. In Illinois, there were 16 different addresses with a history of Barack Obama and Barack H. Obama with two separate Social
Security numbers. One began with 042, while the other began with
364. In California, where Obama attended Occidental College, there
are six addresses with three Social Security numbers, one beginning
with 537, and the other two beginning with 999. There is no address
listed in New York, while he attended Columbia University; however,
in nearby Jackson, New Jersey, there is one Social Security number beginning with 485. In Massachusetts, where Obama attended Harvard
Law School, there are three addresses, each using 042 in the beginning of the Social Security number, which was connected to the addresses in Chicago. The same 042 Social Security number is used again

in 2005, when Obama was elected to the U.S. Senate, in connection with Obama's apartment. However, three years later, Obama used a different Social Security number, beginning with 282, which was verified by the government in 2008 as an address listed at the Senate Office Building. Overall, the one Social Security number most often used was the one beginning with 042. However, 042 was a number issued by the state of Connecticut sometime between 1976 and 1977. During that time, Barack Obama was living in Hawaii, and no records have ever shown him living in Connecticut!

The information provided regarding Barack Obama's Selective Service form and Social Security numbers have been validated. There has been no other information offered or claims that the information isn't true. The serious question is why hasn't Barack Obama been questioned on any of these findings? As there is evidence that his Selective Service form was forged in 2008, shouldn't the valid question be raised that the longstanding doubts regarding Barack Obama's birth certificate could also possibly be a forgery? Why hasn't the media researched the information about his birth certificate, his forged Selective Service form, and his multiple Social Security numbers?

The media had access to all of Governor Palin's history and public records for reporting and publication. If her records had not been made available, an investigation would surely have quickly ensued. However, any and all records of President Obama and his history have been hidden and/or sealed, leaving Americans to question who he really is and what part(s) of his past he is hiding. The media continues to refuse to investigate!

Political Influence

Palin's interest in political service was influenced in her early life by her youth pastor, Theren Horn. Pastor Horn stated to her youth group, "You are called by God for a purpose," and continued, stating, "Some of you will be called to political leadership." Sarah clearly remembered those words, as she had strong faith and trusted God to direct her path in life. She was encouraged in her public service by Todd when she stepped into the political arena on the Wasilla city council as a young mother. She was motivated to do what was right, knowing her decisions would impact the future of her family and community.

The three primary people who had the greatest influence on Obama were Frank Marshal Davis, William "Bill" Ayers, and Reverend Jeremiah Wright.

Frank Marshall Davis had a major influence on Obama's early life, having met Obama sometime between the age of ten and his high school years, while he was living in Hawaii. Obama identified Davis as "Frank" in his biography, "Dreams from my Father: A Story of Race and Inheritance," to conceal his real identity, although he had previously admitted in "social conferences" that Davis had been his mentor. Obama developed a close father-like relationship with Davis, listening to his poetry and seeking advice on college and his career path. Obama wrote in his book that, during his adolescent years, "I could see Frank sitting in his overstuffed chair, a book of poetry in his lap, his reading glasses slipping down over his nose." Obama wrote that Frank was full of "hard-earned knowledge," and "Frank and his old black power dashiki self" gave him advice. Obama wrote that, prior to his leaving Hawaii at the age of 18 in 1979 for Occidental, Davis stated, "You are not going to go to college to get educated. You're going there to get trained....They'll train you to forget what you already know. They'll train you so good, you'll start believing what they tell you about equal opportunity and the American way and all that shit. You may be a well-trained, well-paid nigger, but you're a nigger just the same."

Toby Harndon, a writer for the UK Telegraph, has revealed that the "Frank" mentioned in Obama's book is actually Frank Marshall Davis. Davis is an admitted communist and member of the Communist Party USA, who spied on U.S. military installations in Hawaii for the Soviet Union. He is a radical activist, who edited a communist newspaper, an admitted pedophile, who authored pornographic novels, and wrote poetry in praise of Joseph Stalin.

Two investigative journalists, Herbert Romerstein and Cliff Kincaid, also released two explosive reports on President Obama's ties with communists and other anti-American affiliates. (*See* www.obamaism.blogspot.com.) Their major findings included that Obama has surrounded himself in the middle of two international communist networks—one in Hawaii, the other in Chicago—that have influenced, mentored, and supported his political advancement.

The Hawaii Communist Network, organized and directed from Moscow, was judged a security threat to the United States and was the subject of a congressional hearing on the "Scope of Soviet Activity in the United States." The Congressional Un-American Activities Committee (HUAC) also accused Davis of his involvement in several communist-front organizations. Davis first gained the attention of the FBI when he was a member of the Communist Party's Dorie Miller Club in Chicago. Davis left Chicago and moved to Hawaii, where he became a columnist for the Honolulu Record, a publication which was union-financed and communist-controlled. The FBI followed Davis to Hawaii and observed him photographing obscure beaches in Hawaii, assuming for the purpose of espionage. The Hawaii Communist Party was very dynamic and charged with agitation against the U.S. military bases at every opportunity. Davis was listed by the FBI as an individual who would be immediately arrested if a war broke out between the U.S. and the Soviet Union.

Davis, along with others in the Communist Party, went underground, dividing themselves into independent cells. Davis was known by the FBI to be in a cell called "Group 10." These Communist Party members joined officials within the local Democrat Party, and some in the Hawaiian Democrat Party still operate under those influences today.

Even further disturbing is Davis's involvement as a pedophile. According to Toby Herndon, writing for the UK Telegraph on August 24, 2008, Davis wrote a pornographic book, "Sex Rebel," under the assumed name "Bob Greene," in which he revealed that he and his wife engaged in a sexual "relationship" with a 13-year-old girl named Anne for the purpose of "educating her." He had the audacity to justify his actions, stating he and his wife were seduced by the young girl, and it was the girl who seduced him into sex with her. Davis wrote, "I'm not one to go in for Lolitas. Usually I'd rather not bed a babe under 20. But there are exceptions. I didn't want to disappoint the trusting child. At her still-impressionistic age, a rejection might be traumatic, could even cripple her sexually for life"!

After a reader of "Sex Rebel" revealed the "similarities in style and phraseology" between the pornographic book and his poetry, Davis admitted to changing his identity, writing, "I could not then truthfully deny that this book, which came out in 1968 as a Greenleaf Classic, was mine." He further wrote he "changed names and identities…all incidents I have described have been taken from actual experiences."

The next individual to have a major impact on Obama's political future was William Ayers, who during the 2008 presidential race, Senator Obama referred to as just "a guy who lives in my neighborhood" and "not somebody who I exchange ideas with on a regular basis." Really? Ayers was known as the "unrepentant terrorist," who in a September 11, 2001 New York Times article titled, "No Regret for a Love of Explosives," stated, "I don't regret setting bombs. I feel we didn't do enough." In addition, in a 2001 article in a Chicago magazine, Ayers is pictured stomping on the America flag. Also, in 2001, he stated to the New York Times that the notion of the United States as just a fair and decent place "makes me want to puke."

In the 1960s, Ayers and his lover, Bernardine Dohrn, were leaders of America's first terrorist organization, the Weather Underground. The Weather Underground, which was a Chicago 1960s and 1970s network of communist students, declared war against America for its involvement in Vietnam. The anti-war terrorist organization was responsible for several bombings of government buildings throughout America, including the U.S. Capitol, the Pentagon, the attempted bombing with the goal of killing our military officers in New Jersey, and the bombing of the San Francisco Police Headquarters, killing Sgt. Brian McDonnell and injuring eight other officers. Sworn testimony by former FBI informant Larry Grathwohl states that Ayers and Dohrn themselves were involved in the bombings, either through knowledge and/or planning of the bombing that killed Sgt. McDonnell. Grathwohl details that metal staples from the bomb ripped through Sgt. McDonnell's body, killing him after several agonizing days in the hospital.

While the FBI and police searched for Ayers and Dohrn for several years, they had two children, named Zayd and Malik, both Muslim names. In 1981, they turned themselves in to the police. However, most charges against them were dropped. It is unknown how they escaped criminal prosecution for murder, organized crime, and conspiracy to bomb several government buildings. The only reason I can reference in my research is "prosecutorial misconduct," which Ayers, himself, calls "extreme government misconduct."

Dohrn did serve seven months in federal prison in 1983 after refusing to testify before a grand jury in the investigation of a Brinks truck robbery, in which two New York City police officers and a security guard were killed. According to a New York Times report, Dohrn worked at a shop called Broadway Baby, from which customers' identifications were stolen through payments by check and providing their driver's license numbers. Those identifications were also used to rent getaway cars for those committing robberies between 1979 and 1982. Dohrn refused to cooperate with the police or to provide a signature that was sought by the FBI.

Due to her criminal conviction, Dohrn was refused admission to the New York bar. However, ironically, she was hired in 1989 as a legal clerk in Chicago where her co-worker was Michelle Robinson, who would become the wife of Barack Obama in 1992. Obama also worked as an intern at the same law firm, Sidley & Austin, during the summer of 1989. Meanwhile, Ayers was hired as a professor of education at the University at Illinois in 1987, his office plastered with communist, anti-Israel and pro-Hugo Chavez propaganda.

In 1995, Obama and Ayers began their relationship, which goes far beyond the "just a guy who lives in my neighborhood" statement Obama would like people to believe. Essentially, Obama was an employee of Ayers and served on several boards and committees with him over an eight-year span. Ayers created the Chicago Annenberg Challenge (CAC) in 1995 to reform the Chicago public schools. He placed Obama as the first chairman of the board of directors for the CAC. Obama served on the board for eight years, from 1995-2003, as the board raised $110 million to make "radical" reform, as stated by Ayers, to the Chicago public schools. The specific goal of the reform was to push students to "confront issues of inequity, war, and violence."

Ayers was the board chairman for the nonprofit group, Woods Fund of Chicago, where Obama was a board member and director from 1999-2002. Also serving with Obama on the Woods Fund was Rashid Khalidi, a Columbia University professor, Palestinian activist, and former spokesman for Yasser Arafat of the Palestine Liberation Organization, which was designated a terrorist organization by the American government in the 1970s and 1980s. Rashid Khalidi's wife, Mona, was head of the Arab American Action Network (AAAN), which supports Muslim terrorist organizations, boasts about destroying Israel, and opposes all U.S. immigration laws. (See http://www.eyeblast.tv/Public/Video.aspx?rsrcID=2036.) Obama, in 2001, assisted the AAAN to receive a $40,000 grant from the Woods Fund and again, in 2002, to receive an additional $35,000 grant, while Khalidi held a fundraiser to assist Obama politically.

Just one week prior to the 2008 presidential election, the Los Angeles Times obtained a video of Senator Obama praising Khalidi at a farewell dinner for Khalidi, but refused to release it, knowing the video connection and praise of Khalidi, a spokesman for a terrorist organization, could be damaging to the Obama campaign. McCain spokesman, Michael Goldfarb, responded in a written statement, "Khalidi was a frequent dinner guest at the Obamas' home and, at his farewell dinner in 2003, Obama joined the unrepentant terrorist, William Ayers, in giving testimonials on Khalidi's role in the community. The election is one week away, and it's unfortunate that the press so obviously favors Barack Obama that this campaign must publicly request that the Los Angeles Times do its job make the information public"!

In 1997, both Ayers and Obama participated in a panel at the University of Chicago and, in 2002, Ayers, Dohrn, and Obama, who was then an Illinois state senator, all participated in a conference entitled, "Intellectuals: Who Needs Them"?

Ayers and Obama also together shared an office, served on boards, committees and panels, and worked on donations. Obama even reviewed a book Ayers authored in 1997, "A Kind and Just Parent." Ayers has also admitted twice to being the one who wrote Obama's book, "Dreams from my Father: A Story of Race and Inheritance," which had little to do with the actual events of his life.

Apparently, Ayers returned the favor to Obama. At a March 24, 2011 speech at Montclair State University to the Democratic Society, Ayers got into a discussion with a student about Obama's book, "Dreams from my Father: A Story of Race and Inheritance," questioning, "Did you know that I wrote it, incidentally"? The student asked, "What's that"? Ayers responded, "I wrote that book." Ayers had also given a similar answer to a National Journal reporter, which was reported by World Net Daily (WND) on October 8, 2009. Ayers stated, "This is my quote. Be sure to write it down. 'Yes, I wrote 'Dreams from my Father.' I ghostwrote the whole thing. I met with the president three or four times, and then I wrote the entire book."

Jack Cashill of WND investigated the similarities of Ayers's writing and that of the writing in Obama's book. Christopher Anderson, the author of "Barack and Michelle: Portrait of an American Marriage," reported that Obama was facing a second cancelled book contract and that Michelle advised her husband to turn to Ayers, who was skilled at writing, to complete the manuscript for the editors. However, the media did absolutely no investigation into or reporting on the fraud of "Dreams from my Father: A Story of Race and Inheritance," supposedly written by Obama, yet, admittedly, ghostwritten by Ayers. Even then, Obama has stated that Ayers is just "a guy who lives in my neighborhood" and "not somebody who I exchange ideas with on a regular basis."

Obama also launched his political career from the home of Ayers, when Illinois state Senator Alice Palmer, also a far-left activist and former community organizer with a record of being involved in communist-front activities, hand-picked Obama to succeed her seat.

In an article from Zombie Time, it is revealed that Ayers wrote a manifesto called "Prairie Fire: The Politics of Revolutionary Anti-Imperialism." The manifesto is dedicated to over 200 radicals, including Sirhan Sirhan, who assassinated Robert Kennedy. In the manifesto, Ayers wrote, "We are a guerilla organization. We are communist men and women, underground in the United States for more than four years," and "We need a revolutionary communist party in order to lead the struggle, give coherence and direction to the fight, seize power, and build the new society." Ayers continued, "Our intention is to disrupt the empire, to incapacitate it, to put pressure on the cracks, to make it hard to carry out its bloody functioning against the people of the world, to join the world struggle, to attack from the inside."

As Obama advanced himself into politics, he had the support and endorsement of the Democratic Socialists of America (DSA), of which Ayers is a member. Many of Obama's campaign workers displayed the communist flag featuring Che Guevara, an identified communist leader. Obama had surrounded himself with the Chicago Communist Network, which included identified communists and socialists committed to communist victory in Vietnam and ties to the Castro regime in Cuba. Dohrn and Ayers each have called for socialism in America, stopping aid to Israel, and have traveled to both Venezuela and Cuba to meet with communist officials, which can possibly explain Obama's desire to end the embargo against Cuba.

World Net Daily's Aaron Klien reported that some in the group behind the deadly clashes in Gaza were Ayers, Dohrn, and Jodie Evans. Evans is the leader of Code Pink, a radical activist organization which has also been actively behind clashes with Israel in the Gaza strip through marches and the Free Gaza Movement, a coalition of liberal human rights activists and pro-Palestinian organizations. Further, Ayers, Dohrn, and Evans were involved in provoking the chaos in Egypt to stir up riots after the Egyptian government refused to allow protesters to enter Gaza. Eventually, the government allowed 100 protesters to enter Gaza, but later in February 2011, Egyptian President Mubarak was overthrown by protestors in favor of the Muslim Brotherhood, who were assisted through the efforts of Ayers, Dohrn, and Evans with funding from George Soros.

Ayers is not just "a guy who lives in my neighborhood," and "not somebody who I exchange ideas with on a regular basis," as Obama has stated. He is a radical, unrepentant terrorist, and a danger to America!

Robert Malley, an adviser to Barack Obama, has advocated negotiations with Hamas and providing international assistance to the terrorist organization. It is no wonder that Ahmed Yousef, chief political adviser to the Hamas Prime Minister said, "We like Mr. Obama, and we hope he will win the election."

Barack Obama's third political influence came through his pastor of 20 years, Reverend Jeremiah Wright. Most people seek a pastor who shares similar beliefs, presents himself with a shepherd's heart—a role model with character, love, unity, moral values, and offers spiritual guidance and influence through God's Word. Reverend Wright does not express those characteristics but, instead, preaches Black Liberation Theology, expressing himself with hate and division as a racist man using the pulpit to rant against whites, Jews, and America.

Wright proclaimed on the Sunday following September 11, 2001 that America got what it deserved, as "America's chickens are coming home to roost." He has made other outlandish statements calling America the "U.S. 'KKK' A" and "Not God bless America, but God damn America." These statements are just some of the bitter hatred coming from Reverend Wright. He may claim to be a Christian, but this is not the message of Christianity. This is a mask covering the same type of rhetoric that is proclaimed by the Islamic terrorists who hate America and Israel. As recently as July 22, 2007, Obama sat in Trinity as Wright blamed "whitie" for the world suffering, targeting "white" America and Israel. Also, on July 22, 2007, the "Pastor's Page" in the church newsletter, included a reprinted manifesto by Hamas, a terrorist organization responsible for suicidal bombings. The manifesto defended terrorism as legitimate resistance and refused to recognize the right of Israel to exist, similar to other Islamic terrorist organizations.

Reverend Wright and Trinity honored Louis Farrakhan with a lifetime achievement award and named him Person of the Year. Farrakhan, who is head of the Nation of Islam, is a radical Muslim leader who also pushes Marxist Socialism and has ties to the Black Panther Organization. He has called the white man the "skunk of the earth," "our mortal enemy," and "blue-eyed devil." He has stated, "Allah will destroy America," and called America the "Great Satan." He also called "Judaism" a "gutter religion," that Jews are "bloodsuckers" and denigrated the Holocaust by falsely attributing it to Jewish cooperation with Adolph Hitler. Farrakhan has referred to Obama as "the messiah." Obama and Wright also attended the 1995 million-man march in Washington, D.C., which was organized by Farrakhan.

Racism or hate organizations, such as Obama's church, Louis Farrakhan's Nation of Islam, or the "brain dead" KKK have no place in America or ties to our churches or political leaders, and especially the presidency. Obama cannot say his views are not in line with his former preacher. In a campaign appearance, Obama said, "I don't think my church is actually particularly controversial." The preaching he has chosen to sit under has molded and influenced the attitude and thoughts he has toward America, which could possibly explain his refusal to wear a pin of the American flag or his refusal to put his hand over his heart during the National Anthem.

Wright's racist, hate-based preaching can also give some insight into the thinking of Michele Obama. Michele, during the presidential campaign, stated that she was then proud of her country for the first time in her adult life and wrote in her college thesis that "blacks must join in solidarity to combat a white oppressor."

In spite of this, Barack Obama referred to Reverend Wright as his "mentor" and held him in high regard, having him officiate at his wedding and baptize his daughters. Obama contributed to Wright's church, including a $22,000 donation, and placed Wright on the Spiritual Advisory Committee for his presidential campaign. Obama should have used better judgment and left Trinity rather than attending the church for 20 years. Obama should have sought a spiritual leader of the character of Martin Luther King, who preached against racism and hatred and spoke of equality and a dream for America.

There is absolutely no way this country would have even considered electing John McCain, or any other person as president, if he had spent even one day in association with any racist organization, such as the KKK.

Suppose Sarah Palin had been influenced by a communist being watched by the FBI, who was also a pedophile and wrote pornographic material. Would the media have reported and sensationalized on that? Suppose Sarah Palin had associated with an "unrepentant terrorist," involved in terrorism against America, with whom she sat on several boards and was employed by for eight years. Suppose Sarah Palin had launched her political career from the home of that "unrepentant terrorist." Would the media have reported and sensationalized on that?

Suppose Sarah Palin's pastor was a racist, repeatedly spewed hatred against black people, for only the "White Society" and made hateful statements against America. Would the media have reported and sensationalized on that? The media ignored Obama's political influences, while labeling Sarah Palin as "out of touch," a "right-wing extremist," and "Christian" in an attempt to convince the American people that she was too polarizing to hold the office of vice president or president of the United States of America!

Governor Palin entered the 2008 campaign as an experienced elected office holder of many years—a lady who truly loves America and has surrounded herself with others who are also patriotic lovers of America and our freedoms. Senator Obama entered the 2008 campaign as an experienced community organizer, with a few years of experience as an elected office holder—a man who has surrounded himself with those who proved themselves disloyal to America, who influenced his intellectual development and moral views on the world, causing him to actually arrive at the point of apologizing for the United States of America!

Sam Webb, Chairman of the Communist Party USA, said it best when he stated, "Obama's agenda is the agenda of the Communist Party USA—how nice"! He further stated, "This is a necessary step toward a new society." (*See* www.liveleak.com/view?i=724_1227566786.)

Media, Affairs, and Deception

News agencies are expected to report facts but, in 2008, the "news" was designed to influence public opinion against McCain/Palin and in support of Obama/Biden! The National Enquirer reported falsely that Governor Palin was involved in an extra-marital affair with one of her husband's former business partners, over which the McCain campaign threatened to sue the Enquirer. The New York Times reported falsely, obviously without naming its source, that Senator McCain was involved in an affair with a lobbyist. However, the media did not fully investigate or report the threats to or intimidation of Larry

Sinclair by the Obama campaign. Larry Sinclair, a registered Minnesota Democrat, claimed he and Obama had been involved in homosexual acts and used cocaine together in a limousine and hotel room in 1999.

On June 18, 2008, Sinclair elaborated on his allegations in a 2 1/2-hour press conference at the National Press Club. He provided details of the alleged homosexual encounter between himself and Obama while using cocaine. (Obama did admit his past use of cocaine in his book.) Sinclair elaborated on two separate encounters between himself and Obama between November 3 and November 8, 1999 in Gurnee, Illinois. Both Obama and Sinclair are documented to have been in the Chicago area during that time, as Obama was absent from the Illinois Senate on November 4, 1999 and had, in fact, been in Chicago on November 8, 1999 for a speaking engagement. Sinclair further pointed out that Obama would not provide his cell phone number and telephone records during the alleged time period and actually provided the Chicago Police Department with an affidavit regarding Donald Young, who was a gay choir director at Obama's Trinity Church.

Young was an openly gay man, who was shot and killed in his Chicago home on December 3, 2007. Two other openly gay men, Larry Bland and Nate Spencer, who also attended Trinity, also conveniently died within 60 days of each other—Bland on November 17, 2007, and Spencer on December 24, 2007. Quite curiously, neither Obama nor his campaign said anything regarding the murders, since Norma Jean Young, Donald Young's mother, revealed that Obama and Donald were "close friends." Nor was there ever any questioning of Obama or his staffers by the Chicago Police, which is Norma Young's employer. Ms. Young stated, "There is more to the story," adding, "I do believe they are shielding somebody or protecting someone." While Obama may not have had any association with these murders, any other individual who had been publicly accused of being a closet homosexual during a time when gay men from his church were murdered, would have at least caused the police to respond with some manner of questioning. An investigation would have at least been launched with questioning to gain any and all knowledge, especially when there is a motive involved, such as Senator Obama's desire to be president.

One month later, Sinclair went public about his own relationship with Obama. As a result, Sinclair received several death threats just before his June 18, 2008 statement to the National Press Club. After the press conference, Sinclair was arrested on a felony warrant from Delaware, which was issued by then-vice-presidential candidate Senator Biden's son, Delaware Attorney General Beau Biden. Interestingly, the Delaware charges against Sinclair were later dropped.

I am not personally convinced of Sinclair's story. There are many holes in it, including his admission about being arrested in Colorado on November 8, 1999 and his failure to pass a polygraph test. He also loses much credibility due to his many previous arrests. However, this story is relevant to indicate in no uncertain terms the media's willingness to investigate and entertain false stories regarding Governor Palin and Senator McCain while ignoring allegations made by an actual individual against Senator Obama. Further, Sinclair was correct about the actual facts that three gay men from Obama's church were murdered; however, neither Senator Obama nor his staff were questioned or willingly provided any statements about the murders. Murder is a fact one cannot ignore, and it does raise an eyebrow of curiosity and suspicion.

When Senator Obama was interviewed by ABC's George Stephanopoulos on "This Week" on September 7, 2008, and referred with a slip of the tongue, to his "Muslim faith" and did not correct himself, Stephanopoulos immediately corrected, "Christian faith." Senator Obama indicated Republicans were attempting to scare voters by suggesting he was not Christian. Stephanopoulos responded, "The McCain campaign has never suggested you have Muslim connections... your Christian faith." Senator Obama, quickly responded, "My Christian faith..." Regardless of his religion, the point of this is the media constantly made efforts to present Senator Obama in a more positive

light than Governor Palin. (*See* http://ballotpedia.org/wiki/index.php/
Sarah_Palin, "ABC Double Standard," footnote 62.)

Paul Kane, of the Washington Post, reported on September 2,
2008, that Governor Palin reduced state funding by 20% to Covenant
House, a shelter for troubled teens in Alaska. However, Kane never
contacted the McCain/Palin campaign for an explanation; but, rather,
came to his own conclusions to provide misleading information in an
effort to cause the perception that Governor Palin wasn't concerned
with troubled teens. Had he actually done his job, he would have
learned and should have printed that Covenant House, in fact, does
receive other sources of funding.

Anne Kornblut, of the Washington Post, on September 9, 2008,
solicited "tough" questions from Governor Palin. However, Kornblut
solicited "ridiculous" questions with predicable responses from Senator Obama. While it is definitely appropriate and expected for a reporter to ask tough questions, one would expect the reporter to ask
tough, fair questions of both candidates.

Dana Milbank, of the Washington Post, on October 16, 2008,
made a false claim that, "In cooperation with the Palin campaign, [the
Secret Service has] started preventing reporters from leaving the press
sections to interview people in the crowd," which was an attempt to
smear Governor Palin and her supporters. The false report caused
many liberal sites to run with the false information. The Secret Service
then responded to the media in general that there was absolutely no
such cooperation, and that members of the press are isolated, in fact,
as a matter of course.

Both the New York Times and CNN ran transcripts of the October
2, 2008 vice-presidential debate that were misquoted and unfavorable
to Governor Palin. Those transcripts both quoted the Governor as saying, "And I may not answer the questions that either the moderator or
you want to hear, but I'm going to talk straight to the American people
and let them know my track record also." However, what she actually

said was, "And I may not answer the questions the way that either the moderator or you want to hear, but I'm going to talk straight to the American people and let them know my track record also." The New York Times later corrected the quote; however, CNN did not.

Drew Griffin, of CNN, on October 23, 2008, also misquoted an article, which appeared in the National Review, as having said, "I can't tell if Sarah Palin is incompetent, stupid, unqualified, corrupt or all of the above." The original quote from the National Review, written by Byron York, stated, "Watching press coverage of the Republican candidate for vice president, it's sometimes hard to decide whether Sarah Palin is incompetent, stupid, unqualified, corrupt, backward or all the above. Palin, the governor of Alaska, has faced more criticism than any vice-presidential candidate since 1988 when Democrats and the press tore into Dan Quayle." York was simply pointing out the continuous vicious and unfettered attacks against Governor Palin by the media. CNN later aired a correction for misquoting the article.

US Magazine printed a photo of Governor Palin holding Trig with the headline, "Babies, Lies & Scandal," while US Magazine printed in another edition a photo of Senator Obama standing next to his wife, Michelle, with the headline, "Why Barack Loves Her."

In August 2009, Runner's World, a health magazine, printed an exclusive appropriate photo of Sarah Palin wearing shorts with her arm on an American flag, for its regular "I'm a Runner" feature. In November 2009, Newsweek, a news magazine, proceeded to use that particular photo on its cover, without the permission of the original photographer, instead of a more appropriate photo of Governor Palin in a political environment. Its biased headline read, "How Do You Solve a Problem Like Sarah"? Had Newsweek indicated enough bias? Apparently not, because it added, "She's Bad News for the GOP—and for Everybody Else, Too."

Newsweek's poor taste in the photo it chose to print of Governor Palin caused much controversy. However, Governor Palin herself had the final word, and on her Face book page wrote, "The choice of photo for the cover of this week's Newsweek is unfortunate....When it comes to Sarah Palin, this 'news' magazine has relished focusing on the irrelevant rather than the relevant. The Runner's World magazine one-page profile for which this photo was taken was all about health and fitness—a subject to which I am devoted and which is critically important to this nation....The out-of-context Newsweek approach is sexist and oh-so-expected by now. If anyone can learn anything from it, it shows why you shouldn't judge a book by its cover, gender or color of skin. The media will do anything to draw attention—even if out of context."

Newsweek, however, when printing its cover photo in March 2011 for its "150 Women who Shake the World" issue, chose a professional photo of Hillary Clinton, headlined "Hillary's War—how she's shattered glass ceilings everywhere." Newsweek has consistently shown its political bias to persuade public opinion that "liberal" women are intelligent and the heroes of our next generation, while "conservative" women are reckless, unintelligent, and not savvy enough to serve the United States of America. (See http://www.editorsweblog.org/newspaper/2011/03/newsweeks_new_design_to_focus_on_women.php.)

Governor Palin's supporters also have pointed to questions from the media over whether serving as vice president would interfere with her ability to care for her still-at-home youngest children, including Trig, who has Down syndrome, as evidence of media sexism. Alan Colmes, Liberaland, even posted on August 30, 2008, "Did Palin Take Proper Pre-Natal Care," questioning Governor Palin's actions and decisions at the time she went into labor with her last pregnancy. (See http://ballotpedia.org/wiki/index.php/Sarah_Palin, New York Times: "Fusing Politics and Motherhood in a New Way," September 8, 2008, footnote 63; and "Did Palin Take Proper Pre-Natal Care"?, footnote 64.)

John Zeilger, who produced the documentary, "Media Malpractice," made the following points:

"Barack Obama announced to the media that attacks on his family were off-limits, and the media respected that boundary, but they did not give Palin the same respect which either exposed a sexism or a liberal bias." Zeilger continued, "It is a sad state of affairs when the media uses anonymous blogs as a hard news source. Of course, they only used those blogs as a source to attack Sarah Palin, who was threatening an Obama victory before the media went on attack mode."

Zeilger also pointed out that, "The Katie Couric interview was edited to show Sarah at her worst. Many topics where Palin feels she shined hit the edit room floor. Sarah says she knew the interview was heading in a bad direction after day one, but the McCain campaign insisted she go back for days two and three." (*See* http://www.thesarahpalinblog.com/2009/01/sarah-palin-unplugged.html#ixzz1KNPN5.)

Thousands upon thousands have questioned whether the McCain campaign staff made multiple mistakes in its "handling" of Governor Palin, strongly believing the staff should have allowed Governor Palin to be herself, rather than limiting her on how she could and couldn't interact with the media or what she could or could not say to the public she so energized. Had Governor Palin been "unleashed" and allowed to speak about vital and common sense issues to both the media and the American people, the 2008 election may have had a very different outcome.

As to the 2012 presidential election, media coverage is going to take on an entirely new picture—most likely, again, in favor of the liberal candidates. On May 23, 2011, the White House named Jesse Lee its Director of Progressive Media and Online Response. This newly-created position will maintain President Obama's online presence as he prepares for his 2012 presidential re-election bid. Lee's duties will be dealing with negative or factually incorrect stories about President Obama. In his first tweet in his new position, he included a picture of The Terminator. Lee has worked with the Democratic National Committee's rapid response team, was formerly Online Programs Director under the Obama Administration, and was hired to perform Internet work for the Democratic Congressional Campaign Committee in 2001, working in its online division from 2004 to 2006. In addition, he served as Senior News Media Advisor to former U.S. Speaker of the House, Nancy Pelosi. This new position suggests that the White House will be adopting a more aggressive engagement in the online world in the months ahead. As a side note, Lee's wife, Nita Chaudhary, is one of the people responsible for the 2007 MoveOn.org newspaper ad that portrayed General David Petraeus as "General Betray Us." (*See* http://www.nationalreview.com/media-blog/267916/obama-white-house-creates-new-rapid-response-position-greg-pollowitz.)   (*Also, see* http://en.wikipedia.org/wiki/Jesse_Lee_(politician).)

Handling Media Darts

During the campaign, Governor Palin not only suffered media blow after blow, as the designated media punching bag, with a continuous assault of lies, false reports, deception, and misrepresentations being hurled at her, she also dealt with many internal family issues without once making an "excuse." She had given birth just five months earlier to a child who had his own special needs. Her daughter was pregnant. Her son, Track, had been deployed to active duty in the Iraq war during the campaign. All of these issues had to play on her mind, but Governor Palin remained poised, positive, strong, and proud of her opportunity to serve her country.

Yet, like all of us, Sarah Palin is human, and continued attacks can take their toll. However, Sarah relies on her inner-strength from God, through prayer, to carry her through her daily battles. She stated, "I know He hears me when I just call out to Him, which I do a lot. Oh, yes, I pray. I talk to God every day. I've put my life, so I put my day, into God's hands, and I just ask for guidance and wisdom and grace to get through one situation after another."

Obviously, after the election, Governor Palin was disappointed. However, it is not Sarah Palin's style to seek sympathy. Although she took a relentless beating in the campaign, she showed consistent courage, self-discipline, and self-determination to conquer her battles. She has openly acknowledged that each experience in her life is designed for a purpose, and experiencing that purpose absolutely causes her to become stronger and wiser. Like a prizefighter, Sarah takes punch after punch from all directions, gets up with her effervescent smile and uses each opportunity to punch right back and strike a power knockout.

Yet, the liberal's obsession with her would not end after the election. They not only wanted to destroy her as a politician but, also, as a person to assure she would be irrelevant in any future campaign. They used the legal system to file many frivolous lawsuits against her claiming ethics violations. Sarah realized the repeated attacks against her, the frivolous ethics charges, and lawsuits filed by her political opponents would cost Alaska an extraordinary amount of money and countless hours to refute. Making her decision to resign saved the Alaskan taxpayers a great amount of money and allowed her lieutenant governor, Sean Parnell, to commit his full time governing Alaska. The liberals labeled Governor Palin a quitter after she resigned her governorship. She had served two-thirds of her term, which was the exact percentage Senator Obama served in the U.S. Senate. Sarah Palin was now able to take her message to the people of the United States, to speak about her accomplishments, to write and take a stand on various issues in the media and policies in the government. Sarah became the face for the TEA Party movement, a force to speak out against socialist and expanded government, and on the front line, ready to speak the truth and fight back against the liberal media assaults.

Sarah's personal email account was hacked into during the 2008 campaign. The liberal media then filed a Freedom of Information Act (FOIA) request with the state of Alaska for the release of her official government emails. This has become better-known as the "Palin email dump." On June 10, 2011, 25,000 official emails, in excess of 24,000 pages, were released by the state of Alaska. Contrary to the "sensational dirt" the liberal media so eagerly anticipated to report upon, the emails produced absolutely nothing negative either regarding Sarah personally or her service to Alaskans during her tenure as their governor! In fact, the treasurer of SarahPac, Tim Crawford, stated, "The thousands upon thousands of emails released today show a very engaged Governor Sarah Palin being the CEO of her state. The emails detail a governor hard at work. Everyone should read them."

Even with many media darts still pointing in her direction, Sarah remains thick-skinned. After a despicable attack of personal and vulgar shots at her by Bill Maher in March 2011, Sarah responded back on Facebook, "I won't bother responding to it though, because it was made by he who reminds me of an annoying little mosquito found zipped up in your tent; he can't do any harm, but buzzes around annoyingly until it's time to give him the proverbial slap." Sarah continued, "Friends, too often conservatives or Republicans in general come across as having the fighting instinct of sheep. I don't. I was raised to believe that you don't retreat when you're on solid ground; so even though it often seems like I'm armed with just a few stones and a sling against a media giant, I'll use those small resources to do what I can to set the record straight. The truth is always worth fighting for." Sarah ended her post stating, "Let's just acknowledge that commonsense conservatives must be stronger and work that much harder because of the obvious bias. And let's be encouraged with a sense of poetic justice by knowing that the 'main stream' media isn't main stream anymore. That's why I call it 'lame stream,' and the LSM is becoming quite irrelevant, as it is no longer the sole gatekeeper of information."

Media Aftershocks

Even two years after the 2008 election, the liberal media's obsession with Governor Palin continued. On April 21, 2011, Bobby Eberle reported that a left-wing site, Wonkette, posted "disgusting and hate-filled" writings by author Jack Stuef in response to Sarah's son, Trig, who had just celebrated his birthday on April 18. In a sampling of his writing, Stuef threw out his rhetorical filth stating, "Today is the day we come together to celebrate the snowbilly grifter's magical journey from Texas to Alaska to deliver to America the great gentleman scholar Trig Palin. Is Palin his true mother? Or was Bristol? (And why is it that nobody questions who the father is? Because, either way, Todd definitely did it.) It doesn't matter. What matters is that we are privileged to live in a time when we can witness the greatest prop in world political history."

Stuef continued his hateful rhetoric in reference to Trig's birthday, when he turned three years old, "Oh, little boy what are you dreaming about. What's he dreaming about? Nothing. He is retarded," referring to Trig being born with Down syndrome.

The despicable Stuef continued his insults, but he isn't the only one. There are many liberals who have continued their assaults on Governor Palin and her family, even though the 2008 election has long passed. They have even tried to label her as "unelectable," tooting their own horns as if they have achieved a victory to knock her out as a future leader of America.

MSNBC's Chris Mathews and Cynthia Tucker stated about Sarah Palin that "she's damaged goods." Tucker went further, stating, "I love the fact that this woman is so confident in her ignorance." Mathews followed up, comparing her to Libyan dictator Mummar Gadhafi, stating, "She doesn't know the world around her."

In January 2011, the media and Democratic lawmakers used a tragic event in Arizona, where 22-year-old Jared Loughner shot Congresswoman Gabrielle Giffords and killed many innocent victims. Immediately, Sarah Palin became the media's target of blame, as she had listed several congressional districts across the United States as targeted districts in the 2010 mid-term elections, even though Democrats had previously used the same type of targeting. In the 2004 race, the Democrat Leadership Council used a map featuring a bull's eye mark on certain congressional districts. Yet, the Democrats were not blamed in January 2011. The media also assumed that some conservative must have shot the congresswoman since she is a Democrat, passing immediate blame on the TEA Party movement. Later, it was revealed that Loughner had actually attended a class that taught the radical education program designed by none other than William Ayers, which was funded through the Chicago Annenberg Challenge. Barack Obama was the founding chairman of the Annenberg Challenge board of directors in 1995. If it was necessary to cast blame, with what Loughner learned in that radical class, there was actually more evidence to attach possible ties to William Ayers and Barack Obama as an influence on those senseless killings than there was any evidence that Loughner saw a bull's eye mark three months earlier on Sarah's "Take Back the 20" map and decided on that day to shoot the congresswoman. In fact, Loughner is not even able to think or reason logically, as a judge, in May 2001, ruled him incapable of standing trial due to mental insanity.

In a letter to a newspaper editor, I presented the facts of the shooting:

"The Tragedy after the Arizona Shooting Tragedy"

The news of the shooting of Representative Gabrielle Giffords and the death of six other individuals, including Federal Judge John Roll and nine-year old Christina Greene, was both senseless and tragic. As tragic as this event was, the aftermath was also disturbing. The first irresponsible reports from the left-wing media blamed Sarah Palin and the TEA Party as responsible for the shooting (www.newsmax. com/Headline/gabrielle-giffords-Jared-Loughner) assuming a conservative must have shot the Democrat lawmaker, before it was learned that 22-year-old Jared Loughner, a "left-leaning liberal" and self-proclaimed communist and admirer of Karl Marx, who was a follower of the Communist Manifesto, hated God, religion, and the Constitution as well as advocating the burning of the American flag, was responsible for the murders. Representative Linda Lopez also politicized the event, blaming the TEA Party and American veterans before the real facts were revealed. Loughner was neither a veteran nor a member of any TEA Party, and his attack against Representative Giffords had nothing to do with any conservative movement. As a matter of fact, there is more evidence surfacing that he had ties to the liberal and communist movements. It was reported that on his Facebook page, the shooter was inspired by President Obama and Saul Alinsky, who was a Marxist grassroots organizer and wrote the communist-based book, "Rules for Radicals." Loughner also attended a high school group that provided resources by a liberal group founded by Weatherman terrorist Bill Ayers and funded by President Obama, WND has learned. The group, Small Schools Workshop, has been led by a former top communist activist who is an associate of Ayers. Obama launched his political career from the home of Ayers. (*See* Bill Ayers, communist provided Arizona shooter's curriculum? http://www.wnd.com/?pageId=249429#ixzz1A m7O48CI.)

While the TEA Party and conservatives offered prayer for the families and the victims, as well as a speedy recovery for Representative Giffords, the liberals (both politicians and the media) salivated at the opportunity to use this tragic event to their advantage before knowing the facts that one of their own caused the tragedy.

Frank Aquila, January 2011

More Media Bias

The mainstream media pulled every punch possible to misrepresent Governor Palin and her record while elevating Senator Obama as its "savior" and "messiah" in an effort to persuade public opinion against Governor Palin and for Senator Obama. Throughout the campaign, the media reported on ridiculous, many times nonfactual, information about Governor Palin while not reporting the actual facts about Senator Obama.

The media made a huge issue about Governor Palin's wardrobe, which cost more than $150,000 and was donated to her by the Republican National Committee, with no taxpayer expenses involved. Governor Palin held true to her initial promise and returned all of the items to the RNC. After the election, Michelle Obama, as First Lady, took a personal trip to Spain. The cost of her travel alone was nearly the same as the cost of Governor Palin's returned campaign wardrobe. Michelle Obama traveled on one of the planes that usually serves as Air Force Two, and sometimes Air Force One, which is operated by the Department of Defense, at a cost of $11,351 per hour. So, her 6.5-hour flight to Spain cost approximately $73,781.50, bringing the round-trip travel cost to the United States taxpayers to approximately $147,563.

There has been little reported by the media about the record number of servants who cater to Michelle Obama as First Lady, at an approximate annual taxpayer expense of $1,750,000, including a hair dresser and makeup artist, without taking into consideration the lavish benefits package each attendant receives with their spouse, during a time when most Americans are struggling with their own personal finances.

According to D'Angelo Gore of factcheck.org, there are 26 attendants catering to the First Lady.

The following was the list of White House staff members assigned to the First Lady, published in 2010, including their annual salaries (see http://www.politicsdaily.com/2009/07/06/what-michelle-obamas-staffers-earn/): *

$172,200   Susan Sher (Chief of Staff) **
$140,000   Jocelyn C. Frye (Deputy Assistant to the President and Director of Policy and Projects for the First Lady)
$113,000   Desiree Rogers (Special Assistant to the President and White House Social Secretary) ***
$102,000   Camille Y. Johnston (Special Assistant to the President and Director of Communications for the First Lady)
$102,000   Melissa E. Winter (Special Assistant to the President and Deputy Chief of Staff to the First Lady)
$ 90,000   David S. Medina (Deputy Chief of Staff to the First Lady)
$ 84,000   Catherine M. Lelyveld (Director and Press Secretary to the First Lady)
$ 75,000   Frances M. Starkey (Director of Scheduling and Advance for the First Lady)

$ 70,000	Trooper Sanders (Deputy Director of Policy and Projects for the First Lady)
$ 65,000	Erinn J. Burnough (Deputy Director and Deputy Social Secretary)
$ 65,000	Joseph B. Reinstein (Deputy Director and Deputy Social Secretary)
$ 62,000	Jennifer R. Goodman (Deputy Director of Scheduling and Events Coordinator for the First Lady)
$ 60,000	Alan O. Fitts (Deputy Director of Advance and Trip Director for the First Lady)
$ 60,000	Dana M. Lewis (Special Assistant and Personal Aide to the First Lady)
$ 52,500	Semonti M. Mustaphi (Associate Director and Deputy Press Secretary to the First Lady)
$ 50,000	Kristen E. Jarvis (Special Assistant for Scheduling and Traveling Aide to the First Lady)
$ 45,000	Tyler A. Lechtenberg (Associate Director of Correspondence for the First Lady)
$ 45,000	Samantha Tubman (Deputy Associate Director, Social Office)
$ 40,000	Joseph J. Boswell (Executive Assistant to the Chief of Staff to the First Lady)
$ 36,000	Sally M. Armbruster (Staff Assistant to the Social Secretary)
$ 36,000	Natalie Bookey (Staff Assistant)
$ 36,000	Deilia A. Jackson (Deputy Associate Director of Correspondence for the First Lady)

Three additional attendants to Michelle Obama not reported include Natalie Bookey, a "staff assistant," Johnny Wright, the "first hair-stylist," and Ingrid Grimes-Miles, a "makeup artist."

* The 2010 Report to Congress of White House Staff Members may include updated names and salaries; however, "specific positions" are not detailed.

** Tina Tchen, salary unpublished, second and current Chief of Staff (appointed in January 2011), replaced Susan Sher.

*** Jeremy Bernard, salary unpublished, third and current Special Assistant to the President and White House Social Secretary (appointed in February 2011), replaced Desiree Rogers and Julianna Smoot.

Why would Michelle Obama have such an unprecedented number of staffers during a time when millions of Americans are out of work and struggling to support their families? Over President Obama's four years as president, the taxpayers will have had to pay over $6 million to compensate the First Lady's staff members. Let's clearly recall that the future First Lady stated during the campaign, "For the first time in my adult life, I am proud of my country." I assume she is proud now that the taxpayers are paying for her luxuries.

The mainstream media also never made an issue of any of the following:

1. The $540 Lanvin sneakers the First Lady wore during a stop to provide soup to the needy at a shelter.

2. Whether President Obama actually wrote his own autobiography or if it was, in fact, written by William Ayers, a fact which Ayers has twice admitted.

3. President Obama has a half-brother, who is living in poverty in a Kenyan hut. His aunt is illegally living in Boston on government assistance.

4. President Obama's relationships and associations, including those with known-Marxist ties to Communists, corrupt politicians, racists, self-identified terrorists and criminals, and the full extent, suspicious activity and involvement he had with these people and their influence and relationship with him.

5. President Obama's birth certificate or why it took between two to three years for him to release it. The questions of its authenticity, as it appears to be printed on totally different print stock than other birth certificates during that time period and doesn't contain the embossed seal of Hawaii; or why he has spent up to $2 million in legal fees trying to conceal the birth certificate, as well as all his academic records, and many other documents.

6. President Obama traveled to Pakistan in 1981, during a time when Americans were prohibited from travel and entry into the country.

7. Senator Obama had no record of any significant accomplishments while running for the presidency and had received the endorsement from the Democratic Socialists of America and the Socialists International.

8. President Obama's oversees internet fundraising, including millions of foreign dollars.

9. President Obama had a relationship as an advisor and attorney for ACORN, which was now known to be an organization involved with voter fraud.

10. Barack Obama's possibly-forged Selective Service forms.

11. President Obama has multiple Social Security numbers, which are associated with his many addresses. There are also questions as to why three other people are listed as owners of President Obama's Chicago home, including the attorney to Obama's friend, contributor and convicted felon, Tony Rezco.

12. Senator Obama made donations to Reverend Jeremiah Wright of $23,500 in 2006, which funded a racist pastor, as well as including him on his campaign staff before canceling Wright's appearance at the opening of his campaign.

13. There were three gay men from President Obama's former church, who all suspiciously died within 60 days, including Donald Young, a "close friend" of Obama.

14. The reasons Senator Obama wanted Americans to ignore his Muslim name during his campaign, but proudly professed it during his travel to Muslim nations.

15. The reasons why President Obama criticizes and apologizes for America, while never mentioning her goodness and greatness, or her generosity to the world.

16. The issue as to why Senator Obama refused to wear an American flag pin on himself until the end of his presidential campaign or why he wouldn't place his hand over his heart during the National Anthem.

There are countless questions with no answers regarding President Obama due to his refusal to be honest and the media's lack of effort to provide us the truth. Instead, the media has used every opportunity to have us believe Obama is extremely intelligent, in spite of the fact that he stated he had "visited 57 states" during his campaign. It would seem a person running for president of the United States; a Harvard Law School graduate nonetheless, should know how many states he would be presiding over! Imagine if Governor Palin had made that comment—the media would have immediately thrown darts at her. Instead, they consistently produced false reports, misleading news, and hurled personal and vulgar comments regarding her and her family, even going so far as to report on what cosmetics she was using.

The media minimized the executive accomplishments of Governor Palin and ignored her 80% approval rating in Alaska, which was the highest among all 50 governors in the United States. Instead, it focused on anything and everything possible to promote a negative opinion about her as a vice-presidential nominee, while ignoring and not questioning Obama as a presidential nominee. Governor Palin even stated in USA Today, "I don't blame people for not really knowing what it is, in some instances—what I stand for or what my record is—because if I believed everything that I read or heard in the media, I wouldn't like me either."

The media has always tilted to the left and, according to the Project of Excellence in Journalism, 57% of the news stories about Senator

McCain were considered negative compared to 29% about Senator Obama during the 2008 presidential campaign.

The media's biased reporting was also reflected in a Zogby poll, which indicated those who voted for Senator Obama could not answer questions about any of the candidates. 57% did not know which party controlled congress, even with the 50-50 chance of guessing. 88% did not know Senator Obama stated his policies would bankrupt the coal industry and make energy rates skyrocket. 56% did not know Senator Obama started his political career at the home of William Ayers, the leader of the Weathered Underground, who publicly took credit for bombing the U.S. Capitol, Pentagon and police stations. However, 96% knew Governor Palin's daughter was pregnant and 87% thought Governor Palin said she "could see Russia from her house," even though it was Tina Fey from Saturday Night Live who originated that statement in a comedy sketch.

The media never ridiculed Senator Obama for his claim of world experience, as he laid claim to relatives throughout the world. Perhaps he was referring to his half-brother, who was actually living in poverty in a hut in Kenya, or his aunt, who was living in Boston, in the United States illegally and living on government assistance.

Perhaps if Governor Palin had a brother living in a hut in poverty or a relative living in the United States illegally, the media would have investigated and reported in depth on the information it acquired. Why not? They showed absolutely no hesitation in reporting untruths regarding Governor Palin while covering up the truth about Senator Obama to forward their agenda.

The media's blind eye and refusal to report facts accurately and fairly is actually a black eye to American journalistic ethics and has proven Sean Hannity's statement, "2008 is the year journalism died in America" absolutely correct!

Chapter 5
The Communist Influence on America

"A government big enough to give you everything you want is big enough to take away everything you have." Thomas Jefferson

The Direction of America's Future

The American people must choose the future direction of America. One choice is represented by a vision of the socialist/communist movement of total government control of the people; the other choice is represented by a vision of the TEA Party, where government is "limited," as outlined in the U.S. Constitution. The "TEA" in TEA Party means "Taxed Enough Already." It is also a reference to the Boston Tea Party, when on the evening of December 16, 1773, American colonists, led by Samuel Adams and Paul Revere, dressed as Native Americans and boarded three ships in the Boston harbor. The colonists protested the tax imposed upon them by the British parliament by taking the imported British tea and dumping it into the Atlantic Ocean.

Reference to "limited government" is key to our American philosophy, as our U.S. Constitution limits the power of our central government through the express "right of the people." The government, therefore, can only enact policies and legislation authorized by the people, through their elected representatives. Thus, the government receives its delegating power directly from the people's representatives, making government limited, as opposed to unlimited, in its power over the people. These principles were clearly outlined in the U.S. Constitution by the founders of America.

Communism has so pervasively infiltrated key institutions of the left that much of the Communist Party's platform has been adopted by the Democrat Party, which has been explicitly advocated by President Obama. The TEA Party represents a conservative counter-revolution to that pernicious development; it seeks to restore the ideals of the American founding as the lodestar of political debate. And Sarah Palin has become its champion.

So what exactly is the difference between capitalism, socialism, and communism?

Capitalism is an economic system which allows private individuals, small businesses or corporations to produce products, distribute, and compete for their own economic gain, allowing the free market forces to determine the price of products or services based on the desires of the consumer. This economic system is based on the premise of separating the government from the activities of the private sector. Capitalists believe the free markets are efficient, and the role of the government should be to protect the system without unnecessary regulation or interference by the government.

Socialism is known as the first stage of transition from capitalism to communism, as suggested by the theory of Karl Marx, who is known as the "Father of Communism." Socialists believe there are inequalities that exist in our society, and the profits of production and distribution made by the capitalists should be shared with the community. The government's role, therefore, is to oversee the redistribution of wealth to the community and determine the investment, prices, and production levels. In socialism, the government owns the means of production, economically.

Communism is an advanced form of socialism where the government takes full control of managing all aspects of both the economy and society as outlined in the 1847 book by Karl Marx and Fredrich Engels, "The Communist Manifesto." Each person in the community will have equal status with a rejection of both private property and personal profit. Distribution of goods and services are provided by the government according to the needs of the people. Property would be owned collectively, with government control being centralized over the distribution of property to achieve the abolishment of both the class and the state. Karl Marx stated, "From each according to his ability, to each according to his need."

Obama has shrugged off and laughed at the assertion of socialism; but he has acknowledged he was drawn to both the socialist and Marxist views while attending college.

Obama had written about his college days in his book, "Dreams From my Father: A Story of Race and Inheritance," that "I chose my friends carefully," and that he associated with "the more politically active black students. The foreign students. The Chicanos. The Marxist professors and structural feminists." Obama continues from "Dreams" that, "In search of some inspiration, I went to hear Kwame Toure, formerly Stokely Carmichael of Black Panther fame, speak at Columbia. At the entrance to the auditorium, two women, one black, one Asian, were selling Marxist literature."

While Obama describes himself as choosing his "friends carefully," it is not understood how he then chose to launch his political career in 1995 from the home of the "unrepentant terrorist," William Ayers, (59) who is the former leader of the Weather Underground, a domestic terrorist organization and self-proclaimed communist organization, which Ayers describes as "an American Red Army." (60) Ayers further describes the organization's ideology as, "Kill all the rich people. Break up their cars and apartments. Bring the revolution home, kill your parents." (61) Ayers is also a self-described Marxist and proclaimed in 2002, "I am a Marxist." (62)

Obama also chose Reverend Jeremiah Wright as his pastor for 20 years. Reverend Wright has preached anti-American hate speech, grounded in the philosophy of black liberation theology, which is based on the principles of Marxist ideas.

During the 2008 presidential campaign, Senator McCain accused Obama of being a socialist after Obama himself told "Joe the Plumber" that he wanted to "spread the wealth around," which is a principle of socialism. McCain went as far as to refer to Obama as wanting to become "Redistributor-in-Chief." During the campaign, a 2001 radio interview surfaced and became widely distributed across the internet, in which Obama scolded the U.S. Supreme Court's inability to enact "redistribution of wealth."

The Democrat-Communist Manifesto

The Communist Party of America makes no effort to hide its agenda with regard to turning America into a communist country. Its goal is outlined in the Soviet slogan, "Let us drive out the capitalists from Earth and God from Heaven."

On January 10, 1963, Representative Albert S. Herlong read and listed 45 communist goals—from a book titled, "The Naked Communist," by Cleon Skousen—into the Congressional Record. Goal No. 15 is to "Capture one or both of the political parties in the U.S."

Today's Democrat Party has been successfully captured by the communists and their goal is to fulfill the remaining 45 goals for the takeover of America. It is shocking to see how the Democrat Party has adopted and used many of the following communist goals that were read into the Congressional Record by Representative Herlong:

1. "U.S. acceptance of coexistence as the only alternative to atomic war."

2. "U.S. willingness to capitulate in preference to engaging in atomic war."

3. "Develop the illusion that total disarmament [by] the U.S. would be a demonstration of 'moral strength'."

4. "Permit free trade between all nations regardless of communist affiliation and regardless of whether or not items could be used for war."

5. "Extension of long-term loans to Russia and Soviet satellites."

6. "Provide American aid to all nations regardless of communist domination."

7. "Grant recognition of Red China. Admission of Red China to the U.N."

8. "Set up East and West Germany as separate states in spite of Khrushchev's promise in 1955 to settle the German question by free elections under supervision of the U.N."

9. "Prolong the conferences to ban atomic tests because the United States has agreed to suspend tests as long as negotiations are in progress."

10. "Allow the Soviet satellites individual representation in the U.N."

11. "Promote the United Nations as the only hope for mankind. If its charter is rewritten, demand that it be set up as a one-world government with its own independent armed forces."

12. "Resist any attempt to outlaw the Communist Party."

13. "Do away with all loyalty oaths."

14. "Continue giving Russia access to the U.S. Patent Office."

15. "Capture one or both of the political parties in the United States."

16. "Use technical decisions of the courts to weaken basic American institutions, by claiming their activities violate civil rights."

17. "Get control of the schools. Use them as transmission belts for socialism and current communist propaganda. Soften the curriculum. Get control of teachers' associations. Put the party line in textbooks."

18. "Gain control of all student newspapers."

19. "Use student riots to foment public protests against programs or organizations which are under communist attack."

20. "Infiltrate the press. Get control of book review assignments, editorial writing, policy-making positions."

21. "Gain control of key positions in radio, TV, and motion pictures."

22. "Continue discrediting American culture by degrading all forms of artistic expression. An American Communist cell was told to 'eliminate all good sculpture from parks and buildings, substitute shapeless, awkward, and meaningless forms'."

23. "Control art critics and directors of art museums. Our plan is to promote ugliness, repulsive, meaningless art."

24. "Eliminate all laws governing obscenity by calling them 'censorship' and a violation of free speech and free press."

25. "Break down cultural standards of morality by promoting pornography and obscenity in books, magazines, motion pictures, radio, and TV."

26. "Present homosexuality, degeneracy, and promiscuity as 'normal, natural and healthy'."

27. "Infiltrate the churches and replace revealed religion with 'social' religion. Discredit the Bible and emphasize the need for intellectual maturity, which does not need a 'religious crutch'."

28. "Eliminate prayer or any phase of religious expression in the schools on the grounds that it violates the principle of 'separation of church and state'."

29. "Discredit the American Constitution by calling it inadequate, old-fashioned, out-of-step with modern needs, a hindrance to cooperation between nations on a worldwide basis."

30. "Discredit the American founding fathers. Present them as selfish aristocrats who had no concern for the 'common man'."

31. "Belittle all forms of American culture and discourage the teaching of American history on the grounds that it was only a minor part of the 'big picture.' Give more emphasis to Russian history since communists took over."

32. "Support any socialist movement to give centralized control over any part of the culture—education, social agencies, welfare programs, mental health clinics, etc."

33. "Eliminate all laws or procedures which interfere with the operation of the communist apparatus."

34. "Eliminate the House Committee on Un-American Activities."

35. "Discredit and eventually dismantle the FBI."

36. "Infiltrate and gain control of more unions."

37. "Infiltrate and gain control of big business."

38. "Transfer some of the powers of arrest from the police to so-cial agencies. Treat all behavioral problems as psychiatric disorders which no one but psychiatrists can understand [or treat]."

39. "Dominate the psychiatric profession and use mental health laws as a mean of gaining coercive control over those who oppose communist goals."

40. "Discredit the family as an institution. Encourage promiscuity and easy divorce."

41. "Emphasize the need to raise children away from the negative influence of parents. Attribute prejudices, mental blocks and retarding of children to suppressive influence of parents."

42. "Create the impression that violence and insurrection are le-gitimate aspects of the American tradition; that students and special-interest groups should rise up and use ['] united force ['] to solve eco-nomic, political, or social problems."

43. "Overthrow all colonial governments before native popula-tions are ready for self-government."

44. "Internationalize the Panama Canal."

45. "Repeal the Connally reservation so the United States can-not prevent the World Court from seizing jurisdiction [over domestic problems. Give the World Court jurisdiction] over nations and individ-uals alike."

I need not comment on the extent to which of the 45 points above has been enacted. A simple review of current events in America demonstrates the success in these 45 goals. In fact, there are still Amer-ican intellectuals and elected members of Congress who dream of an eventual one-world government and who view the U.N., founded by communists such as Alger Hiss, the first U.N. Secretary General, as the instrument to bring this about. World government was also the dream of Adolf Hitler and Joseph Stalin. World government was the dream of Osama bin Laden and the 9/11 hijackers.

Socialists began their movement into the Democrat Party in the 1930s. Norman Thomas, who ran for president six times as a socialist, has been attributed to stating, "The American people will never knowingly adopt socialism. But under the name of liberalism they will adopt every fragment of the socialist program until, one day, America will be a socialist nation, without knowing how it happened." Thomas continued, "I no longer need to run as a presidential candidate for the Socialist Party. The Democrat Party has adopted our platform." Thomas made the alleged comment in 1944, after his final attempt at the presidency. Even though his comments have been used through the media and other discussion within political campaigns, there is no verified source that he either made the statement or wrote it.

By the 1960s, many from both the Socialist Party and the American Communist Party had disbanded and became leaders within the Democrat Party. As the Communist Party achieved its goal of capturing leadership within the Democrat Party through the infatuation of communists like Frank Marshall Davis, who used the Democrat Party in Hawaii as an official cover for his front of communist activities, many other Democrats began to wonder what had happened to their party. Former U.S. Senator Zell Miller, a Democrat from Georgia, stated, "The Democrat Party today has gone further and further to the left. It's left me, it's left moderates, and it's left a lot of people who want to support a strong commander-in-chief." (63)

The Communist Party has begun to achieve its goal, transforming the Democrat Party into a socialist party with the philosophy of Karl Marx, who proudly proclaimed, "From each according to his ability, to each according to his need." (64) Using this Marxist philosophy, the Democrat Party has led America toward the socialist path and adopted the goals laid out in the communist plan to take over America.

President Obama has a known history of associates through the Democratic Socialists of America (DSA) and the Communist Party USA (CPUSA). Obama has an admittedly close relationship of "social conferences" with Frank Marshall Davis, a member of the Communist Party, who praised the Soviet's Red Army and mentored Obama at the beginning of his political career, which led him to the endorsement of the Democratic Socialists of America, of which William Ayers is a member. The DSA is the largest socialist organization in America, which may explain why many of Obama's campaign workers display a flag featuring communist hero Che Guevara.

In just a short period of time, President Obama's Marxist views and influence have led the Democrat Party toward fulfilling the remaining 45 goals for the communist takeover of America. Our government has already begun its course to replace capitalism with the socialist government control of some financial institutions and, now, our health care with its believed unconstitutional individual mandate.

Rules for Radicals

The Democrat Party has become the primary organization responsible for coordinating the multi-level movement and efforts to bring socialism/communism to America through the infiltration of radicals into the leadership within the party. One of several means for achieving their goal is through a book called "Rules for Radicals," written by Saul Alinsky, which was published in 1971, just prior to his death in 1972. Alinsky was raised in Chicago and was also a radical Marxist and socialist. He was known as the "Father of Modern America Radicalism," who developed strategies and tactics for other radicals to follow his rules of "social change" through a non-violent revolution against business and the government from the energy, emotion, and agitation of a community organization, organized by the deception and manipulation of the community organizers. Alinsky, himself, was a community organizer; and his modern day followers are Hillary Clinton and Barack Obama.

Alinsky begins his book of deception with a disturbing dedication to Lucifer, the Satanic father of lies, "Lest we forget at least an over-the-shoulder acknowledgement to the very first radical: from all our legends, mythology, and history (and who is to know where mythology leaves off and history begins—or which is which), the first radical known to man who rebelled against the establishment and did it so effectively that he at least won his own kingdom—Lucifer." (65) The dedication to Lucifer is only seen in the original versions of Alinsky's book and has been removed from more modern versions.

"Rules for Radicals" lays out a blueprint for his followers, or organizers, as a guide for them to successfully use deception to bring about "social change." "Change" was also the key code word credo for Alinsky's revolution. He believed in manipulating the people and using the ballot box to wrench power for the communists in order to evoke the "change" he envisioned. Alinsky believed in radical socialism and the redistribution of wealth. He believed in eliminating capitalism and replacing it with socialism, as well as peacefully overthrowing the government and replacing it with communism.

Alinsky believed the roles of the community organizer are to "Agitate, Aggravate, Educate, and then Organize." Alinsky referred to the community organizer as a master manipulator, who must create the issues or problems in the community to persuade people through the "realization" that they are indeed miserable. The community organizer must be charismatic, full of personality, and well-liked—relating to the people through lies and deception to stir up dissatisfaction and discontent in the community. The people are to be led to believe the community organizer is interested in the well-being of "hope" and "change" for the people, thus providing him with the power to lead them. As a result, the people believe his deceptive lies and organize a social rebellion against the government to bring about enough public discontent and chaos to spark a social upheaval in order to collapse the so-called flawed system and bring a new system of "hope" to "change" to their lives.

As Alinsky noted, "A reformation means that the masses of our people have reached the point of disillusionment with past ways and values. They don't know what will work, but they do know that the prevailing system is self-defeating, frustrating, and hopeless. They won't act for change but won't strongly oppose those who do. The time is then ripe for a revolution." The people would be deceived to believe that their misery is the fault of unresponsive government or greedy corporations, which ultimately would allow the government to gain control of the people as they give up their freedoms and liberties through the idea that the new government will save them and end their frustration and hopelessness. The whole idea is to "burn the system down" and replace it with a new one. Alinsky's motto was, "The most effective means are whatever will achieve the desired results," which is to replace capitalism with communism through socialism.

Alinsky writes, "A Marxist begins with his prime truth that all evils are caused by the exploration of the proletariat by the capitalist. From this, he logically proceeds to the revolution to end capitalism, then into the third stage of reorganization into a new social order of the dictatorship of the proletariat, and finally the last stage—the political paradise of communism."

The success of the community organizer is to create mass organization to seize power through the army he creates. The community organizer must recruit through local organizations, churches, service groups, labor unions, corner gangs, or individuals. Alinsky notes, "Change comes from power, and power comes from organization."

It is both accepted and expected that community organizers use deception and lies to achieve their goals. Alinsky wrote, "Integrity is not necessary to activism, but the appearance of integrity is important." Lying was the preferred tactic of Alinsky. He believed if a lie is repeated several times, people will believe it to be true. He taught that if you are caught in a lie, quickly change the lie slightly to make it appear you meant something else. He taught if you are caught in a lie or are losing an argument to personally attack and ridicule your opponent in order to put your opponent on the defensive and alter the debate. He advises to never admit to a lie. He taught that those who run for elected office should tell the people what they want to hear and later, after elected, make excuses or demonize key figures.

An example of demonizing key figures is what the Democrats did to President Bush with the war in Iraq and accusations that Bush misled the American people into war when there were no weapons of mass destruction in order to persuade public opinion against the president. But one must not forget what the Democrats stated about Iraq and the weapons of mass destruction prior to the war.

"If Saddam rejects peace and we have to use force, our purpose is clear. We want to seriously diminish the threat posed by Iraq's weapons of mass destruction program." President Bill Clinton, February 4, 1998.

"Iraq is a long way from [here], but what happens there matters a great deal here. For the risks that the leaders of a rogue state will use nuclear, chemical, or biological weapons against us or our allies is the greatest security threat we face." Madeline Albright, Clinton's Secretary of State, February 18, 1998.

"He will use those weapons of mass destruction again, as he has ten times since 1983." Sandy Berger, Clinton's National Security Adviser, February 18, 1998.

"Saddam Hussein has been engaged in the development of weapons of mass destruction technology which is a threat to countries in the region and he has made a mockery of the weapons inspection process." Nancy Pelosi, former Speaker of the House of Representatives, December 16, 1998.

Then, after President Bush was elected, these prominent Democrats made these comments prior to going to war:

"We know that he has stored secret supplies of biological and chemical weapons throughout his country." Al Gore, former Vice President, September 23, 2002.

"I will be voting to give the President of the United States the authority to use force—if necessary—to disarm Saddam Hussein because I believe that a deadly arsenal of weapons of mass destruction in his hands is a real and grave threat to our security." Senator John Kerry, 2004 presidential candidate, October 9, 2002.

"In the four years since the inspectors left, intelligence reports show that Saddam Hussein has worked to rebuild his chemical and biological weapon stock, his missile delivery capability, and his nuclear program. He has also given aid, comfort, and sanctuary to terrorists, including al-Qaeda members….It is clear, however, that if left unchecked, Saddam Hussein will continue to increase his capacity to wage biological and chemical warfare, and keep trying to develop nuclear weapons." Senator Hillary Clinton, October 10, 2002.

There was a litany of similar statements by prominent Democrats. Each of them knew that Saddam Hussein was a potential threat to America, especially after September 11, 2001. If America were to have been attacked again, President Bush would have been accused of ignoring the threat. America knew Saddam had used weapons of mass destruction. Sandy Berger mentioned Saddam had used them ten times since 1983. Many mass graves were found throughout the country, as Saddam used them on his own people, predominately on the Kurdish people in the northern part of the country. Empty canisters were discovered in a dump that held the destructive chemicals. Saddam refused to allow inspectors to enter the country or refused certain areas to be inspected, and General Sada of the Iraqi military admitted the weapons of mass destruction were secretly delivered into Syria.

The Democrats admitted through intelligence reports, before Bush was president that Saddam was a threat, and they authorized the war. However, as the war seemed to be prolonged in nature and Americans began to become impatient, the Alinsky model of community organizing was put into place. They demonized President Bush, even if they had to lie and make it appear as if they had been against the war all along.

Obama stated that his years as a community organizer were the "best education I've ever had." From 1985 through 1988, Obama worked as a community organizer and taught on the Alinsky method, working for a group called the Developing Communities Project, designed to bring a coalition of black churches together in Chicago with the desired goal for Obama to bring his social reform and change to the community.

Obama also followed Alinsky's instructions to "spread the wealth around" using class warfare of a rigorous class structure, which Alinsky describes as "The Trinity" in "Rules for Radicals." As Alinsky points out that society is divided between the Haves, the Have Nots, and the Have a Little—Want More. The Haves were the upper class and smaller in numbers. Alinsky knew the Have Nots, which were the lower class, would be envious of the Haves making the Have Nots enemies of the Haves and easier to motivate through invoking "hope" as an appeal for their action. Alinsky described the middle class, which is a larger portion of the population, as the Have a Little—Want More. The middle class is the group of people Alinsky knew he would have to "change." Alinsky wrote, "That is where the power is." He taught, "When more than three-fourths of our people from both the point of view of economics and of their self-identification are middle class, it is obvious that their actions or inactions will determine the direction of change." As much disdain as Alinsky had for the middle class with his desire to overturn their identity and values, he would deceive the middle class as a pawn by convincing those in the middle class to seek a desired "change" that he had envisioned. Alinsky invoked "change" on the middle class as a pre-planned appeal to those who Have a Little—Want More, while they were climbing the social/economic ladder. He advised the organizers to understand "the local legends, anecdotes, values, idioms" in order to relate to the middle class so they would side with him in their own destruction. Obama's campaign slogan to target the middle and lower classes with "Hope" and "Change," in an effort to invoke class warfare between the populations against each other was taken directly from the instructions of Alinsky.

Madeline Talbott, a former leader of the Association of Community Organizations for Reform Now (ACORN), used her position to intimidate banks into making high-risk loans to individuals with poor credit. She was known in the community for organizing people through intimidation to create disruptions and was described as a specialist in "direct action." She became so impressed with Obama's community organizing skills and his national effort at Project Vote in 1992 that she invited him to come and train her staff. Obama conducted annual leadership training seminars for ACORN organizers and administrators in the Alinsky method to develop a philosophy to subvert the voting process in favor of liberals, even though ACORN technically had "non-partisan" government status.

By 1995, Obama was hired as an attorney to represent the legal efforts of ACORN, suing the state of Illinois to get the courts to force Illinois to adopt the Motor Voter Law. World Net Daily also reported in 1995 that Obama, who sat on the Chicago Annenberg Challenge with William Ayers, funneled money to many far-left community organizers, including ACORN, through a $50-million grant program.

During the 2008 presidential campaign, the ACORN Political Action Committee endorsed Obama, even though Obama and his campaign denied having any relationship with ACORN, which was known for its illegal voter registration efforts in several states during the 2004 presidential election. By August 2008, the Obama campaign had paid nearly $1 million to Citizens Services Inc. (CSI), which is an "offshoot" of ACORN to "get out the vote." It was later revealed that CSI and ACORN were using the same address in New Orleans. While the voter registration drives were being conducted, propaganda was being handed out in the community instructing people not to vote for any Republican.

By 2009, a congressional committee investigation found ACORN to be involved in criminal activity and "has repeatedly and deliberately engaged in systemic fraud" and "to launder federal money in order to pursue a partisan political agenda and to manipulate the American electorate." Video was also released showing ACORN counselors providing advice on tax evasion to undercover reporters posing as a pimp and a prostitute. Since 1994, ACORN had received more than $53 million from the federal government. Under the Obama stimulus plan, ACORN was to receive $8.5 billion in federal funding! However, due to the discovered fraud, Obama has tried to publicly disassociate himself from ACORN, hypocritically stating, "It had nothing to do with us. We were not involved."

In 2009, David Alinsky, the son of Saul Alinsky wrote in a letter, "Obama learned his lesson well. I am proud to see my father's model for organizing is being applied successfully beyond local community organizing to affect the Democrat campaign in 2008. It is a fine tribute to Saul Alinsky as we approach his 100th birthday."

In 1988, Obama wrote an article honoring Alinsky, which later became a chapter in a book called "After Alinsky: Community Organizing in Illinois." The article Obama wrote in 1988, entitled, "Why Organize? Problems and Promise in the Inner City," was published by the University of Illinois at Springfield, where his writings were from the same philosophy of Alinsky's "Rules for Radicals."

The whole Alinsky model is that the "ends justify the means." Alinsky believed it is not important if you lie, deceive, or manipulate the people; it is important to get the result you are looking for by any and all means. Alinsky believed a man was a fool to tell the truth, when a lie would better serve the immediate purpose.

The Alinsky method has also been used in our schools. From 1999 through 2002, Obama used the Woods Fund with Ayers to help fund the Alinsky Academy, which is a school for community organizing and citizens committed to progressive social change. Now that

Obama is president, it is the time for the communists to gain momentum to accelerate the process of fulfilling those items listed in the congressional record by Congressman Herlong on January 10, 1963. The communists' plan was to gain control of our schools, which goal has been successful in a large part. They actually believe that the children belong to the state. Dr. Mary Jo Bane, who was President Clinton's Assistant Secretary for Children and Families in the Department of Health and Human Services, said, "If we want to talk about equality of opportunity for children, then the fact that children are raised in families means there's no equality....In order to raise children with equality, we must take them away from families and communally raise them." This is point 41 read by Congressman Herlong, which states "Emphasize the need to raise children away from the negative influence of parents. Attribute prejudices, mental blocks, and retarding of children to suppressive influence of parents."

When Obama signed the Health Care Bill, it allowed, under Title V of Obama's "American Affordable Health Choices Act of 2009," H.R. 3200, Subtitle B, School-Based Health Clinics (SBHCs) to allow special interest groups, like Planned Parenthood, to operate inside public schools at the expense of all American taxpayers. Again, more power allowed to the government over our children, while removing the rights of the parents and families over their children.

Jared Loughner, the killer who severely injured Congresswoman Giffords in Arizona, while killing others including a nine-year-old girl and a federal judge, had reported on his Facebook page that he was inspired by President Obama and Saul Alinsky. Loughner also attended a high school group that was provided resources by a liberal group founded by terrorist Bill Ayers and funded by President Obama. The group, Small Schools Workshop, has been led by a former top communist activist who is an associate of Ayers, according to World Net Daily. The whole idea behind these schools is to influence our children with communist propaganda and to influence their minds to support the socialist/communist movement. However, the media tried to influence the American people that conservatives and Governor Palin were the root cause of this tragedy, ignoring the true background and influence of this troubled individual and most likely others like him.

Similarly to Sarah Palin when she was mayor of Wasilla and accused of attempting to ban a book, I also had an issue with a librarian. My problem was with a librarian who was refusing to offer Sarah's book for use in the library, while offering Obama's book for the teenagers to read. As I work in a juvenile institution, I have had the opportunity to talk to many teenage boys about a variety of issues, including politics, about which most know little to nothing. Often, while transporting them to court, I would be listening to Sean Hannity on the radio in the car. They would ask me questions, and we have had some serious conversations about the politicians or issues that were raised on the radio show. One day, when Sarah's autobiography was released, one teenaged boy asked me about Governor Palin. We began to have a conversation about her and her accomplishments. Many of these incarcerated teenaged boys have had a difficult time with women in authority, so it was an opportunity to discuss how any person, whether male or a female, can do a good job as an effective leader. The boys were intrigued about my thoughts of Sarah and asked how they could also read her book. I suggested they ask the librarian.

Our institution has a county-run library. I knew the librarian was liberal, because during the 2008 election, the library had voter registration forms available for the boys who turned age 18 and were eligible to vote. I often saw the boys with their registration forms and asked them with which political party they associated themselves. Most of the time, they advised me they didn't know anything about politics, but the librarian had suggested they register as a Democrat, since that was how she was registered. When the boys went to the librarian and asked her to order Governor Palin's book, she refused, telling the boys she wasn't going to get "that book."

I confronted the librarian about her refusal to order Governor Palin's book. She advised the library had only a certain amount of funds, and she would be wasting funds if she purchased "that book."

She also stated, "None of these boys will ever be interested in reading her book in six months." I pointed out that she had Barack Obama's book available for the boys to read, to which she responded, "Sure, he is the president." I reminded her of the fact she had Obama's book in the library before he was elected president. I pointed out to her that she was not being fair by only allowing liberal books to be available for the boys to read, refusing to also make conservative books available. She then suggested, if I so desired, I could donate Sarah's book, and it would be made available. I continued the conversation, stating she should remain unbiased and make available to the boys books discussing all view points, not just her own personal liberal viewpoint. I also pointed out that each of the boys should not be influenced as to how they should register to vote, but they should be allowed to register independently if they were not familiar with the main parties' political platforms.

Alinsky's key would was "compromise." Today, liberals have transformed "compromise" into "tolerance." The U.S. Constitution gives each American the freedom of speech, but liberal Democrats want to silence anyone who opposes their liberal agenda by limiting their speech. Over the years, liberal Democrats have pushed for people to be "tolerant" and "inclusive" to force guilt on anyone who would be against advancing their political agenda. They know tolerance will lead to acceptance, which leads to imitation, which leads to the lifestyle from one generation to the next. This is most evident with the homosexual movement. The alternative lifestyle led to domestic partnership, which led to civil unions, which ultimately led to the forcing of the gay marriage issue. However, there is no tolerance for people to speak out against their liberal agenda. They expect everyone to be "politically correct," and anyone who voices an alternative opinion should be punished for using "hate speech." Ultimately, liberal Democrats want to punish anyone who dares to voice his or her opposition.

Carrie Prejean was removed as Miss California for expressing her opinion that marriage is between a man and a woman. She has been viciously attacked for voicing her opinion when one of the judges, who was a gay activist, used his position to pose a controversial question on a national stage to advance the gay agenda before millions of viewers. He gave her a low score, causing her to lose the Miss U.S.A. crown. He then blasted her with insulting profanities, causing a firestorm to have her also removed as Miss California, even though she performed all the duties that were required of her and carried out her position in a respectful and dignified manner. No other pageant winner has been treated so poorly.

The liberal Democrats will continue to ask for "tolerance" to promote their liberal agenda and call it "hate speech" to those who block it. They want to have full control over the people in the press and schools to influence their well-orchestrated hidden agenda. The U.S. Constitution gives us our freedom of speech but, like everything else, the liberal Democrats want to take it away from the people if it negatively affects advancing their agenda, even if it means changing the U.S. Constitution to silence conservatives, or using the Fairness Doctrine to silence the alternative media through conservative talk radio.

As a Christian, I do not hate any homosexual, but I hate the sin of homosexuality. It is clear in the Old and New Testament of the Bible that it homosexuality is a sin (Leviticus 18:22 and Romans 1:26-27). The Bible is clear that marriage is between a man and a woman. Liberals have tried to silence Christians by stating there is a separation of church and state. This phrase is a passing statement from a letter written by President Thomas Jefferson, and is not found in the U.S. Constitution. It is, however, quoted as gospel by the liberal Democrats as yet another method to silence conservative speech.

Communism v Christianity

Alinsky believed that Christianity was the biggest threat to his movement of socialism. He believed those with Biblical absolutes and Christian morals had to be crushed as a social force in order for the new face of communism to rise and flourish. Karl Marx stated, "My object is to dethrone God and destroy capitalism."

When Obama ran for the state senate, he wrote, "The right wing, the Christian right has done a good job of building these organizations of accountability, much better than the left or progressive forces have. But it's always easier to organize around intolerance, narrow-mindedness, and false nostalgia. And they also have hijacked the higher moral ground with this language of family values and moral responsibility."

Whittaker Chambers, who was a communist spy, stated, "The communist vision is the vision of man without God. It is the vision of man's mind displacing God as the creative intelligence of the world."

Socialists and communists saw Christianity as a danger to stopping their progressive movement of transferring society. They feared Christians wouldn't join their socialist movement or rely on the need of government, since Christianity relies on Christ.

Communists and those countries that embrace socialism and communism have tried many times in history to proclaim there is no God. They believed faith in God is a deceptive illusion and wanted to remove Christianity from their society.

Christianity is a religion of freedom and democracy, while communism has always viewed Christianity as a crutch for weak people and a threat to the communist movement of government control of the people, since Christians rely more on God than on government. Karl Marx, the communist leader who introduced the Marxist philosophy, also opposed religion. According to Marx, religion prevents the fulfillment of his communist ideas—that communism is the only answer for all the world's problems. Marx believed religion created illusory fantasies for the poor. Therefore, removal of religion was necessary for people to become dependent on government rather than trust in God.

Their goal is to control religion and remove the founding principles of Christianity from our country. Their plan is to "infiltrate the churches and replace revealed religion with "social" religion. Discredit the Bible and emphasize the need for intellectual maturity, which does not need a "religious crutch." This has been largely accomplished through the communist infiltration of the National Council of Churches.

This can explain the church attended by President Obama for 20 years, where his racist pastor and "mentor" spewed American hatred, blaming America for 9/11, and calling America the U.S."KKK" A. Obama went on to state in June 2009, "Whatever we once were, we're no longer a Christian nation." Obama clearly does not know history. America's roots and establishment of government are based on Christianity.

It is understandable how President Obama could develop these feelings, since from his youth; he has been filled with radical communist influences. John Perzzo, in "The Communists Behind Obama's Health Care Goals" (see frontpagemag.com/tag/care), notes "Barack Obama did not conceive of socialized medicine on his own. His acceptance of such a system was cultivated and nurtured by the same types of Marxist revolutionaries with whom he has surrounded himself throughout his entire adult life—and who are now shaping the major policy agendas of his administration." Obama had an admittedly close relationship of "social conferences" with Frank Marshall Davis, a member of the Communist Party USA (CPUSA), who mentored Obama at the beginning of his political career. The CPUSA has developed leaders within the Democrat party to adopt their goals listed in the Communist Manifesto, which support policies to silence Christianity. These policies destroy moral standards and influence through gaining "control of the schools," "infiltrate the press," "gain control of key positions in radio, TV, and motion pictures," "eliminate all laws governing obscenity by calling them 'censorship' and a violation of free speech and free press," "break down cultural standards of morality by promoting pornography and obscenity in books, magazines, motion pictures, radio and TV," and "present homosexuality, degeneracy and promiscuity as 'normal, natural and healthy'."

These policies are well established within the Democrat party, which can explain the Democrat Party platform for supporting homosexual marriages and indoctrinating our children in teaching homosexuality. The Democrat Party passed hate-crimes legislation providing protection for gays and lesbians, bisexuals, and transsexuals making them a protected class. The law would also make negative statements concerning homosexuality, such as calling it a sin from the pulpit, a "hate crime" punishable by law, which is all referenced in the Congressional Record in 1963 as the agenda of the communists by Congressman Herlong through "The Naked Communist," by Cleon Skousen.

In "The Naked Communist," Point 26 instructs the communist to "present homosexuality, degeneracy, and promiscuity as normal, natural and healthy." Point 40 instructs "discredit the family." Obama has been able to accomplish both and then violate the U.S. Constitution, as Point 29 instructs "Discredit the American Constitution by calling it inadequate, old-fashioned," and "out of step with modern need." In February 2011, Obama refused to have the federal government defend marriage between a man and a woman, even though the Defense of Marriage Act was a federal law approved by an overwhelming majority of Congress (342-67 in the House and 85-14 in the Senate) and signed by President Clinton in 1996. Obama, in effect, appointed himself a judge in determining a law as unconstitutional based upon his own feelings or beliefs. While Obama does have the right to not defend a law, it is only if there is no reasonable argument available in its defense. However, this is not the case. There are several arguments available to defend the law of marriage including the will of the people. Imagine for a moment if Governor Palin were president and decided she was not going to have her attorney general defend abortion, since she believes it is morally wrong. The liberal media would have made a huge scene on the issue; but since this concerns President Obama, the media remains silent as he supersedes his authority. What President Obama has done is a dereliction of his duty "to care that the laws be faithful executed" (U.S. Constitution, Article II, Section 3) through his sworn duty to "preserve, protect and defend" the U.S. Constitution.

While Obama and the Democrats have attacked the institution of marriage and refused to defend it, there is one organization that should be criminal and their members thrown in prison. I wrote about them in one of my letters to a newspaper editor:

"The Democrats and NAMBLA"

NAMBLA, the North American Man-Boy Love Association, is a homosexual organization for older men to follow their fiendish desires to be with young boys sexually. This organization is criminal and should be dismantled with its members and organizers thrown into jail. Yet, NAMBLA has a working relationship with the Democrat Party. President Obama appointed Kevin Jennings as the Safe School Czar. Jennings expressed his admiration and praise for Harry Hay, who is a long-time advocate for NAMBLA and the legalization of sexual abuse of young boys by older men.

As an educator, Jennings was approached by a 15-year-old boy who sought his advice about a relationship he was having with an older man. Instead of reporting this felonious act to police or encouraging the boy to talk to his family or seek counseling, Jennings told the boy to "use a condom" with the man. (*See*: www.**thenewameri-can.com**/index.php/culture/education/2386.) This is our Safe School Czar? Jennings also wrote the forward to a book called "Queering Elementary Education," which promotes homosexual doctrine to be taught in elementary school, even to children in first grade. Jennings has already stated he will promote his "homosexual agenda" into our public school curriculum.

NAMBLA made headlines when a 10-year-old boy from Massachusetts, named Jeffery Curry, was abducted by two men who tried to force the boy to have sex with them. When the boy refused to consent to sex with the men, they murdered him by forcing him to choke on a gasoline soaked rag. Then, the men sexually assaulted the dead boy's body. Curry's parents sued NAMBLA, since one of the killers said he was discouraged from following his fiendish desires until NAMBLA encouraged him. Curry's lawyer explained how NAMBLA instructed perverts on how to lure children into sex, citing NAMBLA's publication

"The Rape-and Escape Manual." Its actual title is "The Survival Manual: The Man's Guide to Staying Alive in a Man-Boy Sexual Relationship." The American Civil Liberties Union, which receives a bulk of support from Democrats, including former House Speaker Nancy Pelosi, defended NAMBLA against the parents of the murdered boy. Not one Democrat came out in opposition to the ACLU's defense of NAMBLA.

In the 2001 San Francisco "Gay Pride" parade, Nancy Pelosi walked along side of the NAMBLA advocate, Harry Hay, who has stated, "If the parents and friends of gays are truly friends of gays, they would know from their gay kids that the relationship with an older man is precisely what thirteen-, fourteen-, and fifteen-year-old kids need more than anything else in the world."

NAMBLA is a criminal organization of pedophiles preying on young boys. How can an organization like NAMBLA even exist? Why aren't these men in jail? Who is protecting these boys or even girls from these pedophiles? Where is the national media? How safe are our school children with the hidden agenda of our Safe School Czar? Should the Democrat Party and its leaders walk with or praise and admire the leaders of NAMBLA? Should the Democratic Party give money to an organization that defends NAMBLA? These are just some of the disturbing questions that should be answered.

Frank Aquila, October 2009

Many Democrats are attempting to use the "Fairness Doctrine" as a means to silence Christian and conservative views by forcing conservative and Christian radio talk stations to give equal air time to opposing views. The Federal Communications Commission (FCC) in Washington, D.C. could ultimately use its power to pave the way to stop conservative speech or the preaching of the gospel of our Lord and Savior on the airwaves of America.

There are also attempts to remove all references to God, including the removal of "In God We Trust" from our currency and "one nation under God" in our Pledge of Allegiance. There are even some who wish to remove Christmas as a national holiday due to its ties to Christianity. Democrat Senator Patti Murray, of the state of Washington, refused to recognize the national Christmas tree, referring to it, instead, as a "holiday tree." When I was attending school, children were allowed to have a "Christmas vacation" and "Easter vacation." Today, it has been replaced by "winter recess" and "spring break."

Step-by-step, the goals and plans of the Communist Manifesto are being established to silence Christianity and the moral standards of America. While many may denounce the true plan of the Communist Manifesto, the proponents have not hidden their goals and plans.

During World War II, there was a Nazi concentration camp in Dachau, Germany, with the misleading words welded onto an iron gate, "Arbeit Macht Frei," meaning "Work Makes You Free." This was just a false hope to those who entered this place of death. The new false hope of today is to transfer faith and hope away from God and toward the government. The communists' ultimate goal is to replace "In God We Trust" with "In Government We Trust." Those words would be both frightening and most deceptive.

The Most Dangerous Organization in America

The American Civil Liberties Union (ACLU) is the most dangerous organization in America. It was established by self-proclaimed communist Roger Baldwin in 1920 to "suppress" Christians through a godless revolution and ultimately make America a communist nation. In his book, "Liberty Under the Soviets," he explains, "I was not an innocent liberal. I wanted what the communists wanted....." Baldwin further defined socialism as the means and communism as the goal, stating, "We are for socialism, disarmament, and ultimately for abolishing the state itself...." "We seek the social ownership of property, the abolition of the propertied class, and the sole control of those who produce wealth. Communism is the goal." (*See* http://dianedew.com/aclu.htm.)

On January 17, 1931, a Congressional Committee investigating communist activities in America issued the following in a report: "The American Civil Liberties Union is closely affiliated with the communist movement in the United States, and fully 90% of its efforts are on behalf of communists who have come into conflict with the law. It claims to stand for free speech, free press, and free assembly; but it is quite apparent that the main function of the ACLU is to attempt to protect the communists in their advocacy of force and violence to overthrow the government....Roger N. Baldwin, its guiding spirit, makes no attempt to hide his friendship for the communists and their principles." (*See* www.stoptheaclu.com.)

Goal 16 of the communists, as reported by Congressman Herlong from "The Naked Communist," by Cleon Skousen, is to "Use technical decisions of the court to weaken basic American institutions, by claiming their activities violate civil rights" and Goal 29 is to "Discredit the American Constitution by calling it inadequate, old-fashioned, out-of-step with modern needs, a hindrance to cooperation between nations on a worldwide basis. And replace our nation of 'laws, not men' with royal decree emanating from appointed judges and executive orders. Replace elected officials with bureaucrats."

To accomplish these goals, the Democrats are using the judiciary to appoint judges who are card-carrying members of the ACLU, including Supreme Court Justice Ruth Bader Ginsburg, who was general council to the ACLU prior to her appointment to the Supreme Court. President Obama has appointed several radical judges to key positions in the U.S. Supreme Court, including Sonia Sotomayor and Elena Kagen. He has also appointed Edward Chen, David Hamilton, and Goodwin Liu, whom the Washington Times has labeled as "radical" judicial nominees. This is not surprising, since socialist and communist organizations throughout the world and within America have supported President Obama and the Democrat Party.

Through the courts, the socialists and communists have used the ACLU to fight against America. The core belief of the ACLU has not changed. The ACLU will use the courts to progress toward communism. As Roger Baldwin, founder of the ACLU, stated, "Communism is the goal."

The Bible, Communism, and the New World Order

The goal of the New World Order is to make America part of the global society. You cannot fully understand the New World Order without also understanding references from the Bible. Very few people like to discuss religion or politics, so when you combine the two, it is certain to bring out even more passionate disagreements.

Louis Farrakhan, who is the head of the Nation of Islam, has referred to Obama as "the messiah." Obama is not the messiah. The only Messiah there will ever be is Jesus Christ, as his birth, life, and resurrection fulfilled many Biblical prophecies. Obama has a view of the New Age world, Israel, and his philosophy of socialized/communist government that does lead us toward fulfilling other Biblical prophesies. Nearly 5,000 prophecies are listed throughout the Old and New Testaments of the Bible, with nearly 90% of those prophecies fulfilled to date.

One of those recent prophecies occurred on May 14, 1948, when Israel became an accepted nation, after 2,000 years, when God promised Israel would return to their land again. (Jeremiah 16:15, 30:3) The nation of Israel is written as God's Holy Land from Genesis (Genesis 12:3) throughout the Bible to Revelation, with many references pointing to an invasion of Israel (Ezekiel Chapters 38 and 39) by Persia (Iran) and Gog of the land of Magog, which is Russia, as well as many other countries aligned together to eventually set the world against Israel in the Battle of Armageddon.

Today, Russia is aligned with Iran, as Iran vows to "wipe Israel off the map." Conflicts are occurring as Israel is hated by the Arab nations, who are vowing to take back "their land." America has supported Israel; but under the Obama administration, Israel does not have that security, leaving her to defend herself. However, the Bible states a great leader will arise, who will bring peace on earth. This person will reign as the Anti-Christ, putting the final touch of the New Age World Government, which is the "'666" discussed in Revelation 13:18, according to the Christian religion.

Obama has the New World Order vision to bring America toward a European-style socialized/communist government; essentially moving us toward a one-world controlled government. He has become the first U.S. president to ever be made chairman of the United Nations Security Council, in violation of the U.S. Constitution. CNN has already reported him as "The President of the World." The current economic condition in the world, as well as the devaluation of the American currency also moves us closer toward a one-world currency. So far, many of the European countries have given up their currencies for the Euro. Now, with the framework being established to have America join the globalization, the Amero, which is a currency combining the American dollar and the European Euro, is the next step toward a one-world currency, prophecy of the "666" in Revelation Chapter 13, where no one without the mark of the beast (666) in a global economy will be able to buy or sell products.

Once the socialist/communist globalization is established, it will be nearly impossible to reverse its course. As the government seizes control, society will rely on the government. Even the laws of our U.S. Constitution are not safe, as judges appointed by Obama will have lifetime appointments to give authority to international law rather than interpret laws based on the U.S. Constitution.

America has changed and "we the people" forgot what made this country great. We have become a "me first" society, taking what we can from the government. But the Bible also warns of such a society: "For men will be lovers of themselves, lovers of money, boasters, proud, blasphemers, disobedient to parents, unthankful, unholy, unloving, unforgiving, slanderers, without self-control, brutal, despisers of good, traitors, headstrong, haughty, lovers of pleasure rather than lovers of God." (II Timothy 3: 2-4) We have become a moral-less society, teaching tolerance rather than what is right and wrong. We have removed God and glorified evil. "Woe to those who call evil good and good evil." (Isaiah 5:20) For those who discredit prophecy, most prophecies are fulfilled, and the few remaining are beginning to align themselves perfectly.

Karl Marx introduced his 10 Planks of the Communist Manifesto in 1848:

1. Abolition of property in land and application of all rents of land to public purposes.

2. A heavy progressive or graduated income tax.

3. Abolishment of all right of inheritance.

4. Confiscation of the property of all emigrants and rebels.

5. Centralization of credit in the hands of the state, by means of a national band with state capital and an exclusive monopoly.

6. Centralization of the means of communication and transport in the hands of the state.

7. Extension of factories and instruments of production owned by the State, the bringing into cultivation of waste land, and the improvements of the soil generally in accordance with a common plan.

8. Equal liability of all to labor and the establishment of industrial armies, especially for agriculture.

9. Combination of agriculture with manufacturing industries; gradual abolition of the distinction between town and country by a more equitable distribution of population over the country.

10. Free education for all children in public schools.

The Communist Party USA has stated, "The future is socialism" and "capitalism is the enemy." Sam Webb, Chairman of the Communist Party USA said it best when he stated, "Obama's agenda is the agenda of the Communist Party USA—how nice!" and "is a necessary step toward a new society." (See www.liveleak.com/view?i=724_1227566786.)

Lenin stated, "The best revolution is a youth devoid of morals." Sadly, Americas have become brainwashed through liberal propaganda while they remain too indulged in their sin to recognize the socialist/communist transformation of our society with a complete subversion of our U.S. Constitution and an end to representative sovereign government as we know it. "We the People" will be replaced by "We the Government," which is the whole communist idea.

As author and philosopher Ayn Rand said, "The (U.S.) Constitution is a limitation on the government, not on private individuals.… It does not prescribe the conduct of private individuals, only the conduct of the government.…It is not a charter for government power, but a charter of the citizens' protection against the government."

The Importance of the TEA Party

Governor Sarah Palin was the face of the TEA Party's first national convention in February 2010, with her face on the cover of the program for the event and as its first ever keynote speaker. Whether or not Governor Palin or the TEA Party feels that Sarah is the face of the TEA Party movement, they share a lot in common, primarily "fiscal responsibility" and "limited government."

The TEA Party movement began its successful national presence in 2009. It became the largest grassroots political movement in America since the anti-war movement of the 1960s. The TEA Party movement was not a Republican movement; but it is the conservative movement of Republicans, Democrats, and Independents to return America to the values and principles outlined in the U.S. Constitution. With its broad appeal throughout America, the TEA Party movement became even larger than the liberal movement of the 1960s.

While the liberal movement of the 1960s influenced Alinsky to write "Rules for Radicals," where he admitted to teaching radicals to lie, manipulate, and use deception where the "ends justify the means," the conservative movement of the TEA Party exploded through a "silent majority," who recognized their government as reckless and violating individual freedoms and liberties as guaranteed by the U.S. Constitution. The movement was fueled by a Democrat-controlled congress, senate, and president, who were ignoring the will of the people. The movement was also against the out-of-control spending and the expansion of the government power and control over the people. As a result, the Republican Party made historic and substantial gains in the congress, setting a modern-day record of 70 congressional seats that changed representation. The Republicans made gains in both the senate and many state legislatures throughout the country, including 11 governorships, despite the liberal media's attempted influence to paint the TEA Party as a bunch of racists. The TEA Party also sent a strong notice to Republicans, who were becoming mini-Democrats, that they must return back to their conservative principles or face a challenge of being removed from office.

In Sarah's book, "America by Heart," Sarah references the TEA Party movement when she wrote, "This is the central political struggle facing America today, being played out right here....[TEA Party opponents] want something more from government....[TEA Partiers] are the ones paying the bills."

Sarah energized the movement at several rallies throughout America, including a rally organized by Glenn Beck which attracted 500,000 people. Sarah's influence and power on the movement mobilized the people to respond to this power conservative movement uniting people throughout the nation to fight back against their government's irresponsibility and intrusion. Leaders organized the people to attend town-hall meetings to express their outrage to their representatives. They also organized protests on Tax Day, April 15th, and 1,000,000 marched on Washington with very little media exposure. Conservatives are not going to be quiet any longer. They are uniting to save America and striking fear into those in government. Thomas Jefferson stated, "When governments fear the people, there is liberty. When the people fear the government, there is tyranny."

The TEA Party is actually divided into two separate organizations—The TEA Party Patriots and the TEA Party Express, which is also referred to as the political action committee called, Our Country Deserves Better (OCDB), both of which are non-partisan to support conservatives and those who believe in "fiscal responsibility" and "limited government."

The TEA Party Patriots' motto is "Ordinary citizens reclaiming America's founding principles." They claim to have over 1,000 local chapters throughout America to provide "logistical, educational, networking, and other types of support" to TEA Party groups around the country. They have also developed a "Contract for America," similar to the 1994 Republican Contract, which share some of the same core principles and goals.

The TEA Party Express, or (OCDB), promotes conservative candidates and has coordinated cross-country rallies through a bus convoy, as well as numerous other rallies across America "to oppose the out-of-control spending, higher taxes, bailouts, and growth in the size and power of government." They are also non-partisan and sophisticated in their political operations and coordination of members as well as providing financial support to conservative candidates.

The original Boston Tea Party was more than a protest against taxes; it was a revolution of independence and liberty against a tyrannical government. The founding fathers were distrusting of a centralized government with too much overreaching power and authority over the rights of the individual citizens. They had just finished a war fighting a tyrant government that wanted to impose total control. They wanted independence. They wanted a government that represented the will of the people, limited government control and offered individual freedom. Thomas Jefferson stated, "A government big enough to give you everything you want, is big enough to take away everything you have." Jefferson also warned of the nanny state, where the government should supply the needs of their citizens. Often, it is referred to as a cradle-to-the-grave dependency on the government to fulfill all of the citizens' needs and care for them. Jefferson stated, "The democracy will cease to exist when you take away from those who are willing to work and give to those who would not."

Limited for Liberty

"Limited government" is a key term in the traditional American philosophy that teaches our government must be limited in order to preserve and safeguard the power of individual liberty for the people. The Declaration of Independence summarizes the government's power as limited "to secure these rights" to protect the people. The U.S. Constitution refers to "limited" as a basic law to control the government's power through representation for the people. Therefore, the U.S. Constitution can only be changed, as intended by the framers and adopters, through amendments, through the representatives of the people. Therefore, the U.S. Constitution is the "supreme law of the land" as the people's fundamental law to limit the powers of the United States government.

The founders warned many times, in both public and private writings, that strict enforcement of the constitutional limits of the power of the federal government is essential for the protection of liberty for the people. Here are some of the other statements by the founding fathers of America:

"Most bad government has grown out of too much government." ~ President Thomas Jefferson.

"It has been said that all government is an evil. It would be more proper to say that the necessity of any government is a misfortune. This necessity however exists; and the problem to be solved is, not what form of government is perfect, but which of the forms is least imperfect." ~ President James Madison, who is also known as the father of the U.S. Constitution, 1833.

"When government fears the people there is liberty. When the people fear the government there is tyranny." ~ Thomas Jefferson.

"The two enemies of the people are criminals and government, so let us tie the second down with the chains of the Constitution so the second will not become the legalized version of the first." ~ Thomas Jefferson.

"Freedom is lost gradually from an uninterested, uniformed, and uninvolved people...." ~ Thomas Jefferson.

"Children should be educated and instructed in the principles of freedom." ~ President John Adams, 1787.

"Those who would give up essential liberty to purchase a little temporary safety deserve neither liberty nor safety." ~ Benjamin Franklin, 1759.

These are just some of the statements written or spoken by the founding fathers of America. Even George Washington refused to make himself a king, knowing that the government should always have the authority by the people with three equal branches of government—executive, legislative, and judicial—to check and limit the powers of each other. Individual liberty is essential for effective limitations of government power.

It is easy to be a popular leader when you offer everything to people using someone else's money. Too often, we have become a society that depends on our government and expects it to give us more. That was not the intent of the framers of America. A real leader stands for what is right even when what is wrong, for the moment, seems popular. Sarah Palin is that leader, and she has lived it throughout her life. She stands on principle. She exceeded the expectations of the people at every level of government within which she served. She walked away from a position and a six-figure salary as the commissioner of the Alaskan Oil and Gas Conservation Commission based on the unethical violations that occurred. She fought against corruption within her own political party. She took on Big Oil, leading to drilling in Point Thompson, while cutting earmarks, reducing taxes, eliminating special governor perks, and achieving an approval rating above 80%. She resigned as governor to save the state of Alaska hundred of thousands of dollars as well as countless hours her staff would have needed to refute the numerous frivolous ethics charges and lies by political operatives that were all ultimately dismissed—all simply alleged to sabotage her and her reputation.

Instead, Sarah went to the people and delivered the message of an ethical woman who really loves America, beyond just her adult life, and became a voice for the conservative revolution of the TEA Party, endorsing its message of "limited government" and "individual freedom" for all America. Even though Sarah cautions the movement to be about any one leader or politician, the people look to her to lead the course to fight back and expose the truth. Sarah has the "ability to capture the spirit of the conservative grass roots," according to Wall Street Journal reporter Susan Davis.

Sarah has taken her message to the people, who are still mostly unaware of her accomplishments and positions of various issues. Sarah has written several opinions and commentaries about the unrest in Libya, the protests in Wisconsin, the dangers of the ObamaCare legislation, Obama's budget proposals, tax policies, the death of Osama bin Laden, specifics of Obama's energy legislation and many other issues.

Sarah went throughout the country supporting and endorsing numerous congressional, senatorial, and gubernatorial candidates who stood for the same principles outlined in the U.S. Constitution and endorsed by the TEA Party. She also started her "Pink Elephant Movement" to support several female conservative candidates throughout America.

After the 2010 election, Sarah addressed the Republican freshmen members of Congress in a letter of congratulations. Sarah penned,

"When you take your oath to support and defend our Constitution and to faithfully discharge the duties of your office, remember that present and future generations of 'we the people' are counting on you to stand by that oath. Never forget the people who sent you to Washington. Never forget the trust they placed in you to do the right thing."

Sarah then went on to explain, "Republicans campaigned on a promise to reign in out-of-control government spending and to repeal and replace the massive, burdensome, and unwanted health care law President Obama and the Democrat congress passed earlier this year in defiance of the will of the majority of the American people." She pointed out, "You've also got to be deadly serious about cutting the deficit" and "check the growth of spending on our entitlement programs."

Sarah continued to touch many other issues including taxes, border security, foreign and national security. Sarah, reminding the new congress to be cautious, stating, "When the left in the media pat you on the back, quickly reassess where you are and readjust, for the liberals' praise is a warning bell you must heed." Sarah finished, "May your work and leadership honor their faith in you," referencing the voters who sent them to Washington.

Sarah feels at ease with Middle America and showed up at several rallies throughout the county. She made several speaking engagements and addressed various national, state, and local issues across America, including the farmers' inability to receive water for their farm land in the Central Valley of California due to environmentalist protection of a "three inch fish." Sarah also visited Israel and India.

Sarah became an author to provide America a view of her life in her autobiography called "Going Rogue," which became a best seller. Another best seller, "America by Heart" allowed the American people to feel a more personal side of Sarah.

Sarah made several media appearances, including the "Oprah Winfrey Show" and hosted her own television show called "Sarah Palin's Alaska," while working as a political commentator at FOX News.

In all, Sarah has humbly experienced the benefits of America. She has made herself more available to the American people while being the voice of the principles the framers of America foresaw as the success of America with "limited government," "individual freedom," and "life, liberty and the pursuit of happiness."

Chapter 6
Solutions for the Restoration of America

"Now, no one expects us to agree on everything, whether in Juneau or in Washington. But we are expected to govern with integrity and good will and clear convictions and a servant's heart." ~ Sarah Palin

Wake Up, America!

The Democrat Party and the American people have been successfully hijacked by communists and socialists in the Saul Alinsky ["Rules for Radicals"] model of lies, deception, and manipulation. The liberal media has assisted this hijacking. Conservatives and capitalists in the Republican Party have failed in exposing these lies and relaying their alternative message to the American people. Instead, many Republicans have become lighter versions of the socialist-Democrat Party, caught in the Alinsky code word of "compromise," while they exchanged their own principles and values, appearing to be "moderates," in order to chase votes. That is not to say that every conservative should be molded as a cookie-cutter image of each other. However, it is vital for conservatives to share and make evident their beliefs and principles by standing together on core issues concerning the original intent of the U.S. Constitution in our government.

Governor Palin and the TEA Party have warned the Republican Party of this socialist transformation and compromise. By becoming a mini-Democrat Party, moderate Republicans are not going to provide the American people a legitimate, or even fair, alternative. The Republican Party needs to take a strong stand, reintroducing itself to

Americans as a conservative party intent on protecting the U.S. Constitution, without hesitation, and consistently act in exposing lies, fraud, and communist connections in the Democrat Party. It must stop compromising capitalism and conservative values and, instead, return as the continuation of the foundation of what made America great. "We the people" must wake up and recognize the issues that have caused erosion in America. I wrote about this issue in one of my letters to an editor with updated statistics as of June 2011:

"Wake Up, America"

A major problem in America is we have lost our identity. The early immigrants who came to America loved America and did not call themselves Italian-Americans, Spanish-Americans, Irish-Americans or Asian-Americans. They called themselves Americans, adapting to one culture and one language to love one country—America. Those immigrants did not expect anything from America but appreciated the opportunity to pursue happiness without government interference. They were willing to fight for America. They fought and were willing to die for liberty and freedom during the world wars. Americans from all cultures and both political parties came together in nationalism and unity. America was strong and powerful.

However, through the generations, the many descendants and modern immigrants have become spoiled and dependent upon America, wanting to know what America is going to do for them. There is less loyalty and appreciation for America. We have now become a nation of multiculturalism where, through diversity, our government has to adapt to each language, lifestyle, and culture, rather than the modern-day immigrants adapting to America. Today, we have allowed an Islamic woman to have her driver's license photo issued wearing a burka because not doing so offends her belief. Our children are being required to learn about several different cultures while the importance of U.S. history has become less significant. We cannot survive as a nation being all things to all people. This diversity really has created disunity which is destroying the strength of our culture. Today's American multiculturalism has allowed and tolerated those who are loyal to their own culture and not America. Americans should not have to adapt to every other culture of immigrants; instead, every immigrant culture needs to adapt to America. It is that one culture which is our strength where everyone is proud to be an American.

Most Americans also believe English should be our official language; but our politicians ignore the voice of the people. Fifty-three countries have declared English as their official language, yet America, ironically, adapts to every other language. We have not given any of these other cultures a reason to assimilate into our culture since our government makes every effort to become all things to all people.

The government has decided to unconstitutionally mandate health care coverage on all Americans, while congress exempts themselves from that same government mandate. Our federal government has expanded its influence and controls into the banking, mortgage, and now the health care and insurance industries, even though our government has already run Social Security, Medicare, Medicaid and twelve other entitlement programs into bankruptcy. America had no national debt less than 100 years ago; but now our government has a national debt approaching $15 trillion, of which each citizen's debt share is approaching $50,000, and each taxpayer's share is over $130,000, according to www.usdebtclock.org. To get an idea of $1 trillion, if our congress saved $1 million a day, it would take 2,740 years to pay off $1 trillion and 41,100 years to pay off $15 trillion. This does not include interest or the $4 trillion of unfunded liabilities from Social Security that the government has loaned itself to pay for other government programs. It is now projected that the national debt will be $23 trillion by 2020 and, with the government takeover of health care and the retirement of the baby boomers, the Government Accountability Office projects a stunning $53 trillion in "unfunded liabilities"" over the next several decades, with no money available for Social Security, Medicare, and Medicaid by 2040.

America has become broke due to poor management. Our government still can't figure out how to secure our borders, which costs our government $113-$338.3 billion each year in services and benefits to illegal immigrants based on various reports. The government does not know how to balance a yearly budget to control spending. In 2009, the congress raised government spending an astounding 24% and then froze $15 billion in discretionary spending in 2010 to deceive the American people into believing that they were being fiscally conservative. This would be the same as a family that makes $50,000 a year living on a budget of $62,000 a year and going into debt $12,000 each year without cutting expenses. The only difference is our government is spending trillions beyond its means. The government's only solution has been to raise taxes or fees on Americans, while our government continues to give billions to other nations, such as Egypt, which vote against America 80% of the time, or waste billions of dollars of taxpayers' money to fight AIDS in Africa, while millions of taxpaying Americans suffer from heart disease and battle cancer. The needs of our military veterans have become an afterthought, even though they deserve the absolute best resources for their unselfish sacrifice in serving America.

Common sense would also be for our local, state, and federal governments to set aside money for a national emergency or natural disaster, such as a major earthquake, which experts claim is a matter of "when" and not "if" it will occur. We need to lay down our global burden and rebuild America. We should not be the welfare department to the world while neglecting our own country. We should not give compassion to 15-20 million illegal immigrants and no compassion to the over-burdened American tax-paying families. (Resources being used to feed, school, incarcerate, and provide health care for many of these illegal immigrants are substantial sucking our taxpayer resources, which is one reason California cannot pass a balanced budget, and only 40% of high school graduates can read at a fourth-grade level!)

Activist judges have ignored the will of the people, as well as our history, culture, the Constitution of the United States of America, the Declaration of Independence and every other founding document, and to remove God from American public life. The founding fathers were clear that we are "endowed by our Creator with certain unalienable rights." The ACLU has passed on the lie of "separation of church and state." This phrase is not even in the Constitution. It was a separation intended to protect government from control by religion and to protect religion from control by government—not to build a confrontational wall to keep government and religion separated. Separation from God was never intended by our founding fathers.

Political parties of change will not secure our borders, force employer verification or stop taxpayer funding to illegal immigrants. These progressive, global thinkers are traitors who tolerate the behavior that is destroying our society.

In 1907, President Theodore Roosevelt stated, "There can be no divided allegiance here. Any man who says he is an American, but something else also, isn't an American at all. We have room for but one flag, the American flag…we have room for but one language here, and that is the English language…and we have room for but one sole loyalty and that is a loyalty to the American people."

No matter where our ancestors came from, we are all Americans. We need to stop dividing Americans against each other. Be proud of your heritage but love America and your opportunity to pursue the American dream.

Frank Aquila

Ten Solutions for the Restoration of America

So what recommendations do I have to restore America and create an American reawakening?

1. National Security

Although there are many vital issues concerning us as Americans, our federal government's first obligation is to protect us from America's enemies. Al-Qaeda is, obviously, the most familiar enemy, having planned and carried out several attacks against our homeland, including those on September 11, 2001.

Information obtained by our intelligence agencies is our first line of defense against terrorist attacks. It would be unwise and a tremendous mistake, with the death of former al-Qaeda leader, Osama bin Laden, to move into a comfort zone, believing we cannot be attacked again. Especially in light of the fact that bin Laden has already officially been replaced by Egyptian-born Ayman al-Zawahri, who has vowed to take revenge upon the United States and "the West." Al-Qaeda, which coordinated its efforts to attack America's homeland, is only one of several international terrorist organizations. We should remain constantly aware of their magnitude and ability to attack us again. The 9/11 Report's recommendations should be accepted and implemented. Vital to our security is the realization of how vulnerable we remain and the provision of all tools necessary to allow law enforcement agencies across the country, in addition to the National Security Agency (NSA), the ability to work together in preventing future terrorist attacks on America.

Osama bin Laden and al-Qaeda declared war on America in 1996. There was little, if any, media attention drawn to it at that time, but the international terrorist organization was real as were its threats. We must continue to place close, vigilant attention to enemy terrorist "chatter" around the world in order to stay on top of what they are planning and be able to take preventative steps to control any threat to America. The jihadists within terrorist organizations are sophisticated in their ability to spread messages to followers and plans to involved individuals. They recruit other jihadists and plan terrorist attacks using the internet, satellite television, and even computer games. Al-Qaeda is known to be located in many countries, including Canada, China, India, Philippines, Serbia, Sweden, Thailand, Yemen, throughout Europe, the Middle East and, not surprisingly, even within America, with home-grown jihadist terrorists being raised here.

Since 2001, most Democrats have refused to recognize the threat of these terrorists. The Obama administration was openly hesitant in identifying terrorists as "terrorists," instead referring to them as "enemy combatants," even referring to their terrorist acts as "man-caused disasters." Since they have refused to recognize the terrorists for who they are, most Democrats have eroded the tools used by the Protect America Act (PAA) and the Foreign Intelligence Surveillance Act (FISA) to combat against these terrorists, claiming our intelligence agencies use these preventative intelligence procedures against the American citizens, even though no evidence has ever been provided to support these accusations.

When the Terrorist Finance Tracking Program, which tracked the financial transactions of terrorists, was leaked to the media in 2006, the Democrats asserted that then-President Bush was using the program to spy on individual Americans, in a blatant effort to politically rally the American people against the president. We have lost the ability of our intelligence to utilize the Terrorist Surveillance Program, which allowed and authorized telecommunication companies the ability to assist the U.S. government in monitoring terrorists. The telecommunication companies ceased cooperation with our government after threats of investigations by congressional Democrats, which led to the understanding that these companies could face disabling lawsuits.

The Democrats have also consistently interfered with the interrogation, investigation, and prosecution of suspected or alleged terrorists, including weakening efforts to gather information of foreign terrorist plots by providing them the protection of the U.S. Constitution. Democrats have pressed to provide terrorists the same rights as "lawful combatants" under the Geneva Convention—in spite of the fact that the terrorists totally ignore the laws of war as required by the Convention. Further, our CIA investigators have even undergone criminal investigation for their interrogation "tactics" and destruction of CIA videotapes of terrorists. As a result, our intelligence and investigation community have suffered internal/personal risks in carrying out their responsibilities in gathering vital, and even lifesaving information, without facing investigation themselves. Unfortunately and justifiably, U.S. intelligence officers have become so fearful of lawsuits, legal liability, or congressional investigations that many feel forced to purchase professional liability insurance.

During Senator Obama's campaign for president, he stated his first official presidential act was to close Guantanamo Bay, a prison island used to house 245 hardened terrorists. Upon election, he and his Attorney General, Eric Holder, together attempted to grant these hardened terrorists U.S. constitutional rights, including Miranda rights, to prevent them from "self-incrimination." They went so far as to propose transporting alleged terrorists to American soil in order to provide them trials under American criminal law, as opposed to rightly trying them under military tribunal law—a court action conducted by the military without the same constitutional protections we, as Americans, receive.

Also, orders of President Obama and Attorney General Holder severely infringed upon our government's successful methods of interrogating terrorists, ordering the cessation of all enhanced or advanced interrogation procedures, including the much-maligned water boarding, which was successfully used on Khalid Sheik Mohammed, the mastermind of the September 11, 2001 attacks. Water boarding—an aggressive interrogation technique always carried out under medical supervision—has successfully been employed in the past by the CIA, usually as a last resort and only in a few instances. This technique has absolutely been proven to push terrorists to the point of providing vital information regarding their associates' involvement in and planning of attacks, to seek information with the ultimate goal of saving lives of Americans in our homeland and in foreign countries.

Unfortunately, many terrorists were released from Guantanamo and allowed to return to their home countries, or ones which would accept them. It has been proven many immediately returned to either once again wage war on our military on battlefields or plan new attacks against American interests. With all of this having taken place, great credit must be given to our intelligence agencies which gathered information finally leading to the death of Osama bin Laden. I wrote about this issue in one of my letters to an editor:

"Death of Osama bin Laden"

The death of Osama bin Laden (OBL) was a great day for America and the families of the men, women, and children who were murdered on September 11, 2001. There are many people who deserve credit for achieving this historic accomplishment, including President Obama, President Bush, the CIA, and the Navy Seals for killing the leader of an evil organization that affected all in America.

President Bush deserves credit for initiating the process of gathering information through the approved efforts of enhanced interrogation at Guantanamo Bay, a prison camp for suspected terrorists. Bush further approved water boarding to gather more intelligence on al-Qaeda, which Obama's CIA director, Leon Panetta, admits was an essential piece of information that led to the messenger, who lived with OBL in the compound, which had been built in 2006.

President Obama also deserves credit for approving the military plan to capture or kill OBL. However, if Obama had initiated the policies he desired when he campaigned, we would not have killed OBL. During the campaign, Obama had promised to close Guantanamo Bay and also stop all enhanced interrogations or water boarding of terrorists. Even the word "terrorist" was forbidden to be used by the Obama administration. Instead, the terrorists were called "enemy combatants," and a terrorist act was called a "man-caused disaster." Then Obama and his Attorney General, Eric Holder, wanted to provide constitutional rights to these terrorists, try them on U.S. soil, and provide them Miranda rights, which are rights given to American citizens. This idea by the Obama administration was insane. America is at war with an enemy that does not deserve the same constitutional rights our soldiers have sacrificed their blood to protect. It is a good thing that the Navy Seal who shot OBL saw him as a threat and shot him so he did not have to provide him Miranda rights.

Another major mistake by the Obama administration was providing intelligence to the enemy. After OBL's death, our government proceeded to announce we had collected his computer files. This was foolish information to provide to the media and the enemy. We should have kept that information secret and stated that we had OBL, but did not obtain any other information. We allowed the enemy to move, missing further opportunities to get further al-Qaeda commanders. Now, those commanders can regroup and alter their strategy and locations, knowing we had their prior addresses.

Another disturbing piece of information was the Obama administration's desire to provide a religious funeral for OBL. OBL received his religious rites on the deck of the U.S.S. *Carl Vinson* aircraft carrier. In accordance with Islamic practice, OBL was washed and wrapped in a white linen sheet before his burial at sea within 24 hours of his death. So many survivors of 9/11 were not provided the same closure in saying good bye to their loved ones. Further, the White House even refused to provide the American people a photo of OBL in death, since it did not want to incite the Muslim world. Obama has become too concerned about the feelings of the Muslim world when, instead, he should show more concern about the feelings of the American people.

Frank Aquila, May 2011

Ironically, it was the killing of Osama bin Laden that revealed how ridiculous the Obama administration's terrorist policies are. Barack Obama has stated water boarding is "never acceptable" because it contradicts America's values. So, does the Obama administration believe it is acceptable to actually kill bin Laden, as compared to water boarding a few other terrorists who wage war against America and, most likely, are holding on to knowledge that could save American lives? The Navy Seals performed a tremendous service to our country, and the majority of Americans are relieved bin Laden is no longer alive. However, this analogy can be used to demonstrate the inconsistency of the liberal position and explain the need to support our intelligence officers' use of enhanced interrogations. Further, it is troubling that many of our intelligence officers' were just recently investigated, while others face prosecution by Attorney General Holder, for using the enhanced interrogation measures which Holder and Obama deem "unconstitutional." What actually should be unconstitutional is our government refusing to allow our intelligence agencies and officers to employ measures in gathering information to prevent the threat of terrorist organizations within and outside of America.

According to the U.S. Constitution, Article II, Section 1, before [a president] enters the execution of office, the following oath or affirmation must be taken: "I do solemnly swear (or affirm) that I will faithfully execute the office of President of the United States, and will to the best of my ability, preserve, protect and defend the Constitution of the United States."

In addition, elected and appointed officials and judges of our federal government must answer the following question prior to undertaking their respective constitutional duties: "Do you solemnly swear that you will support and defend the Constitution of the United States against all enemies, foreign and domestic; that you will bear true faith and allegiance to the same; that you take this obligation freely, without any mental reservation or purpose of evasion; and that you will well and faithfully discharge the duties of the office on which you are about to enter? So help you God?" In response to their oaths of office, these officials answer, "I do," but do they really mean it?

It is appearing more and more obvious that, especially in the Obama administration era, the cause of freedom and the oaths of office have become a mere, rather than sincere, formality. More and more members of our administrative, legislative, and judicial branches of government are failing to "support and defend the Constitution of the United States" and "bear true faith and allegiance to the same." Our Constitution is being misinterpreted, violated, abused, and "shoved under the carpet," thus causing us to gradually lose our freedoms and national security.

Our executive and legislative branches must be committed to our intelligence agencies, including the NSA, and fully understand we are in an ongoing war against terrorism. Again, they must be supplied with and allowed to use any and all tools in order to identify, contain and, ultimately, defeat the terrorists, preventing future terrorist attacks. These tools should include wiretapping (without warrants) on suspected terrorists inside and outside of the United States via telephone and email communications, internet activity, and medical, financial, and any other transactions or records. The NSA also must be allowed to gather all possible foreign intelligence and broaden its discretion regarding immigration in order to detain and deport immigrants suspected of terrorist-related acts. Attacks and prosecution of our intelligence officers and U.S. companies, which have assisted our government in preventing such attacks, must be stopped. Our goal as a nation must change to prevention by, rather than prosecution of, our intelligence officers.

While some wrongly suggest this compromises our liberties in America, all wiretapping without a warrant was performed on foreign terrorist suspects outside of the United States. Any similar action involving terrorist suspects within America would continue to require a warrant issued by a judge.

Again, al-Qaeda is not the only foreign terrorist threat to America. There are other terrorist organizations, including the Islamic Jihad Union, Islamic Movement of Uzbekistan, and the Eastern Turkistan Islamic Movement. There are also other nations that pose an ongoing serious threat to our country, including North Korea and Iran. Unfortunately, Barack Obama has eliminated our missile defense system, which was developed to intercept any missile heading toward America. Instead, we are using technology to fund a future mission to the moon or Mars. The forefront of our technology must be developed to protect America in these dangerous times and not seek some wild space adventure. While it should be our government's highest priority to protect America and the American people from harm, these governmental policies have placed America in danger of future attacks and harm.

2. Border Security

For purposes of "immigration" and border security in this section of solutions, it is essential to differentiate between "immigrants" and "aliens." "Immigrants" enter the United States legally and either maintain their legal presence according to immigration law or become naturalized citizens. However, "illegal aliens" are not immigrants. When a person illegally enters, is illegally smuggled into the United States, or violates their visa restrictions, that person is not an immigrant or visitor but an "illegal alien," subject to deportation under existing federal immigration law.

Our federal government has turned a blind eye to America's borders. Open borders affect America's national identity, security, and economy. We must have closed borders in order to be able to separate our identification of legitimate American citizens versus illegal aliens and whether or not those aliens are friendly or actually enemies of America. President Bush overlooked the perfect opportunity to shut down our borders after September 11, 2001, at which point his position should have been to prioritize them as a national security issue.

According to various statistical reports, it is estimated there are between 7-20 million illegal aliens living in America at an estimated annual cost to American taxpayers of between $113-$338 billion for services and benefits. The U.S. Border Patrol admits its agents only apprehend one of every five people illegally entering America, while ranchers who actually live along the border believe the number is more accurately one out of every ten!

While many Americans assume these illegal aliens enter our country to pursue the American dream, that is, in fact, not the case. In Texas, Border Patrol agents have discovered Iranian currency, Islamic prayer rugs, Arabic clothing stating "martyr" and "way to immortality," while one piece of clothing showed a jet flying into a skyscraper.

It is a dangerous mistake for Americans and our government to assume these illegal aliens are all from Mexico or Central America. Approximately 10% of those apprehended by the U.S. Border Patrol are from the Middle East. Rene Noriega, a spokesperson for the Border Patrol, stated there is a 42% increase of non-Mexican aliens, with Border Patrol agents apprehending people from all over the world, including from the former Soviet Union, Asia, and the Middle East.

According to the federal Enforcement Integrated Database, 125 illegal aliens were apprehended, in New York alone, between fiscal year 2009 through April 20, 2010, including two Syrians, seven Sudanese, and 17 Iranians, all of whom illegally entered America from countries the U.S. government classifies as state sponsors of terrorism. According to a Homeland Security Investigation Subcommittee 2006 report, "Members of Hezbollah, the Lebanon-based terrorist organization, have already entered the United States across our southwest border."

WSB-TV, Florence, Arizona, reported on the "population breakdown" of illegal aliens detained at one facility. Although most of the 395 males behind bars were Mexicans, several were from Afghanistan, Iraq, Iran, Lebanon, Nigeria, Pakistan, Somalia, Sudan, and Yemen.

Even further disturbing is the number of terrorist suspects who have been apprehended after illegally entering America. In 2005, James Loy, who was then-Deputy Secretary of Homeland Security, stated, "al-Qaeda leaders believe operatives can pay their way into the country through Mexico and also believe illegal entry is more advantageous than legal entry for operational security reasons."

Mahmoud Youssef Kourani, pled guilty in 2005 to providing material support to terrorists. He also raised cash for Hezbollah and secured his visa by bribing a Mexican diplomat in Beirut. Egyptian Ayman Sulmane Kamal, who used the alias Miguel Alfonso Salinas, was detained in New Mexico in 2006.

In 2006-2007, then-National Intelligence Director Mike McConnell stated that at least 30 Iraqis were apprehended. In an interview with the El Paso Times, he stated, "There are numerous situations where people are alive today because we caught them."

The Department of Homeland Security issued an intelligence report on Somali Mohamed Ali, who is a suspected member of al-Shabaab, a Somali-based al-Qaeda ally. (66)

Ahmed Muhammed Dhakane was arrested in Brownsville, Texas, for "a large-scale smuggling enterprise" designed to sneak several members of al-Ittihad al-Islami, a Muslim-extremist organization, and Eastern Africans through the Mexico border into Texas.

Terrorists are fully aware of the fact our nearly 2,000-mile border with Mexico is unmonitored in vast regions. They realize they have a better chance of entering America through that border, rather than entering through our legal visa process, in order to conduct and spread their terrorist activity. These terrorists coordinate with "coyotes," who are human smugglers, paying them $30,000-$50,000 per person, to smuggle them illegally into the United States.

U.S. officials will neither confirm nor deny that terrorist organizations are coordinating with either Los Zetas or MDC, two major Mexican drug cartels. These cartels use "coyotes" and "narco-militarists," known drug runners, and could easily assist, through various drug corridors in the transport of bombs, dirty suitcases, and other weapons of mass destruction and their components into America. The Obama administration has shown great weakness and backed away from such claims in an effort to avoid angering the Mexican government. However, former Mexican national security adviser, Adolfo Aguilar Zinser, has stated, "Spanish and Islamic terrorist groups are using Mexico as a refuge."

There are reported to be several terrorist cells of foreign terrorist organizations (FTOs) in Mexico which are being funded through Iran, including al-Qaeda, Hezbollah (Party of God), Hamas (Islamic Resistance Movement), and the Revolutionary Armed Forces of Columbia (FARC). The Department of Homeland Security has reported that terrorist cells are believed to be in America as well. Eduardo Medina Mora, the former director of Mexico's Center for Intelligence and National Security, has stated that the possibility of an al-Qaeda attack, launched from Mexico, against America "could not be ruled out."

The MDC gang in Mexico is responsible for thousands of murders, including gruesome attacks, which included beheadings and other terrorist-style killings, as well as bombings similarly used by the Islamic terrorist networks in the Middle East. That cartel is also known to have kidnapped and murdered Americans on both sides of the Mexican/U.S. border.

In Brownsville, Texas, a homemade improvised explosive device (IED), which resembled bombs used against U.S. troops by terrorists in the Middle East, and is used as well by Mexican drug cartels, was discovered off U.S. Highway 77. This discovery caused the U.S. Department of Interior to post signs near the Sonoran Desert National Monument reading, "TRAVEL NOT RECOMMENDED," issuing a warning to the public that it was an "active drug and human smuggling area."

In 2007, Daniel Joseph Maldonado, who has ties to Somalia, was arrested in a terrorist training program and returned to Houston for prosecution. KHOU-TV reported, "They had plans for him to come back to the United States and recruit female suicide bombers."

Steven McGraw, head of the Texas Department of Public Safety, advised Congress that the drug cartels are as barbaric as al-Qaeda. Tom Horne, Attorney General of Arizona, has suggested the United States designate the Mexican drug cartels as foreign terrorist organizations, but his suggestion was rejected by the federal government. Ben Anderson, a retired U.S. military colonel, stated, "There is only one way to handle this. In a world now filled with bio-warfare agents, backpack nuclear devices, and chemical weapons like Sarin gas, we must militarize the border. There is no other way to stop the flow."

When people illegally cross into other foreign countries, such as North Korea, Iran, Afghanistan, China, Venezuela, or Cuba, they face a number of consequences, being branded a spy, including arrest or even death. However, in America, we have "sanctuary cities" which protect illegal aliens. America's national security and sovereignty are at risk. Our federal government doesn't even have verifiable statistics as to the number of terrorists OR illegal aliens now in our country, causing our own citizens to live under the threat of murder, kidnapping, and drug and gang violence due to political posturing in Washington, D.C.

Illegal aliens have increased America's crime rate. Approximately 30% of the federal inmates are illegal aliens, which costs our government, and American taxpayers, billions of dollars on incarceration. Millions of pounds of drugs are confiscated by federal, state, and local police each year, and the cost of deportation is billions more. There are many unsolved crimes, including murders, due to the extraordinary presence of illegal aliens, and nearly one million sex crimes are attributed to illegal aliens.

Due to the basic refusal of the federal government to seriously enforce immigration law, Arizona attempted to protect its own citizens. The state passed legislative guidelines to enforce federal immigration laws. Police agencies were granted the authority to verify citizenship when detaining suspects in order to determine whether they were in that state legally. The Obama-Holder administration fought against the legislation through the Justice Department's attorney, Tony West, who, unknown to many Americans, had formerly represented terrorists who sought to fight against America. West was ultimately able to block much of the legislation, claiming Arizona had no right enforcing federal laws. Those who supported the Arizona law were deemed "racists" for supporting its legislation. The Obama administration has made it perfectly clear it is waging war against those who want to protect our borders. This is an outright affront against those who respect the rule of law and wish to keep America safe and secure. Contrary to the Obama administration's beliefs and unfair allegations, these people are not racists.

In fact, Barack Obama, in the political mode of Alinsky, outright lied in order to make it appear the government is protecting our borders. On May 10, 2011, in El Paso, Texas, Obama stated, "We have strengthened border security beyond what many believed was possible." He also cited increases in the amount of fencing, aerial surveillance, the number of border agents, National Guard troops, intelligence analysts, and deportations of illegal aliens. He further went on to deceive the American people, blaming "border-security-first Republicans" for the lack of reform on immigration. Audaciously, he stated, "I want everyone to listen carefully to this. We have gone above and beyond what was requested by the very Republicans who said they supported broader reform as long as we got serious about enforcement. All the stuff they asked for, we've done. But even though we've answered these concerns, I've got to say I suspect there are still going to be some who are trying to move the goal posts on us one more time." When Obama stated "move the goal posts," an audience member yelled, "They're racists." Obama made no correction or rebuke to that ridiculously untrue outburst!

Barack Obama envisions "using" the Hispanic people for future votes. He is making every effort to paint Republicans, who favor protecting our borders, as racists. He is also making every effort to get Republicans to buckle under pressure to allow legislation for amnesty (the Dream Act) for those in America illegally. This is an outright attempt to promote the Democrat political philosophy, as a strategy to increase the ethnic voting block and gain political contributions through emotional pandering.

Barack Obama further stated in his May 10, 2011 El Paso speech, "They wanted more agents on the border. Well, we now have more boots on the ground on the southwest border than at any time in our history. The Border Patrol has 20,000 agents—more than twice as many as there were in 2004, a build-up that began under President Bush and that we have continued. They wanted a fence. Well, that fence is now basically complete." In actuality, legislation was passed five years ago to build a 700-mile double-layer border fence along the southwest border, which promised legislation has not been enforced. In May 2011, the Department of Homeland Security admitted that just 5% (36.3 miles) of the double-layer fencing was complete. Compare this to the 2009 report of the Government Accountability Office (GAO), the investigative arm of Congress, which revealed in early 2009 that only 32 miles of double-layer fencing had been built. That means, despite President Obama's deceptive assertions, only 4.3 miles of double layer fencing has been built since he became president! As well as being deceitful, this is woefully inadequate. (See http://nation. foxnews.com/border-fence/2011/05/10/obama-claims-border-fence-basically-complete-its-only-5-finished.)

Texas Republican Representative Lamar Smith responded to Obama's speech, stating, "It is clear President Obama is in full campaign mode, but his words do not match his record. He continues to ignore the facts. Mexican cartels have increased their presence inside the U.S., the data on spillover crime and violence is 'underreported' and that between 70% and 90% of Texas's 1,200-mile border with Mexico is still not under operational control."

Barack Obama does not like or encourage enforcement of our current immigration laws. With his blessing, his administration has chosen to ignore most of the laws and refuses to arrest illegal aliens. However, Obama deceitfully conveys the appearance of enforcement of the laws with Immigration and Customs Enforcement (ICE) targeting illegal aliens who are "violent offenders and people convicted of crimes." Police departments in "sanctuary cities," like San Francisco, refuse to work with federal immigration authorities, and some continue to shield illegal juveniles if they have family or are enrolled in school.

When the U.S Justice Department was asked why it was suing the state of Arizona in the summer of 2010 for enforcing immigration law, but not going after sanctuary cities for failing to enforce the law, Attorney General Eric Holder's spokesman responded to The Washington Times, "There is a big difference between a state or locality saying they are not going to use their resources to enforce a federal law, as so-called 'sanctuary cities' have done, and a state passing its own immigration policy that actively interferes with federal law."

One justification of creating sanctuary cities is often under the guise of protecting "immigrant rights." But remember, illegal aliens are not immigrants who temporarily or permanently reside legally in the United States! A 1996 federal law, the Illegal Immigration Reform and Immigrant Responsibility Act (IIRIRA), requires local governments to cooperate with the Immigration and Customs Enforcement (ICE) division of the Department of Homeland Security. In spite of IIRIRA, many large and small cities have adopted so-called "sanctuary" policies, which instruct city employees not to notify the federal government of the presence of illegal aliens living within those communities. Ironically, "sanctuary" policies also do not distinguish between legal resident immigrants and illegal aliens, thereby allowing illegal aliens benefits of taxpayer-funded government services, in addition to overlooked and increased crime.

Formal sanctuary cities, or safe havens, have written general or specific resolutions, ordinances or administrative policies adopted by local government bodies. Sanctuary policies are also safe havens for "terrorist cells," as their activities are less likely to be detected by law enforcement. These sanctuary cities' public records are open and subject to requests by citizens and the media. The list of formal sanctuary cities/states within the United States includes, but is not limited to:

Chandler, Mesa, Phoenix, and Tucson, Arizona; Bell Gardens, City of Industry, City of Commerce, Cypress, Davis, Downey, Fresno, Lakewood, Los Angeles, Long Beach, Lynwood, Maywood, Montebello, National City, Norwalk, Oakland, Paramount, Pico Rivera, Richmond, So. Gate, San Diego, Santa Clara County, Santa Cruz, San Francisco, San Jose, Santa Maria, Sonoma County, Vernon, Watsonville, and Wilmington, California; Aurora, Commerce City, Denver, Durango, Federal Heights, Fort Collins, Lafayette, Thornton, and Westminster, Colorado; Hartford and New Haven, Connecticut; DeLeon Springs, Deltona, Jupiter, Lake Worth, and Miami, Florida; Chicago, Cicero, and Evanston, Illinois; Wichita, Kansas; New Orleans, Louisiana; Cambridge, Chelsea, and Orleans, Massachusetts; Portland and the State of Maine (large numbers of illegal aliens travel to Maine to seek public benefits and valid Maine drivers' licenses, which are then used to legally drive in other states); Baltimore, Gaithersburg, Mt. Ranier, Montgomery County, and Takoma Park, Maryland; Ann Arbor and Detroit, Michigan; Minneapolis, St. Paul, and Worthington, Minnesota; Reno, Nevada; Camden, Fort Lee, Hightstown, Jersey City, Newark, North Bergan, Trenton, Union City and West New York, New Jersey.

The list continues as follows: Albuquerque, Aztec, Rio Ariba County, and Santa Fe, New Mexico; Albany, Bay Shore, Brentwood, Central Islip, Farmingville, New York City, Riverhead, Shirly/Mastic, Spring Valley Village, Uniondale, and Westbury, New York; Carrboro, Chapel Hill, Charlotte, Chatham County, Durham, Raleigh, and Winston-Salem, North Carolina; Columbus (misdemeanors), Dayton, Lima, Oberlin, and Painesville, Ohio; Oklahoma City and Tulsa, Oklahoma; Ashland, Gaston, Marion County, Portland, and State of Oregon (1987 law prohibits local/state law enforcement from using state resources when capturing illegal aliens, and law enforcement is allowed, but not required, to "exchange information" with ICE if an illegal alien is arrested); Philadelphia, Pennsylvania; Providence, Rhode Island; Austin, Baytown, Brownsville, Channelview, Denton, Dallas, El Cenizo, Ft. Worth, Houston, Katy (rethinking sanctuary for illegal aliens who commit felonies), Laredo, McAllen, and Port Arthur, Texas; Salt Lake City and the State of Utah (illegal aliens can live/work in the state, as of May 2011, with police to refrain from inquiring about legal status unless someone is stopped/arrested for serious misdemeanors/felonies); Alexandria, Fairfax County and Virginia Beach, Virginia; Burlington, Middlebury, and the State of Vermont; King Co. Council and Seattle, Washington; Madison, Wisconsin; and Jackson Hole, Wyoming.

In addition to formal sanctuary cities/states, "informal sanctuary cities/states" exist. In these instances, state or local governments have not actually adopted legislation opposing the ICE enforcement of immigration laws in those venues. These are not actually documented on paper and are more difficult to confirm, as public records aren't available. Informal sanctuary cities/states are evidenced by the manner in which a local government reacts with ICE regarding an illegal alien after determining the suspect involved in a misdemeanor or felony may likely be, or in fact is, an illegal alien.

As the Obama administration has chosen to overlook enforcement of our government's immigration laws, citizens in formal or informal sanctuary states and local communities are taking steps to combat illegal alien crime. When successful, after contacting state and federal representatives and senators, attending local community public meetings, demanding change/repeal; removal of sanctuary-state/city status encourages illegal aliens to move away from those areas. Crime is then significantly lowered, citizens' quality of life is improved, and their economic tax burden is decreased. (*See* http://www.ojjpac. org/sanctuary.asp.)

Obviously, while our government has ignored securing our borders over many years, millions of illegal aliens have entered the United States to seek employment opportunities. Illegal aliens suppress Americans' wages while returning billions of dollars back to their countries of origin. However, this influx is costing the American economy and taxpayers billions of dollars for services and benefits provided to these illegal aliens and their children, known as anchor babies, born in America. In addition to employment, they receive American taxpayer-provided social benefits, including subsidized rents or loans to purchase homes, the federal program of Women, Infants, and Children (WIC), welfare, social services, food stamps, Medicaid, health care, primary and secondary education, and free school lunches. Illegal aliens enjoy American government representation and protection and, now, some states are even allowing them preferential treatment over American citizens in college, including tuition breaks.

A 2001 California law provides that any student who attends a California high school for three years and graduates can qualify for in-state college and university tuition. Illegal aliens who qualify must swear they will seek to become U.S. citizens. While California faces a devastating budget crisis, according to attorneys for out-of-state students, it spends more than $200 million each year subsidizing tuition for illegal aliens. According to a lawsuit filed by The Immigration Reform Institute (IRLI), U.S. citizens who reside outside of California may pay up to $100,000 more to earn a degree than illegal aliens paying the California in-state resident fee. Opponents of California's illegal alien in-state tuition policy have stated California is unlawfully discriminating against U.S. citizens in favor of illegal aliens, adding the case involves a question of great national importance.

As the federal government holds jurisdiction over immigration law, Congress has enabled tuition battles to grow by lack of action. In 1982, a Supreme Court opinion mandated states to provide illegal aliens access to K-12 education in public schools. However, the absence of comprehensive federal immigration policy has allowed states to impose their own rules with regard to attendance at public colleges and applicable tuition rates.

In addition to California, the following states have enacted similar in-state tuition breaks to illegal aliens: Illinois, Kansas, Maryland, Nebraska, New Mexico, New York, Texas, Utah, Washington, and Wisconsin. (*See* http://www.reuters.com/article/2011/06/06/us-usa-immigration-education-idUSTRE7553KV20110606. *See also* http://www.ncsl.org/default.aspx?tabid=13100.)

In summary, immigration is a complex subject that affects our national security, economy, and politics. A border fence alone will not solve the problem of illegal immigration. There must be interior cooperation with federal, state, and local agencies enforcing the laws and deporting all illegal aliens who are involved in any violations of law. There must also be penalties placed upon those who knowingly hire illegal aliens. Organizations for amnesty, such as Fair Immigration Reform Movement (FAIR), National Council of La Raza (NCLR, Mexican American Legal Defense & Education Fund (MALDF), and League of United Latin American Citizens (LULAC), move tirelessly against the enforcement of existing laws against illegal aliens, including criminals, claiming that policy would "make it harder to build trust in the communities."

There should be a pathway to citizenship for immigrants who have abided by the law and have the education and skills to hold a job. However, these people should not be able to supersede those who have gone through the immigration process legally. There must be a penalties involved. There should also be a guest worker program. Those cities in America, such as sanctuary cities, which do not abide by the laws, should automatically lose federal funding until they show evidence they are abiding by federal immigration laws.

Unfortunately, the Democrats' only solution is granting blanket amnesty to millions of illegal aliens, regardless of whether we, in fact, know who they are or what their purpose is in being here. According to the Washington Examiner, "[Senator Dick] Durbin (D-Illinois) told Senator Jon Kyl [R- Arizona] on FOX Sunday News program that, if the GOP passed the Dream Act, Democrats would be willing to talk about reducing the country's spending habits." Durbin continued, stating, when it comes to granting amnesty to millions of illegal aliens, "we're not giving up."

3. Correct the Erosion of the Middle Class

While the Democrats negotiate deals, using the economy as a game chip for their other policies and agenda items, the American people are struggling to make ends meet in the damaged economy, with the American middle class, especially, being eroded. Government spending is out of control, and the American people are being expected to make up the shortfall, causing them less financial security.

Our economy is facing many threats that could potentially cause an economic implosion. The American dollar has been devalued. While unemployment remains over 9%, more and more American jobs are being sent to foreign countries. Growing numbers of people are on government assistance. Gasoline prices and fuel, in general, are skyrocketing. The national debt continues to grow larger and larger, forcing congress to continue either to raise the debt ceiling or severely cut overall government spending. Adding to the burden on both the government and the people are government agencies' job-killing regulations and congressional mandates that will be implemented by the health care reform legislation. Social Security, Medicaid, and Medicare are on the verge of collapse. The housing crisis has caused thousands of Americans to either lose their homes or face that prospect in the near future. European countries and American states, like California, are defaulting on their debts. Illegal immigration adds an even larger burden on the American economy. America faces constant threats from terrorist organizations. The expanding Middle East conflicts in themselves, and as they apply to Israel, have an effect on the global economy. The American people are burdened with several tax schemes, including the prospect of "Cap and Trade," and there is rampant corruption within corporate America, Wall Street, and unfortunately, even our government.

As the American economy continues to struggle against future cardiac arrest, our government's overall policies and lack of financial restraint are causing a growing number of American families to become victims, falling from the middle class into government dependency. Slowly, America is well on the road to becoming a second-rate country which is working its way toward third-world status.

The reality is that many global economic problems and issues are beyond America's control. However, America's congress can relieve and rectify many of our economic problems by limiting federal government involvement, control, and spending. The opposite of limiting federal governmental involvement, control, and spending is its insistence on the expansion of government policies, services, and "bailouts," such as a socialist government takeover of health care, mortgage industries, General Motors, and other entities "too large to fail," increasing government spending in the process. Obviously, the Obama administration and congress have failed miserably in its policies and legislation. Rather than enacting policies to strengthen our teetering economy and seriously move toward recovery, it has stubbornly insisted on allowing it to either remain in the same dire condition or worsen!

In addition, our government has created a financial crisis with Social Security. Funds that were supposed to be set aside for availability to retirees of future generations was irresponsibly added as a surplus amount of money in the government's general fund. As a result of this mismanagement, significant changes must now be made to finance Social Security for people who have paid into the system their entire working years and are, justifiably, expecting those funds to be available for their own retirement.

Our government has engaged non-stop in unethical increased spending of borrowed money from future generations, essentially from money that doesn't even exist. This has caused the American dollar to experience devaluation, raising the valid concern of inflation on every product and service Americans purchase. Compounding inflation and the escalating economic struggles Americans are facing is the rising cost of fuel and gasoline. Businesses must deal with the increased cost of producing and transporting a product, which increases, of course, are then passed along to American consumers.

On February 9, 2011, Federal Reserve Chief Ben Bernanke announced that China's holding of U.S. Treasury Bonds stands at $2 trillion. This actuality is not based upon China's relationship with America being friendly but, rather, for their business and trade negotiations. How long must America rely on China to hold our debt? Standard & Poor's already downgraded its outlook on America's debt from "stable" to "negative" in the spring of 2011. China announced its intention to reduce its amount of investment in the U.S. dollar, while PIMCO, which is the largest bond fund holder in the world, is now shorting U.S. government bonds.

There are currently more Americans receiving income and assistance from our government than there are Americans paying taxes into the government coffers. In May 2011, former speaker of the house, Newt Gingrich, called Barack Obama "the most successful food stamp president in American history."

Americans' total home mortgage debt is approximately five times larger than it was 20 years ago. Americans are borrowing on their future with credit card debt eight times larger than it was 30 years ago. Americans' household incomes currently being spent on food and gas now stand at 23%.

Economic principles and common sense indicate that the American government cannot continue to sustain this excessive amount of debt. If continued on the same course, a breaking point will arrive where America will lose her power and influence in the world and become, of necessity, a socialist nation—one class of poor people relying on the government with their absolute forfeiture of individual rights. The result of a financial collapse of this nature would allow our government to gain control over everything, including real property, reducing the American people to renters reliant upon our government rather than enjoying our personal freedom of being property owners.

It is essential to bring a screeching halt to our out-of-control government spending as well as reducing and limiting expanding government influence on the American people. Globalists are very concerned about the real possibility of Americans waking up to current reality and arising against our government, potentially imposing an armed revolution against our government, by taking advantage of our freedoms and rights allowed under the Second Amendment of the Constitution, the right to bear arms. This possibility causes tremendous fear in the minds of many progressive liberals, including Barack Obama, who have made attempt after attempt to reduce, or outright eliminate, the freedom and right of Americans to bear arms.

The late U.S. Senator Ted Kennedy (D-Massachusetts) called for a "war against individualism," and Secretary of State Hillary Clinton stated, "We must stop thinking of the individual." Karl Marx would have been extremely proud of those statements as well as the road America is now forging in the formation of a one-class American citizenry.

Imperative to stopping our government's road to the destruction of America is for the American people to reject increased and unnecessary government intrusion into our lives. This intrusion is slowly but surely taking away our individual freedoms allowed us under the U.S. Constitution in exchange for "free" services the government deceitfully promises to provide us in return for those losses. Spending must be reduced in a drastic and responsible manner. Each of us must be relentless in educating our fellow citizens, including young people, and make unrelenting demands on our elected representatives that Americans insist on returning to all the individual freedoms upon which the United States of America was founded!

4. Keep America First

Capitalism in America's business has always been a symbol of our unique greatness. America has always been a capitalistic society in which any person having an idea could market it and achieve success through hard work. This is a principle America has always espoused and which has caused America to be the leader in inventions and achievements throughout the world.

However, individual capitalism is a demon in the minds of socialists, who believe in government control. It is both in the Alinsky model and the Communist Manifesto to attack business as the cause and blame for those in the lower class not being able to achieve. An example of this socialist way of thinking was evidenced when Barack Obama blamed the oil companies for high energy costs. He instructed Attorney General Eric Holder to "root out" cases of fraud and manipulation within the oil and gas industries. Obama proceeded by stating, "We are going to make sure that no one is taking advantage of the American people for their short term gain." In fact, regardless of how deceptive this statement was, it is the government's lack of a comprehensive energy policy, utilizing our country's vast sources of energy, which has caused the energy surge in gasoline prices. Obama is not taking responsibility. Instead, he constantly attempts to shift the blame away from himself and lay it on businesses.

American businesses already pay the second-highest corporate tax rate in the world, just behind Japan. All American businesses, both large and small across every industry, pay 35%-41.6% in combined taxes to the state and federal governments, with Obama attempting to raise it even higher—by 5%! How much longer will the United States remain the world's largest economy? Nearly 50% of our states impose a higher corporate tax rate than top-ranked Japan, and every one of our states impose a tax rate higher than fifth-ranked France. Significant concerns exist as to whether American businesses can continue to remain strong with the burdens our government place upon them.

Union demands and mandates placed by the government and retirement programs have also added to the burden on businesses in America. The exorbitant number and ridiculous nature of government regulations are killing businesses and jobs, as well as causing us to pay more for products and services. To cite just one example, there are 15 government agencies overseeing our food-safety laws! While we all are in agreement of food safety laws, do we really need so many duplicative agencies regulating our food safety laws alone *and* duplicative agencies overseeing and regulating each of our other industries?

As a result of exorbitant taxes, union demands, and overbearing government regulation oversight, the number of American companies moving their facilities and outsourcing jobs to foreign business-friendly countries has increased the numbers of Americans who are losing those jobs that most likely will never return to our country! India is just one example—it is now absorbing former American programming, engineering, telemarketing, and customer services jobs.

America's unemployment rate continues to remain around 9%, with it being even higher (approximately 16%) when discouraged, no-longer seeking workers are taken into consideration, according to the Bureau of Labor Statistics. However, even these high unemployment rates can be deceiving since middle-class American jobs are being replaced by low-income jobs. The middle class is approximately 41% of the American work force. 17,000 Americans holding college degrees are performing jobs requiring a lower skill level than associated with their degrees.

Consumer prices in America have increased by 2.7%, while wages have only increased by 1.7%. In addition, American citizens are feeling the additional crunch of increasing health care, education, gas, and essential goods costs, which is, in fact, imposing hidden taxes on the people.

The American government must cease playing the class warfare game with our citizens. American jobs need to be returned to America, and both the North American Free Trade Agreement (NAFTA) and Central American Free Trade Agreement (CAFTA), which both political parties enacted into law, need to be eliminated. Most of us are believers in free trade, but we also believe in the sovereignty of our nation and that all trade should be fair. America should have never even considered trucks originating from foreign countries driving on American highways, let alone allowed the practice.

In order to return American companies to America, our congress should lower all tax rates on every "American-only" company, essentially allowing tax breaks to every small business in America, in order to create incentives and encourage businesses to employ more American workers. Larger companies making decisions to expand into foreign nations should be required to pay the highest tax rate.

Our congress also needs to decrease the overwhelming tax burden, thus, indirectly, the debt obligations of American taxpayers. If our congress did actually reduce tax rates imposed on Americans, people could more easily eliminate their own personal debt and again begin to make purchases, feeding economic growth. In one of my letters to an editor, I pointed out the amount of taxes our government takes from the people:

"The Government Should be Audited"

Every year, around the first week in May, is known for being the beginning of Tax Freedom Day, where all of your income from January through the first week in May is technically taken in one way or another from the people to supply government spending. President Obama stated when elected he was not going to sign any bill filled with pork (payoffs). Yet, even with a Democrat-controlled congress, he has approved more than 14,000 of wasted government spending amendments with no fiscal accountability. Then President Obama promised that 95% of Americans would get a tax cut; but this has been a lie as everyone has had their taxes increased in one way or another. *(See* www.**colony14.net**/id52.html.)

Congress has wasted our tax dollars for their own luxury. When Nancy Pelosi was Speaker of the House, she wasn't happy with the USAF C-20B jet, so she ordered a big 200-seat, USAF C-32, Boeing 757 jet, even though former Speaker of the House, Newt Gingrich, flew commercial most of the time. The fuel cost alone of Pelosi's jet was $60,000 one-way from Washington D.C. to San Francisco. This means "we the people" paid $480,000 per month and $5,760,000 annually just on her fuel costs alone! It doesn't sound like she was too concerned about global warming. This does not include over $100,000 used by House

Speaker Nancy Pelosi for "in-flight services" of food and liquor or $2.1 million paid annually for military escorts. (*See* http://www.wnd.com/index.php?fa=PAGE.view&pageId=123472.) Just to remove Pelosi as House Speaker and take away her taxpayer-funded jet would be reason in itself not to vote for any Democrat. Yet, congress wants us to trust them and believe they know how to spend our tax money. Congress wasted $6 million in stimulus money awarded to a California contractor under federal investigation for overcharging San Diego for cleanup after the 2007 wildfires. A Denver developer received $13 million in tax credits to help build a senior housing complex, despite being sued as a slumlord for running decrepit, rodent-infested apartment buildings in San Francisco, and Kentucky awarded $24 million to a contractor on trial for bribery. This is just some of the wasted money just blown away. (*See*, http://www.freerepublic.com/focus/f-news/2444651/posts/.)

Our government should be audited. Spending is out of control, and our government needs to cut spending. Families have to live within budgets and so should our government, without burdening the people with taxes, fees, tolls, fines, or whatever else the federal, state, county, and local governments can think of to take money from the people in order to continue to spend wastefully. Unfortunately, "we the people" have blindly elected our representatives who have laid a large tax burden on us while bankrupting programs such as Social Security that is supposed to be available for the American people who have paid into the system their entire working lives. These same policies caused the 2008 financial crisis and are the same policies that will create the perfect economic storm for the future economic problems of America.

America was not bankrupt 100 years ago. We had no debt, and taxes were low. While we have increased our national debt, we have also invented new taxes that did not exist 100 years ago including: Accounts Receivable Tax, Building Permit Tax, Capital Gains Tax, State License Tax, Cigarette Tax, Corporate Income Tax, Dog License Tax, Employment Tax, Estate Tax, Excise Tax, Federal Income Tax, Federal Unemployment Tax, Fishing License Tax, Food License Tax, Fuel Permit Tax, Gasoline Tax, Gift Tax, Hunting License Tax, Inheritance Tax, Inventory Tax, Liquor Tax, Luxury Tax, Marriage License Tax, Medicare Tax, Personal Property Tax, Property Tax, Real Estate Tax, Social Security Tax, Road Usage Tax, Sales Tax, Recreational Vehicle Tax, School Tax, State Income Tax, State Mortgage Tax, State Unemployment Tax, Telephone Federal Excise Tax, Telephone Federal Universal Service Fee Tax, Telephone Federal, State and Local Surcharge Tax, Telephone Minimum Usage Surcharge Tax, Telephone Recurring and Non-recurring Charges Tax, Telephone State and Local Tax, Telephone Usage Charge Tax, Utility Tax, Vehicle License Registration Tax, New Vehicle Sales Tax, Used Vehicle Sales Tax, Watercraft Registration Tax, Well Permit Tax and a Workers Compensation Tax. This does not include other numerous state, county, and local taxes, tolls, fees, and fines invented by our government to take money from the people.

Yet, the Democrats have attempted to impose even more new taxes such as a ticket tax on movies and concerts. iTunes Tax on music, Tractor Tax, Fertilizer Tax, Carbon Tax, Sports Utility Vehicle Tax, Internet Tax, a return of the Death Tax and even a Garage Sale Tax that would require people to report profits from items sold to neighbors. The Democrats have also introduced a Global Tax, International Tax, Bullet Tax, Bottled Water Tax, Plastic Bag Tax, Toilet Paper Tax, and a Windfall Tax, which places a special tax on all stock market profits, including retirement funds, 401Ks and mutual funds. This does not include a Mileage Tax to go with the increased taxes placed on gasoline. Then there is the hoax of global warming of Climategate (*see* http://online.wsj.com/article/SB100014240527487043424045745766832167 23794.html), which has been used to scam the American people to push forward the liberal environmentalist agenda, as well as the cap and trade tax and world tax the people of America would be required to pay.

The Democrats have targeted the tax provisions under the Bush administration's Economic Growth and Tax Relief Reconciliation Act of 2001 to let them expire and raise taxes on the American people. Currently, if the tax rates expire, the top-tier personal income tax rate will rise to 39.6% from 35%. Lower-income families will revert back to 28% from 25%. The 28% bracket will increase to 31%, and the 33% bracket will increase to 36%, while the special 10% bracket is eliminated.

Since President Obama and Nancy Pelosi teamed up, government spending has increase by $1 trillion over the next decade, while they plan to raise taxes on the American people by $1.4 trillion. (*See* http://www.heritage.org/Research/Budget/bg2249.cfm.) They will also add $1.6 trillion to the national debt just in 2010, and on February 4, 2010, congress approved $1.9 trillion of an additional debt ceiling to $14.3 trillion. (*See* www.marketwatch.com/story/house-approves-19-trillion-debt-limit-increase-2010-02-04.) This large expansion of governmental waste has become Democrats spending on steroids. According to the Heritage Foundation, President Obama's budget would run $7.6 trillion in deficits and more debt than all other presidents in American history—from George Washington through George W. Bush—combined. As a result of these deficits, net interest spending would reach $840 billion in 2020.

America needs to audit itself and the wasteful spending it does. We cannot spend our way out of recession or borrow our way out of debt, and no country has ever **taxed** its way into prosperity. We need to cut spending, stop all pork attachments to bills, adopt a balanced-budget amendment and approve the line-item veto to hold every president accountable to those items approved in the budget or a bill.

Frank Aquila, April 2010

5. Energy Independence

Although energy may be the main solution for solving America's problems, it may also be the central problem in America. Our government has limited our ability to become energy independent and, as a result, gasoline prices in America have soared. On the day of Barack Obama's inauguration, gasoline prices averaged $1.83 per gallon nationally. In two short years, prices have more than doubled. Could this really be the energy plan of the Obama administration? In 2008, Energy Secretary Steven Chu stated his desire to boost gasoline prices to the $7-$9 per gallon European levels. Obama followed Chu's statement that he would prefer a "gradual adjustment."

High-energy costs affect the American people and businesses and, thus, the economy. The American people are not only struggling with the high cost of fuel, but businesses need fuel to operate and produce consumer products, thus additional costs are passed on to consumers. American Airlines lost $436 million during the first quarter of 2011 due to high energy costs. At some point, a company like American Airlines will either be forced to cut services or raise ticket costs to the consumer or both. In the end, it is the entire American population that struggles with the high price of energy.

When a father once discussed with Barack Obama how the high cost of gasoline was affecting him and his family, Obama responded, "I know some o' these big guys, they're still drivin' their big SUVs. If you're complaining about the price of gas and you're only getting 8 miles a gallon, you know…," and continued, laughing, "you might want to think about a trade-in."

Republican Mississippi Governor Haley Barbour responded appropriately, stating, "Instead of changing policies, President Obama is trying to blame the American people for skyrocketing gas prices by saying they should trade in their cars."

In spite of the Obama administration's attempt to pass blame onto the energy industry, it can't hide from the truth. America is dependent on foreign oil. Currently, 70% of the oil we use in America is imported from foreign nations. However, we have the ability to become energy independent and drastically lower the cost of oil, as there is more oil in America than in all of the Middle East combined. There are abundant oil and natural gas reserves in the Outer Continental Shelf off the California coast, the Alaska National Wildlife Refuge (ANWR), and many other locations throughout America.

In the Colorado Rocky Mountain Region, the Green River Formation, which spreads through Colorado, Utah, and Wyoming, there is an estimated two trillion barrels of untapped oil, which is the equivalent of eight times the amount of oil in Saudi Arabia alone.

Does it make sense for a rancher who lives on a large dairy farm to travel to the grocery store to purchase his milk? America has oil and natural gas reserves to be energy independent for more than 200 years! It is also estimated that gasoline prices at the gas pump could drop as low as $.60 to $1.20 per gallon, excluding taxes, if we explored and extracted our own oil. Tapping and refining these resources alone would lift the American economy, assisting both consumers and promoting business growth.

If our executive and legislative branches of government would allow America to move into a position to place her own oil on the world market, stabilizing our economy, we could re-fund Social Security, pay off our national debt, and place millions of Americans at work in the oil and gas industries.

On the other hand, Governor Palin is responsible for the Alaska Gasline Inducement Act, the largest private-sector infrastructure project ever accomplished in North American history! Governor Palin is also responsible for legislation, the Alaska Gasline Inducement Act (AGIA), which brought greater progress to a transcontinental natural gas pipeline than her state's administrations of the previous 30 years. In addition, Governor Palin supports renewable energy sources, as well. She is responsible for the development of a plan to cause 50% of Alaska's energy to be produced from renewable sources by 2025. Equally as important, Governor Palin understands how energy independence is vital in the protection of America's dollar as the global reserve currency and its effect on countering increasing commodity prices. Americans should seriously, without hesitation, and quickly take Governor Palin's advice: "drill, baby, drill"!

6. Health Care Reform

The Affordable Health Care Act, the reform package known as ObamaCare, was ruled unconstitutional by U.S. District Judge Roger Vinson on January 31, 2011. Judge Vinson ruled that "the entire act must be declared void." Ultimately, the final decision will be rendered by the U.S. Supreme Court. The reasoning behind the "unconstitutional" ruling is the mandate which forces all American citizens to purchase something, in this case, health care insurance. The U.S. Constitution limits the federal government from such mandates.

While America's health care delivery system was not perfect and needs reform, it is still considered the best quality health care in the world. However, through forced mandates of socialized medicine, many doctors have already begun to and will continue to leave the medical profession. Obviously, statistics and common sense indicate a lesser quality of health care and bureaucratic panels will result. One of the greatest functions of these government-regulated panels will be to determine what services, if any, a patient would be allowed to receive. Further, ObamaCare raises taxes by $500 million and creates an added burden on businesses, which are allowed to opt out under the Act and pay a per person fine to the government. It is estimated that 50% of corporations and businesses will opt out of ObamaCare, forcing their employees into a public health care pool. For some smaller businesses, this would be more economical than providing their employees with health coverage. Knowingly and deceptively, Barack Obama and most Democrats in congress assured Americans, "You will not lose the health care you currently have." Unfortunately, this Affordable Health Care Act will now preclude millions of Americans from receiving the health care coverage they need.

Former Speaker of the House Nancy Pelosi stated to the American people prior to passage of the Affordable Health Care Act, "But we have to pass the bill so that you can find out what is in it, away from the fog of the controversy." Now, as Nancy Pelosi promised, every day we are learning more and more about the health care coverage in ObamaCare. The over 2,000-page proposed legislation was forced to a vote before congress had ample time to review the final actual specifics in the bill. While this Act forces both business and individual mandates on all Americans, congress and the president exempted themselves from the legislation. As of May 2011, the amount of waivers granted by Health and Human Services Secretary Kathleen Sebelius is 1,372 nationwide, with more than 3 million people enrolled in plans affected by these waivers granted to labor unions, large corporations, financial firms, state, and local governments. House Minority Leader Nancy Pelosi, who rushed the vote, has recently received three dozen waivers for businesses in her own congressional district, including restaurants, nightclubs, and hotels.

Meanwhile, Governor Palin responded to the process and numbers of waivers of the mandate granted by the Obama administration as "unflippinbelievable" and "corrupt"!

All of us would agree there is a tremendous need for improved health care delivery and availability in America; however, the answer is not total and unconstitutional government control of our health care system. Instead, America needs free market solutions to provide better health care coverage and delivery, including tort reform, deregulation of the health care industry, and allowing more competition and availability of health care insurance and services between the individual states—across state lines.

Wisconsin Republican Representative Paul Ryan has proposed a health care plan that would not only improve upon our current system but also assist certain Americans by eliminating government influence over the system and reduce government spending on it. Naturally, Democrats oppose the proposed changes, even though they project a $5.8 trillion savings from current government spending projections. Not only would this improve upon health care delivery, at a reduced consumer and government cost, but would assist the federal government in balancing our budget.

Under Representative Ryan's proposed plan, those who retire prior to 2022 would not, in any way, be affected. People, who retire beginning in 2022, would be provided vouchers equal to Medicare costs. Those Americans would then be allowed to shop for their own private health insurance plans, which would be approved by the government, to fit their individual needs. At no point would benefits be slashed. The increase in Medicare spending by the government would be slowed down, as Medicaid would then be transferred to the individual states for control, providing the states authority to effectively manage the program.

It is obvious our government's priorities are not seriously considered and dealt with when we are sending billions of taxpayer-dollars to Africa to prevent AIDS, while our own American citizens die of heart disease and cancer. Our government needs to reprioritize where and how it spends our money. Our government must make the American citizens its priority and must re-evaluate its investment of taxpayer-money to benefit our own citizens by assuring our own health care systems continues to remain the best in the world.

The answer to America's health care reform is a free-market solution and individual choices without government interference or regulation.

7. Military, Veterans, and Their Families

The United States government should be providing free services and assistance to our military members, veterans, and their families. These individuals have literally placed their very lives and limbs on the line to secure our safety and protect the freedoms we take for granted in America. Their families have also sacrificed and endured heartache and pain while supporting our active-duty military members and veterans.

However, our veterans have been sorely overlooked by our government. Statistics of the U.S. Department of Veterans Affairs (VA) indicate that, on any given night, there are an estimated 107,000 homeless veterans and 1.5 million other veterans considered at-risk of homelessness due to poverty, lack of support networks, and dismal living conditions. Many of our veterans suffer from mental illness, alcohol and/or substance abuse, or other disorders. It is estimated that 23% of the homeless population in the United States are veterans who can't afford housing. 76% of our veterans experience substance abuse or mental disabilities, including post-traumatic stress disorder (PTSD). Another 140,000 are incarcerated in federal and state prisons according to a May 2007 Bureau of Justice Statistics report.

Our government should not provide one cent toward any foreign aid until it provides for our military veterans and their families. These veterans need our government to provide them the necessities to succeed when they return to the civilian population in the United States. They are intelligent—91% of those veterans in prison have a high school diploma or GED, and 89% of our homeless veterans have received an honorable discharge from the military.

In light of their vital and sacrificial contributions to the United States, a top priority of our government should be to assist our veterans in finding employment that coincides with their civilian counterparts, including job assessments, skill training, education, and placement assistance. They should receive assistance in obtaining safe and secure housing. Efforts should be made to provide them a supportive network and environment free of alcohol and drugs. Medical needs and coverage of claims must be offered and completed in a timely fashion for each veteran and their eligible family members. Those who qualify for military retirement income should be exempted from taxes.

Our current military members, veterans, and their families deserve and have earned the right to be treated with genuine respect and appreciation for their sacrifice and service—not only from their fellow American citizens but also the government of the United States of America.

8. Education

The future of America is determined in large part by the education of our children. Unfortunately, according to the Ad Counsel of High School Statistics, as of April 13, 2010, 7,000 students in America drop out of school every day. This accounts for 2.5 million students who will not complete high school every year.

We need to do more for our schools and students, in addition to setting higher standards of public school education. The federal government's only role should be to recommend minimum standards expected for students in our public schools. The individual states should be allowed to meet or exceed those standards.

According to the Ad Counsel, 65% of the students who dropped out of school were not motivated to apply themselves to responsible, hard work. While most teachers are professionals and perform an outstanding job in teaching our children, American schools have slowly gotten away from the basics that should be taught in our classrooms—reading, writing, and arithmetic. Today, our teachers are being required to teach a multitude of subjects outside the main core of subjects—driver's education, foreign languages, sex education, consumer education, career planning, peace as an option to war, recreation education, drug and alcohol education, parenting education, computers, ethnic education, global education, multicultural/nonsexist education, sexual abuse education, death education, gang education, bicycle safety education, as well as other basically nonessential educational programs and subjects.

While each of these classes may have some value and be necessary for our children to learn, we have shifted the time and responsibility for teaching reading, writing, and arithmetic, which has caused many students to fall behind in these core subjects. Can our students today write a cogent essay, spell without spell check, or solve simple math without a calculator? Most of our students are not being challenged in school to achieve their maximum potential. We have lowered the bar either to justify and assist those who have fallen behind or to influence our children with liberal propaganda, both of which present major problems within our education system. Many teachers are including in their curriculum viewing such topics as Al Gore's documentary, "An Inconvenient Truth," presenting it as fact, without providing any alternative views, challenging students to make up their own minds based on one theory only. These methods create and increase problem in our education system.

We need to establish and maintain high standards and motivate all students to apply themselves responsibly. They need encouragement. The return of discipline and respect for teachers, allowing them to actually teach in their classroom, is essential. Teachers need proper equipment and fair salary compensation more along the lines of corporate or government trainers.

Students who are genuinely at risk or who wish to seek a vocational profession should be offered more vocational training and guidance in these areas. Although, these programs should not replace basic education courses, they could easily become part of specialized training and job skills to prepare these students for a productive future.

Parental involvement and school competition choices are also essential for students to achieve success. Parents should be allowed the option of using school vouchers to select the specific school they believe their children should attend, whether public or private. This creates competition and incentives for schools to be successful and allows parents who cannot afford private or individual education for their children the choice of enrolling their children in schools that best fit their children's needs and skills.

American families are the real solution. Unfortunately, too many of our families are broken, and the children of those broken families suffer. In one of my letters to an editor, I discussed the problem of schools, our children, and our broken families:

"Our Broken Families"

The American family is our nation's most precious commodity, and it is also the most endangered species. Today it is commonly recognized that over 50% of marriages in America end in divorce, with its highest acceleration occurring in the 1960s. This high U.S. divorce rate has meant that approximately one million American children per year have been affected by divorce. Today, it is even more common that people have decided it is better to live together without making the commitment of marriage, and a growing number of children are living with unmarried parents. The results have been destructive to our children.

According to the U.S. Department Bureau, Historical Statistics of the United States, criminal arrests of teens (14-17 years old) are up 150% since 1950. Teen suicides (15-19 years old) are up 450%. Child abuse is up 2,300%, and illegal drug use of teenagers is up 6,000% since the 1950s. Just recently, in March 2008, the Centers for Disease Control reported 25% of teenage girls have a sexually transmitted disease. Today, we live in a society where casual sex is expected, and 20% of pregnancies end in an abortion.

In 1962, the year prayer was removed from our public schools, top educators listed among their top complaints children standing out of line, not placing paper in waste paper baskets, and chewing gum in class. By comparison, just recently the top educators listed among their complaints gang warfare, teen pregnancy, drugs, assault, and threats against teachers and other students.

The results of our moral decline and social problems have occurred from a lack of a structured family, which is why some children have turned to gangs for a family identity. Other children have turned to alcohol and drugs. Many children have faced physical or sexual abuse. Some teens have become confused about their sexuality, turning to homosexual behavior and some forms of mental illness can also be linked to deteriorating family life. Some children have given up all together and committed suicide.

Our families must return to working together. Families provide the atmosphere where love and marriage of the next generation takes place. Our government should encourage moral behavior by enacting policies that support and encourage our families to stay together. Being a leader means making tough decisions to do what is right to save America and the American family.

Strong families just don't happen. They are built though love, understanding, and commitment. Parents are charged with this responsibility to be involved with their children, teaching them right and wrong, including discipline with love. Parents need to be involved in their children's activities, including church and education. Our children should not be raised by the government but, rather, raised by loving parents to break the cycle of our broken families.

Frank Aquila, December 2008

9. Morality Matters

Nations reflect the character of their leaders. America is heading toward a moral meltdown as many of our leaders live a life of immorality and corruption. We have become a nation that glorifies what is wrong and looks down upon what is right. In the Bible, Isaiah wrote in Isaiah 5:20, "Woe unto them that call evil good and good evil." We have lowered moral standards and values in our society and, as a result, America is drowning in crime, corruption, substance abuse, violence, sexuality immorality, unfaithfulness, child abuse, and perversion.

President George Washington warned, "Reason and experience both forbid us to expect that national morality can prevail to the exclusion of religious principle."

In a 2010 Gallup Poll, 76% of Americans indicated the belief that America's moral values were declining. (67)

The foundations of American society have been traditional marriage, the family, and concern of core family values. Today, marriage has become degraded and less important. As a result, many children are living in broken homes without the structure and guidance of both a mother and father. Even marriage itself has been redefined in many states. Marriage has always been a "religious ceremony," established in the Bible by God, between one man and one woman who become joined together as one. Yet, the homosexual movement has moved consistently forward, one step at a time, in an effort to redefine the definition of marriage to include any two people.

While the divorce rate rises and the American family unit is broken down, sexual immorality has increased. Our children are experimenting with drugs and sex at earlier ages, and 18% of U.S. women obtaining abortions are teenagers. As noted in a previous letter, the Centers for Disease Control and Prevention reports that one out of every four girls between the ages of 14 and 19 actually has a sexually transmitted disease. So many of these young girls (and boys) are confused about their sexuality and lack parental guidance. They lack self-respect and self-esteem. Our children are being taught—and allowed—to glorify what is, in fact, wrong through the music and television industries and have very few positive role models to follow.

We have become a nation that protects the guilty while ignoring the scars of the innocent victims. Thousands upon thousands of criminals have been able to avoid incarceration, which has resulted in many innocent Americans losing their lives and others becoming victims of a system that does not protect their rights.

America's founding fathers wrote the U.S. Constitution to ensure that the government's role would be a protector of the people's rights, not a destroyer of them. However, the rights of victims have become a shadow of the rights of the accused. Our laws provide those accused of crimes to avoid self-incrimination and the legalities of knowing their rights before questioning. While most of us agree with these rights to assure the innocent are not prosecuted, those who are actually guilty of crimes are not receiving just sentencing. Instead, criminals have been provided multiple opportunities to avoid incarceration. We are doing an injustice to the criminal justice system when we allow criminals to go unpunished or receive a punishment that is less than what is deserved.

In one high-profile case, Richard Allen Davis kidnapped 12-year-old Polly Klass from her Petaluma, California home at knifepoint in front of two of her friends. He then sexually assaulted Polly before killing her. Davis was convicted of murder. However, he had been previously sentenced to 16 years in prison for an earlier kidnapping and was released after only serving 8 years. Had he served out his entire previous kidnapping sentence, Polly Klass would still be alive, and millions of taxpayer-dollars would not have been wasted on the cost of sending this convict back to prison.

In another high-profile case, James Jordon, the father of famous NBA basketball star Michael Jordon, was fatally shot in the chest in North Carolina. The murderers were Larry Demery and Daniel Green. Demery, who had three previous arrests for theft, robbery, and forgery, was awaiting trial for bashing a store clerk in the head during a robbery. Green was on parole after completing two years of a six-year sentence for attempting to kill a man with an axe, which caused the victim to lapse into a coma for three months.

In a letter to the newspaper, I discussed not only the death penalty but, also, Obama's attempt to apply international law over the guidelines of the U.S. Constitution:

"Death Penalty: A Constitutional Right"

Adria Sauceda was a 16-year-old girl, who had her life cut short after she was kidnapped, raped, and brutally murdered by Humberto Leal, who was in America illegally. When young Adria's body was found, her skull had been crushed by a 30-40 pound rock with blood spattered around her body. She had bite marks on her cheek, neck, and chest and her right eye had been poked out. A 14-16 inch broken stick with an attached screw had been stuck into her private area, with investigators having determined she was alive during the insertion. One prosecutor described the scene as, "I've never seen that kind of mutilation of the body." There was no shortage of evidence, and Leal was found guilty of murder and lost every appeal to avoid the death penalty of murder under special circumstances of this hideous act.

On July 7, 2011, Leal was rightfully executed and admitted to the murder of Adria; but not before President Obama attempted to stop the execution based on in international law, ignoring the due process in the U.S. Constitution, the right of the state, and the emotion of the victim's family. Obama appealed a stay to the U.S. Supreme Court to stop the execution, which the court denied by a 5-4 decision with all four liberal justices ignoring the U.S. Constitution, attempting to impose international law and legislate their own liberal philosophy from the bench to have international law supersede the U.S. Constitution and remove the death penalty. Liberals have been slowly removing the death penalty from society. They have mocked the justice system and clogged it with numerous state and federal appeals. They removed previous forms of execution claiming it was inhumane, which caused many states to use lethal injections. Liberals in California are attempting to remove the death penalty claiming it costs too much money, sparing the lives of most hideous murderers, including Richard Ramirez, known as the "Night Stalker" and Richard Allen Davis, who kidnapped and brutally murdered Polly Klass. The liberals established the high-cost system of numerous appeals only to now use it as an excuse to dismantle the process, ignoring justice for the victim's family.

Obama's agenda is to remove the U.S. Constitution as the "Supreme Law of the Land" and force America to abide by international law. Even President George W. Bush was wrong in 2005, when he agreed with an International Court of Justices allowing 50 other individuals born outside of America to be granted new trials to determine if their consular rights were violated, which the Supreme Court over-ruled.

While Obama could have pardoned Leal or commuted the sentence, he would have faced a backlash from the American people. He, instead, will stack the court with liberal judges who will advanced his socialist agenda progressing toward an international government bound by international laws, shredding the U.S. Constitution and the rights of the American people. If he has his way next time, the murderer will not be executed.

Frank Aquila, July 2011

As the crime clock ticks, there is a crime in America every two seconds, and criminals are not being incarcerated until they commit serious crimes. And even the serious crimes are being plea-bargained and reduced. Many more crimes are not even prosecuted. According to statistics by Morgan Reynolds, of Texas A&M University, 500,000 burglaries take place each month in America. Only about half (250,000) of them were reported, and approximately only 35,000 arrests were made by the police. About 30,450 of those burglars were tried for their crimes, 24,060 were convicted, with 6,010 sent to prison, while the remainder were given an alternative sentence. The results of the study show that crime really does pay for the criminals. Of the report's 500,000 burglaries per month, only 6,000 burglars were sent to prison.

According to a 1992 Justice Department publication, "The Case for More Incarceration," it was reported that incarceration is more cost-effective than allowing criminals to remain un-incarcerated. When criminals are incarcerated, crime rates go down. When habitual criminals are allowed out of jail, they continue to commit crime, which is extremely costly to taxpayers in additional police services and prosecution. There are multiple increased offenses against law-abiding victims and taxpayers, as well as the additional insurance costs to cover the criminal activity.

Rehabilitation should only be provided in certain cases to those who deserve the opportunity after a first-time offense while assisting the rehabilitating offender with job development or substance abuse treatment. Chronic, habitual offenders with multiple convictions should serve the full extent of their sentences.

The American people should have the right to full protection, including our constitutional right to bear arms. Our government should in no way limit these rights. Our victims deserve a "Victim's Bill of Rights" that allow them the protection they need from criminals. Our government needs to prosecute to the fullest extent of the law those who are a menace to society in committing their criminal acts.

Unfortunately, this is not the case in America today. In a clear case of voter intimidation on Election Day in 2008, Minister King Samir Shabazz and Jerry Jackson, both of the New Black Panther Party, were both actually clearly caught on tape committing felonies and acts of voter intimidation in violation of the 1965 Voting Rights Act. Both men, dressed in paramilitary garb, brandished a nightstick at a Philadelphia polling place entrance and pointed it at white voters shouting racial slurs, including, "You are about to be ruled by the black man, cracker"! This group is also caught on tape with vile racist comments calling for the murder of white people and their babies.

The Justice Department, as a result of this incident, filed a civil suit against the New Black Panther Party and three of its members. However, under the Obama administration, Attorney General Eric Holder dropped all charges against the New Black Panther Party and two of its members, with only Shabazz being barred from displaying a weapon within 100 feet of a Philadelphia polling place for three years, which action is already illegal under the law. In essence, there were no consequences or punishment meted out by our own Justice Department.

Barack Obama, as a specialist in voting rights, is fully aware of voter protection laws. In 2007, as a United States senator, he introduced a bill to protect Americans from such intimidation, increasing the criminal penalty from one to five years in prison. However, this Justice Department ruling is not surprising in light of the fact Obama is known to have had associations with those who encourage civil disobedience rather than peaceful assembly.

In May 2011, the Obamas hosted a poetry celebration at the White House and invited Lonnie Rashid Lynn Jr., better known as Common. During a 2007 HBO appearance, Common called for the burning of President Bush stating, "Burn a Bush cos' for peace he no push no button, killing over oil and grease, no weapons of mass destruction, how can we follow a leader when this is a corrupt one"?

Common is also associated with Barack Obama's ex-pastor, Jeremiah Wright, and performed in 2007 at the Trinity United Church of Christ. It is unheard of to invite an individual to attend a White House event who has previously promoted threatening lyrics, in a so-called song or poetry, against a former president. Common has also made threats against police officers stating, "I got the black strap to make the cops run. They watching me. I'm watching them." Common continues, "When we roll together with a strapped gun, we're going to be rocking them to sleep."

Common also wrote "A Song for Assata," Joanne Chesimard, who renamed herself Assata Shakur. Chesimard is a domestic terrorist, wrapped in crime and anti-social behavior. In 1973, she was convicted of executing Trooper Werner Foerster with his own gun after he was already shot. Dave Jones, of the New Jersey State Trooper Fraternal Association, stated, "And after she shot him, she kicked him in the head to the point that, hours later, after he was picked up, his brain was still part of the remnants on her shoe."

In 1977, Chesimard was convicted of first-degree murder, assault, and battery of a police officer, assault with a dangerous weapon, assault with intent to kill, illegal possession of a weapon, and armed robbery. She was sentenced to life in prison.

Common also performed in a Def Poetry Jam rhyming session supporting another convicted cop-killer, Mumia Abu-Jamal, stating, "We all children of Allah, keep on Fliers say 'Free Munia' on my freezer."

Is this unsettling or disgusting to anyone? The moral decay of our nation rests with the leaders we elect to public office. We must insist that our leaders, as well as their associates, set the example by their character. It is a shame and beyond belief when we as a nation are expected to be a color-blind society while, in the meantime, our leaders excuse those who exude racism and hatred and actually invite them to the People's House!

10. Protect the United States Constitution

Americans and our government must protect and preserve our U.S. Constitution and the laws governing this nation. While some are encouraging our government to rely on the United Nations or international laws, we must shield ourselves from such influence to preserve the sovereignty of our nation.

America is a sovereign nation and our laws must not be subject to foreign interference or influence. Our laws must be supreme and absolute, enabling our nation with the ability and power to govern itself. America was established by people who fought in wars and negotiated land deals to establish our borders and a government "for the people."

Unfortunately, both political parties have broken down our sovereignty. NAFTA, CAFTA, and multinational corporations are destroying the sovereignty of America. Through open trade agreements, again favored by both political parties, America has begun the process of eliminating our borders with Canada and Mexico. Many Republicans view this as beneficial for free markets, while Democrats view it as an opportunity for power and control. Both are dead wrong. When our borders are eliminated, we will lose the sovereignty of our nation!

The current push by Barack Obama is for a comprehensive immigration, or amnesty bill that would include a mandate to encircle Canada, America, and Mexico inside a new outer border called a "common security perimeter," while presenting anyone against this amnesty as a racist. Already those who support Arizona enforcing laws similar to the federal immigration laws are considered racists, while terrorist organizations and drug cartels establish their roots in and around the American border. Federal laws are being broken, and the federal government is ignoring those laws and lawbreakers. Instead, Obama's Attorney General, Eric Holder, sued Arizona to prevent it from enforcing its duly legislated and enacted immigration law. Unbelievably, Mexico actually filed five lawsuits against the State of Arizona, *in our federal court system*, to prohibit Arizona from preventing illegal aliens from entering Arizona, by claiming Mexico's interests and its citizens' civil rights were being jeopardized! And, as though Mexico's suits alone were not troubling to the rights of American citizens, Bolivia, Colombia, El Salvador, Guatemala, Nicaragua, Paraguay and Peru filed similar lawsuits, claiming violation of their citizens' civil rights. Exactly whose civil rights are being violated by Arizona's attempt to enforce the rights of its own citizens against illegal aliens when the American government refuses to do so?!

There are presently two proposed bills in the United States Congress, H.R. 4321 and S. 3932, that would mandate changes to the American borders in a coordinated effort with Canada and Mexico. The goal is to allow the free flow of commerce and people to move beyond the current internal borders throughout North America. Those who are in support of eliminating our national sovereignty and internal borders are using this breakdown of our borders as their means to achieve their goal.

Ten CEOs from Canada, Mexico, and America met at the U.S. Department of Commerce and established the North American Competitiveness Council (NACC) in order to establish, plan, and advise laws and policies for a future integration of trading in North America. The CEOs would offer their "advice" to the leaders in the North American continent. They published their Task Force for "Building a North American Community," and the United States State Department announced, "Establishment by 2010 of a security and economic community for North America is an ambitious but achievable goal that is consistent with this principle and, more important, buttresses the goals and values of citizens of North America..."

The United States Department of State's website, through a link to the Council of Foreign Relations' website, lists the goal of the NACC which states, "The governments of Canada, Mexico, and the United States should articulate as their long-term goal a common security perimeter for North America." The statement continues, "Its boundaries will be defined by a common external tariff and an outer security perimeter within which the movement of people [cheap labor], products, and capital will be legal, orderly, and safe."

Policies of NAFTA, CAFTA, and these multinational corporations are undermining our borders and opening the door for future policies that will cause the destruction of the sovereignty of America without the American people ever becoming aware of it until it is accomplished!

Our government leaders, lawmakers, and those appointed to the judiciary have ignored the laws that made America great. They have twisted the U.S. Constitution and even used foreign law as a basis to change the laws in America.

Many of our judges have ignored the U.S. Constitution. Some in our judiciary have also attempted to accept Sharia Law, which are the laws that guide the Muslim religion. In November 2010, Oklahoma voters overwhelmingly passed a referendum to amend the Oklahoma Constitution to prohibit Sharia Law from being enforced in their state. Almost immediately, before the secretary of state could certify the referendum, Judge Vicki Miles-LeGrange, who was appointed by President Clinton, issued a restraining order against the state, effectively placing the voice of the people on hold.

Judge Miles-LeGrange reasoned that banning foreign law would inhibit the practice of the Islamic religion and lead to excessive government entanglement with religion. In no way was the referendum a ban against the practice of a religion. It was a ban against using such foreign or religious law as a substitute and/or basis of determining a court decision under the Oklahoma Constitution.

In New Jersey, another judge ruled Sharia law superseded New Jersey state law on spousal rape. The danger that exists is, once these laws are established and upheld, a precedent is set for other judges upon which to refer in making their judgment in other cases. Fortunately, the ruling by the New Jersey judge was reversed on appeal; however, it remains a disturbing thought that an American judge would rely upon foreign or religious law to render a decision in a United States court.

U.S. Supreme Court Justice Elena Kagen, who was appointed by Barack Obama, refused military recruiters on the campus of Harvard Law School while she served as dean, but allowed Muslim recruiters who were seeking to implement Sharia-compliant financing into the university. Kagen ignored the rights of the U.S. Constitution, because she disagreed with the military's stance against the "Don't Ask, Don't Tell" policy, which prevented homosexuals in the military from being open about their sexual preferences. Kagen stated, "I abhor the military's discriminatory recruitment policy," describing it as "moral injustice of the first order."

It is deeply troubling when an individual appointed as a justice on the U.S. Supreme Court can use her power and influence to violate those laws in the U.S. Constitution with which she does not agree while supporting foreign or religious laws with which she does agree.

Ironically, while Sharia law and principles are being championed in Dearborn, Michigan, which has a strong Islamic community, four Christians were illegally arrested for passing out free copies of the Bible on public property. The U.S. Supreme Court ruled in a 5-4 decision against a public religious display of the Ten Commandments, even though Moses and the Ten Commandments appear in three separate locations within the Supreme Court building itself.

Barack Obama has also used foreign law to support his agenda. Obama has sought the approval of the United Nations as his basis of approval to seek military action in Libya without consulting congress as required by the U.S. Constitution. Libya did not pose a legitimate threat against America to justify the military attack without congressional approval. Obama knew this. In 2007, Obama was asked to comment on the possibility of President Bush attacking Iran. Obama responded, "The president does not have power under the constitution to unilaterally authorize a military attack in a situation that does not involve stopping an actual or imminent threat to a nation."

He has abused his authority of the office of the president by using "executive orders," which are not mentioned in U.S. Constitution, (68) as a means of advancing his agenda, even though the role of the president under the U.S. Constitution is not to make laws but to approve or disapprove those laws enacted by congress. Article I, Section 1, of the U.S. Constitution begins, "All legislative powers herein granted shall be vested in a Congress of the United States." Article II, Section 3, states that the president "shall take care that the law be faithfully executed." In 2010, then-White House Chief of Staff Rahm Emanuel stated, "We are reviewing a list of presidential executive orders and directives to get the job done across a front of issues."

Barack Obama has also excessively used "recess appointments," appointments of government positions by the president without congressional approval, to appoint people, who are known to be radical and would not be approved in a senate confirmation hearing.

One such appointment was for James Cole, who was installed as a deputy attorney general under Eric Holder. Cole compared the terrorist act on September 11, 2001 to a drug trade and believes civilian courts are the appropriate trial venue for those involved in terrorist attacks.

Barack Obama has made a large number of similar appointments of people who are influencing our government and his decisions. In October 2009, I wrote an article listing the Czars Obama has chosen as his inner-circle of advisers, who did not receive senate confirmation:

"Obama and His Czars"

The people President Obama has chosen to be in his inner-circle should cause concern for all Americans. He has chosen "czars" to be his personal advisors on various issues. These are people who are whispering in his ear and influencing his decisions. These czars have not received any senate confirmation and carry radical and extremist views that should disqualify them from any service in government, especially as a top advisor to the president.

Let us consider the views of these "czars" influencing President Obama:

Afghanistan Czar
Richard Holbrooke is an ultra-liberal who is anti-gun, pro-abortion, and for the legalization of drugs.

Aids Czar
Jeffery Crowley is a homosexual, gay rights activist, believes in gay marriages, and special status for homosexuals, including free health care for gays.

Auto Recovery Czar
Ed Montgomery is a black radical, anti-business activist, and advocates affirmative action. As an instructor, he taught that U.S. businesses have caused world poverty. He is a board member of ACORN. He is also a member of the Communist DuBois Club.

Border Czar
Alan Bersin is a former failed superintendent of San Diego. He served as the Border Czar under Janet Reno who promoted keeping the borders OPEN to illegal aliens.

California Water Czar
David Hayes, Sr. is a member of radical environmental organizations, and ironically, has no experience in water management.

Car Czar
Ron Bloom is an auto union worker with anti-business views, has worked to force U.S. auto workers out of business, and currently sits on the board of Chrysler, which is now auto union-owned.

Central Region Czar
Dennis Ross believes U.S. policy has caused Middle East wars, for which President Obama apologized to the world, and is anti-gun and pro-abortion.

Domestic Violence Czar
Lynn Rosenthal is an anti-male feminist who supports male castration.

Drug Czar
Gil Kerlikowske is a devoted lobbyist for every restrictive gun law proposal, believes no American should own a gun, and supports the legalization of drugs.

Economic Czar
Paul Volcker headed the Federal Reserve under President Carter, when the U.S. economy nearly failed, and is a member of the anti-business "Progressive Policy" organization.

Faith-Based Czar
Joshua DuBois is a political black activist for Black Nationalism and a former anti-gun ownership lobbyist.

Great Lakes Czar

Cameron Davis is a Chicago radical, anti-business environmentalist, and a former ACORN board member. Davis blamed President George Bush for "poisoning the water that minorities have to drink." Again, ironically, he has no experience or training in water management.

Green Czar

Van Jones recently resigned. However, President Obama still originally chose this member of the American Communist Party, the San Francisco Communist Party, and black activist who also expressed anti-white and other racial and radical views.

Guantanamo Closure Czar

Daniel Fried is a rights activist for foreign terrorists and believes America caused the war on terrorism.

Health Czar

Nancy-Ann DeParle is a strong proponent of health care rationing.

Information Czar

Vivek Kundra controls all public information, including labels and press releases, while monitoring all private internet emails.

International Climate Czar

Todd Stern is anti-business, a strong supporter of the Kyoto Accord, and pushed for cap and trade while blaming American businesses for global warming.

Intelligence Czar

Dennis Blair stopped the U.S. guided missile program as "provocative" and was chairman of the ultra-liberal "Council on Foreign Relations," which blames American organizations for regional wars.

Mideast Peace Czar
George Mitchell has stated Israel should be split into "2 or 3 smaller, more manageable plots" and is anti-gun and pro-homosexual.

Pay Czar
Kenneth Feinberg was chief of staff to Ted Kennedy and became wealthy with the payoffs to 9/11 victims.

Regulatory Czar
Cass Sunstein is a liberal activist judge, believing free speech needs to be limited for the "common good," and has ruled against personal freedoms, including private gun ownership many times.

Safe School Czar
Kevin Jennings is a homosexual activist who wrote the forward to a book called Queering Elementary Education, which promotes homosexual doctrine to be taught in elementary school, including first grade. He has stated he will promote his "homosexual agenda" in our public school curriculum.

Science Czar
John Holdren is by far the most disturbing of all of the Czars. He has advocated the formation of a "planetary regime" that would use a "global police force" to enforce totalitarian measures of population control, including forced abortions and mass sterilization programs conducted via the food and water supply. According to Front Page Magazine and other sources, Holdren considers overpopulation as mankind's greatest threat, and he and his co-authors have advocated some of the following proposals in his book, "Ecoscience":

1. Forcibly and secretly sterilizing the entire population by adding infertility drugs to the nation's water and food supply.

2. Legalizing "compulsory abortions," which forces abortions carried out against the will of pregnant women, as is commonplace in Communist China where women who have already had one child and

refuse to abort the second are kidnapped off the street by the authorities to forcibly abort the baby.

3. Forcibly taking away babies from unwed mothers or teenage mothers by the government and put up for adoption. Another proposed measure would force single mothers to demonstrate to the government that they can care for the child, effectively introducing licensing to have children.

4. Implementing a system of "involuntary birth control," where both men and women would be mandated to have an infertility device implanted into their bodies at puberty and only have it removed temporarily if they received permission from the government to have a baby.

5. Permanently sterilizing people whom the authorities deem have already had too many children or who have contributed to "general social deterioration."

6. Formally passing a law that criminalizes having more than two children, similar to the one-child policy in Communist China.

Stimulus Accountability Czar
Earl Devaney promoted removing guns from Americans, believes in open borders to Mexico, and blames U.S. gun stores as the cause of the drug war in Mexico.

Sudan Czar
J. Scott Gration believes the U.S. has done little to help other countries and advocated higher taxes on Americans to support the United Nations.

Tarp Czar
Herb Allison was a Fannie Mae CEO who used real estate mortgages to back up the stock market which led to the U.S. recession.

Terrorism Czar

John Brennan is an anti-CIA activist who suggested the disbanding of the U.S. military and open dialog with terrorists.

Technology Czar

Aneesh Chopra again, ironically, has no technology training, is an anti-doctor activist and believes in government health care and salaried doctors.

Urban Affairs Czar

Adolfo Carrion, Jr. is a millionaire "slum lord" from the Bronx, N.Y., who advocates higher taxes to pay for minority housing and health care.

Weapons Czar

Ashton Carter wants all private weapons destroyed and supports a U.N. ban on firearm ownership in America.

WMD Policy Czar

Gary Samore is a former U.S. Communist who wants America to destroy all WMD programs unilaterally, as a show of good faith to the world.

These are the people President Obama has chosen to be in his inner-circle as close advisers. These people are not only disturbing—they are frightful. None of them had a confirmation hearing and each one receives a salary of $158,500-$172,200 of our taxpayer money. President Obama comes across as a moderate when he speaks; but he has demonstrated he chooses radicals as his friends and advisers. Remember Reverend Jeremiah Wright, who was President Obama's pastor for 20 years? He made outlandish statements calling America the "U.S. 'KKK' of A" and shouted, "Not God bless America; but God damn America." As soon as then-candidate Senator Obama saw this as a problem in his campaign, he distanced himself from the reverend. Then there was adviser Robert Malley, who advocated negotiations with Hamas and providing international assistance to the terrorist organization. In addition, there was William "Bill" Ayres, the organizer of the Weather Underground, who declared war on America in the 1970s with such terrorist actions as bombing the U.S Capitol, the Pentagon and a police headquarters, killing an officer. He was ironically quoted on September 11, 2001 in the New York Times, stating, "I don't regret setting those bombs. I feel we didn't do enough." President Obama also has an admittedly close relationship of "social conferences" with Frank Marshall Davis, a member of the Communist Party USA (CPU-SA), who mentored Barack Obama at the beginning of his political career, which led him to the endorsement of the Democratic Socialists of America (DSA), of which Bill Ayers is a member. Then there was Nadhimi Auchi, an Iraqi billionaire, who was convicted of corruption in France and ripped off the food for oil program related to Iraq. Auchi assisted Senator Obama in the purchase of his million-dollar mansion in a suspicious real estate deal with political fundraiser, Antoin "Tony" Rezko, who was convicted of 16 counts of fraud and federal corruption charges. Rezko gave $250,000 to Senator Obama's campaign and used Barack Obama's state senate office.

Is this the change America really wanted? Can we trust the people who advise President Obama? Can we trust the government with more control on our lives? Can we really trust President Obama? These are the serious questions America must answer. No wonder our founding fathers believed in "limited government," since big government has always brought on corruption.

Frank Aquila, October 2009

The history of czars in America goes back to the first czar appointed by President Franklin D. Roosevelt in 1933. Each president since then has had czars, with only Presidents Dwight Eisenhower and Ronald Reagan having one czar only. President Eisenhower appointed a missile czar and President Reagan appointed a drug czar. However, President Obama has the most appointees who were not confirmed by the United States Senate. This is unconstitutional. Article II, Section 2, of the United States Constitution states that the president may nominate "other public Ministers...by and with the Advice and Consent of the Senate." These excessive presidential appointments, outside of congressional approval, are an abuse of power and surely were never the intent of the Founding Fathers.

The late West Virginia Democrat Senator Robert Byrd expressed concern, writing to Barack Obama that, "The rapid and easy accumulation of power by the White House staff can threaten the Constitutional system of checks and balances. At the worst, White House staff have taken direction and control of programmatic areas that are the statutory responsibility of senate-confirmed officials."

However, on March 30, 2011, Senator Chuck Shumer introduced Senate Bill 679, "The Presidential Appointment Efficiency and Streamlining Act," which is legislation that would grant the president the sole power to appoint people to positions of his choosing within our government. It reduces the number of presidential appointments that would require approval by the senate, thereby ignoring the requirements of checks and balances of presidential appointments through the guidelines of the U.S. Constitution by both the senate and president.

Our United States legislators must go back and reread the U.S. Constitution and protect it. We need to limit the governmental responsibilities and demands on the people by electing leaders who believe in the U.S. Constitution and love America. We need leaders who appreciate our independence and great religious and political freedoms provided by Almighty God. We need leaders who promote individual liberty, responsibility, and the policies of capitalism. We cannot compromise our freedom, independence, or liberty. We must remember how and why America became the great country that was once the envy of the entire world, without a king, dictator, or government control. We were a sovereign nation of immigrants who loved America and fought and died for our freedoms. America was a country "of the people," "by the people" and "for the people" and our best days are still ahead of us if our government will trust "the people."

The Republican Alternative

Recently and consistently, both the Republican Party and the TEA Party have been portrayed by the liberal media and the Democrat Party as a collective group of evil and racist people. The liberal and communist influences that have hijacked the Democrat Party have been successful in using the Alinsky model of lies, deception, and manipulation on a large segment of the American population to actually believe the Democrat Party is the party of "good," while the Republican and "tea baggers" are "bigots" and "racists." The Democrats have encouraged class warfare and allegations of racism in order for fear to grab hold onto various groups of the American population in an effort to openly demonize those who are part of the conservative movement.

Ironically, those who relentlessly demonize conservatives very much appear to be "disciples," or followers, of Saul Alinsky, who personally and brazenly dedicated the original edition of his book, "Rules for Radicals," to Lucifer—the "father of lies."

Alinsky instructed his followers to utilize and promote lies, deception, and manipulation, writing, "Integrity is not necessary to activism, but the appearance of integrity is important." Lying was his preferred tactic. Alinsky believed in a peaceful change to "burn the system down" and build a new one where people would not notice the destructive goal of his movement. His motto was, "The most effective means are whatever will achieve the desired results."

Many conservatives have fallen into this trap set by Alinsky. They have sold their conservative values, in order to appear more moderate, for the sole purpose of votes. Every Republican and conservative does not agree 100% on every issue. However, it is essential for those conservatives in the Republican Party to maintain the core principles of the U.S. Constitution. Republicans cannot become a party of "big government." They must return to the core principles of "limited government" established in the U.S. Constitution. If legislation or policies are in violation of the U.S. Constitution, Republicans and conservatives must openly stand and vote against them.

The Republican Party must firmly redefine itself as the alternative to the socialists and communists within the Democrat Party. The Republican Party will lose credibility if its candidates appear to merely be mini-Democrats taking part in a milder socialist agenda. Republicans must stand strong on principles that are right and stop compromising on those principles in order to appeal to liberal Democrats. The Republicans must consistently prove, by their actions, that they believe in conservative and capitalistic principles as the alternative to the very evident liberal, progressive, socialist, and communistic influences on America today.

In a letter to an editor, I wrote what America would be like—conservative-style:

"America—Conservative-Style"

The Republican Party has had some great conservative leaders who have formed history in America. From President Abraham Lincoln to civil rights leader Martin Luther King to President Ronald Reagan, each believed the conservative principles of individual freedom and individual responsibility.

America is the greatest country in the world. While Republicans and Democrats battle their political platforms of conservatism and liberalism for the future direction of America, I have written my own thoughts of America, conservative-style.

No nation can survive without strength and security. Our nation should always have the necessary resources of strength for our military to achieve victory in any battle. Our borders should also be secure to know each individual entering or leaving America.

We must always remember the moral fabric of America that we are a nation "endowed by our Creator," giving each of us rights to "life, liberty and the pursuit of happiness," where government should be limited and our leaders should be fiscally responsible, limiting taxation and government bureaucracy.

President George Washington stated, "It is the duty of all nations to acknowledge the Providence of Almighty God, to obey His will, to be grateful for His benefits, and to humbly implore His protection and favor." October 3, 1789.

President Ronald Reagan stated, "If we ever forget that we are One Nation Under God, then we will be a Nation gone under."

We need to keep "under God" in our Pledge of Allegiance, "In God We Trust" on our currency, and allow a moment of silence in school, where children can pray silently, if they choose.

The American flag should be protected with a constitutional amendment, and English should be the official language of America, where we, from many cultures, must adapt as one into unity, yet still respecting all.

Federal regulations should require each person receiving a driver's license be a United States citizen, and each citizen should be required to use a state license or identification card to vote, preventing voter fraud. Federal funding should be cut off to any sanctuary city which does not allow law enforcement to verify citizenship through valid identification.

Our CIA and FBI should be able to use necessary means, such as surveillance through the Patriot Act, to gather important information to assist our military and protect America from potential terrorist attacks.

We should provide opportunities of assistance for those in need, without allowing them to become "dependent' on government assistance, but encouraging "independence" of accomplishment to achieve their dreams, where less government is the best government.

People should have their "own" right to invest in their "own" retirement. Personal health care should be reformed with health savings accounts in the private sector where people can choose their own doctor without interference of government bureaucracy. Foreign governments should be billed for those who are here illegally with the savings provided to our veterans and their families to get the best health treatment available. All veterans should be given job security and tax deductions for housing and college education for their children. Those who served their country (and their families) should be given highest priority, as all veterans and their families sacrificed themselves for America. America needs to sacrifice herself for our veterans.

Free trade should only occur if it is fair trade, where every effort should be made to keep business and jobs in America. Teachers should be paid a professional salary and teach our children reading, writing, and arithmetic—not homosexual propaganda, which has drifted into our grade-school curriculum.

Parents should have notification of all medical procedures on their children, including parental notification of an abortion. Abortions should be a last resort as a mother's personal choice when her health is truly at risk or rape but not used as a form of birth control.

We are a nation that is "by the people" and "for the people," where our government leaders are representatives "of the people."

"A wise man's heart is at his right hand, but a fool's heart at his left." Ecclesiastes 10:2

Frank Aquila, March 2010

The Republican Party now, more than ever, has the responsibility to stop playing defense and reveal the truth of the Democrat Party's goals. This may prove to be a real challenge with the liberal media opposing it at every step. However, the Republican Party can join forces with the TEA Party in a battle to inform and persuade Americans about the true threats those in the Democrat Party have, in fact, placed upon America and her citizens.

In bringing to light Alinsky's encouragement of his followers to persuade Americans through deception and lies, the Republican Party needs to persuade the people through truth and information. It is our duty to truthfully inform Americans about who Alinsky was, as well as his destructive influence on America through the Democrat Party. The Republican Party must inform the people about the infiltration of communists in the Democrat Party and this specific threat to America. The Republican Party must also stand on the principles of the U.S. Constitution and be the alternative to the socialist/communist direction of the Democrats. The Republican Party must expose the Democrats for the destruction of those core issues concerning America, including our economy, health care, borders, energy, sovereignty as a nation, and the protection of the U.S. Constitution. The Republican Party must reveal to the American people that it is the party of President Abraham Lincoln, President Ronald Reagan, and Reverend Martin Luther King, Jr.

While the task may seem steep, the Republican Party, with the assistance of conservative talk radio and the TEA Party movement, can truthfully deliver its beliefs and stands to the American people. It must encourage U.S. Constitution-loving Americans to stand together and fight back against the successful tactics of compromise to destroy America that have been brought about one generation at a time.

The local influence of the Republican Party should be to actively involve the community in the party. This was my goal when I formed the South San Joaquin Republicans. I worked to create an organization that reached out to the local community, invited them to meet their area representatives and learn how they could get involved in one of the various Republican or conservative organizations. I committed to provide resources for those who desired to run for local political office and greater access to meeting those in their local community. I worked to provide support for local community residents who felt politically isolated and didn't know how to get involved. Meetings were strategized to meet only three times a year—January, May and September—to allow everyone an opportunity to become excited about the next meeting and continually inform members of any events in the community that would provide an atmosphere allowing family involvement in the political process.

Political Judeo-Christians

God is neither Republican nor Democrat, but the Bible teaches us that God never compromises right for wrong. Therefore, God teaches us to maintain a high standard of morality, and it is our moral and civic duty to vote for people who represent these high standards of morality and personal character. In Exodus 18:21, God admonishes us, "Moreover, you shall select from all the people able men, such as fear God, men of truth, hating covetousness; and place such over them to be ruler of thousands, rulers of hundreds, rulers of fifties, and rulers of tens."

America was founded as a Judeo-Christian nation and still remains blessed as the greatest nation in the world. However, our leaders and laws have attempted to erode our Judeo-Christian foundation. James Madison was known as the father of the U.S. Constitution and established our three equal branches of government—executive, legislative and judicial, using Isaiah 33:22 as its model, "For the Lord is our Judge, the Lord is our Lawgiver, the Lord is our King; He will save us."

It is the obligation of Judeo-Christians to become actively involved in our political process and fully understand the issues. Very unfortunately, too many Americans ignore the issues concerning their personal futures and the future of America. God states in Hosea 4:6, "My people are destroyed for lack of knowledge." We must unceasingly seek knowledge, remain informed, and be able to boldly speak out in public against those who use policies and discrimination to silence us by labeling Judeo-Christian speech of morality as "hate speech."

The Republican Party, TEA Party, conservatives, and individual Judeo-Christians are labeled with names, such as "right-wing extremists" and worse in an effort to make us appear to be out-of-the-norm members of American society. These tactics are also an attempt to silence conservatives from speaking out against our government's policies. Legislators are removing our individual liberties and our freedom to express our Judeo-Christian beliefs.

If the majority of Americans continue to remain silent, those who are evil will gain hold of public offices, which is exactly what the God warns us in Proverbs 29:2, "When the righteous are in authority, the people rejoice; but when a wicked man rules, the people groan."

2012 Presidential Predictions

The 2012 presidential election will be very difficult even though, by all accounts, Barack Obama should handily lose re-election. First, the majority of American voters consider themselves "center-right" in their political leanings. According to a June 2009 Gallup survey, 40% of Americans describe themselves as conservative, 35% describe themselves as moderate, and 21% describe themselves as liberal. Barack Obama didn't hide his liberal agenda or his desire to expand the federal government. Secondly, and historically, no president since Franklin Delano Roosevelt has been elected for a second term when the economy was in such a critical condition and unemployment was higher than 8%.

The U.S. economy is struggling to avoid a financial crisis as Standard & Poor's altered its outlook on the U.S. debt from "stable" to "negative," and our national debt continues to rise beyond $14 trillion. Approximately one out of every four dollars the U.S. government borrows goes to pay the interest alone on our national debt. Barack Obama lied to, or at the very least misled Americans, in his 2008 presidential campaign, claiming he would no longer accept any "earmarks" or additional spending, despite having a Democrat-controlled congress during his first two years in office. Barack Obama placed an unconstitutional individual mandate in his government-controlled health care bill that will cause further debt to our economy. He sank nearly an additional $1trillion into our already down-spiraling economy through the stimulus package. He and his congress claimed this would prevent unemployment from exceeding 8%. Despite that failed stimulus legislation, the U.S. unemployment rate continues to exceed 8%, remaining around 9%, while the rate of those who are underemployed is approximately 17%. The average length of those on unemployment is now at an all-time-high record of 39.7 weeks, which according to the New York Times, "is the longest unemployment spell since the Labor Department started keeping track in 1948." (*See* http://economix.blogs.nytimes.com/2011/06/03/average-length-of-unemployment-at-all-time-high/.) Home values have drastically and continually dropped nationwide, with some communities appearing to be "ghost towns," with half their homes vacant. The federal fund interest rates are near 0% on the interest the government charges banks, and our government has run out of options to grow the economy and control the likelihood of inflation or stagflation that will grip the economy for generations to come. Already, we have experienced the price of goods and services increase, while the U.S. dollar continues to sink on the world market. The American middle class is being sorely eroded, and more and more Americans are receiving some sort of government assistance.

Barack Obama lacks any energy policy that promotes or permits expansion for the oil and natural fuel sources in America, causing gasoline prices to soar during his presidency to as high as $5 per gallon, on April 19, 2011, in Washington, D.C.

Barack Obama presents himself on the world stage apologizing for America. He has refused to negotiate fairly with Israel, causing even further turmoil in the Middle East. Instead, Obama aligned himself with the Palestinians, with whom he has had past friendly relations; who are anti-Israel and desire Israel to give up her land and return to her 1967 borders. Obama has also taken military action against Libya, which posed no actual threat to America or America's interests.

So why is there concern about the possibility of an Obama 2012 victory? The media will do everything they can to elevate Obama to get him re-elected. They have a lot invested in him. They ignored his past disturbing connections and relationships and his lack of a documented personal history. Instead, they trumpeted him to the American people as an intelligent, charismatic, polished, young black man who was going to save America through his promised "hope" and "change." The American populace bought into that media coverage, despite the National Journal's report that Barack Obama was the most liberal member, during the short time he served, in the United States Senate. And, of course, the media told us that if anyone did not vote for Obama they were racist.

The mainstream national media will continue to carry the water for Barack Obama, offering themselves as his personal media center and delivering the messages he wants the American people to hear. No matter who wins the 2012 Republican presidential nomination, the media will attempt to politically assassinate the nominee in the same ferocious style they attacked Governor Palin in the 2008 campaign!

Barack Obama himself will sink up to $1 billion into his re-election campaign and use the Alinsky tactics of lies, deception, and manipulation to get the American people to believe in him and his promises yet once again. He will take no responsibility for anything. He will continue to blame the troubled economy on President Bush, even though his policies have created a larger economic problem for America. He will blame the oil companies for the rise in the cost of gasoline even though he has no domestic energy policy. He will attempt to cause the American people to believe he is the one who is diligently working to assist in a recovery of further "hope" and "change."

Barack Obama will continue to rely on his large base of liberals, primarily the uninformed youth and many in the black community. He will continue to push amnesty for those who are here illegally as a means to attract the large Hispanic vote. He has made deals with the labor unions and other large corporations, exempting them from ObamaCare, to continue to receive their support.

However, Barack Obama will have a problem in 2012. The American people have been awakened to his socialist agenda, a fact which was reflected in the 2010 mid-term elections. The Obama agenda was widely refused by the American people, who voted out many in the Democrat Party in Barack Obama's own words, a "shellacking." The Republican Party was energized by the conservative movement of the TEA Party. This time, however, it is imperative that the Republican nominee be someone who is not just focused on the issues but willing and able to expose Barack Obama's failed, non-stop socialist agenda he has attempted to usher into America during his first term. The Republican nominee must be someone who doesn't attempt to make friends with the media but rather, has the fighting spirit to do what is right and speak the truth to the American people. The Republican Party needs someone who exhibits sincere integrity and has the ability to excite and motivate the conservative base to unite together in fighting against the arsenal of the Obama/DNC/media machine in order to halt America from sliding into the grip of total government control.

The answer for America, the American people, and the Republican Party is Governor Sarah Palin. Governor Palin is the only one who can generate power and excitement to motivate the conservative base. Other potential Republican nominees are fine candidates. However, it is Governor Palin whom the liberal establishment has and continues to fear the most. This is why the liberal media has continued to focus their attention on every move she has made since 2008. They have done everything to destroy her politically and personally by attempting to persuade public opinion that she is not inteligent. However, the repeated lies have grown tierd on the American people and there is no more ammo for them to shoot. While other politicians appear to lack the true courage and fortitude to say and do what is right for America and her future, for fear of personal assaults from the media, Governor Palin has consistently proven she is in no way afraid to stand up and verbalize the truth regarding the socialist and dangerous road Barack Obama continues to take America down. Governor Palin has a gentleness and kind spirit about her, but also a toughness of steel with the ability to deflect the non-ending barrages of mocking and criticism directed her way. She has taken her message directly to the American people using Facebook, Twitter, and other social media networks. Governor Palin is the one who generates large crowds wherever she travels. In spite of the media personal attacks to destroy her, she remains in high demand on the talk show circuit and invitational speeches. She has written two best-selling books, was involved in a popular television series depicting her life in Alaska, promoting her beautiful and beloved state, as well as the subject of a recent film documentary, "The Undeafeated," depicting her experience and accomplishments as Governor of Alaska. Governor Palin continues to dominate search engine inquiries as the only American politician who generates a comparable interest as President Obama. She has established a large conservative network of supporters and pro-Palin networking organizations that would be able to challenge the capability of the Obama team.

Her nomination would immediately bring life into the Republican Party, which has struggled in recent years with a lack of funding and volunteers, due to its watered-down conservative platform, which has drifted toward playing catch up with the Democrat Party. The Sarah Palin networks, organizations and the TEA Party movement were all responsible for turning out the conservative base in the 2010 election with conservative candidates. Those same organizations and networks would assist the Republican Party in further fundraising and volunteers capable of motivating the conservatives to again turn out in the 2012 election. Currently, no other candidate has the ability to raise funds and fire up the conservative base to assist other candidates running for political office than Sarah Palin. After his 2010 re-election victory in Georgia, Republican Senator Saxby Chambliss called Sarah the "great future in the GOP" and stated that "when she walks in a room, folks just explode," referring to the excitement and power she generates.

Sarah Palin is not your ordinary politician. Her roots are an average woman who lived an average life in America, pursuing the American dream. She did not attend an Ivy League school, thinking she was better than anyone else, or abuse any elected or appointed position to exhort money from corporations or businesses. Sarah lived a humble and normal life as a wife and mother, who joined the PTA so she could be involved in improving her children's education. She was elected to local government on the city council and as mayor of the fifth largest city in Alaska. She was appointed to chair the Alaska Oil and Gas Conservation Commission, making $124,000 a year. Sarah fights for what she believes in, even if it adversely affects her career. She resigned from the Commission position due to ethical violations by the other chairmen on the Commission. Sarah never hesitated to expose fraud within businesses, Alaskan politics, and within the Republican Party. She ran against a governor with significant power in Alaska and defeated him based on her honesty and ethical background. Sarah is everything people would hope for in a politician—experienced, ethical, has the ability to connect with normal "grassroots" Americans, and the ability to lead by example. Sarah bleeds American pride in her own unique patriotic spirit, is willing to fight for what she believes is right, regardless of any and all obstacles lined up against her, and has the courage to place her own credibility and reputation on the line to battle for America and the American people.

For those who have any doubts as to whether Governor Palin could win the Republican nomination and presidency of the United States of America, due to wounds inflicted by the media's personal assaults on her, they need to look no further than Governor Ronald Reagan. Reagan was the underdog after he won the Republican nomination in 1980 and was down 25% against President Jimmy Carter in a March 31, 1980 Time Magazine poll. Yet Reagan used his vision, charisma, and conviction to win over the America people and became

President Ronald Reagan. Like President Reagan, Governor Palin understands the problems that confront America. She understands that "government is not the solution but is the problem" and, if not fixed, it will lead America toward a "road to ruin." She believes in removing unconstitutional governmental regulations. She stands strongly against the restrictions of ObamaCare, which adds an additional burden to the American economy, destroys future medical standards, and limits availability to our elderly or those with special needs. She understands that America is being shackled by high debt and out-of-control spending. She believes the federal government needs to lower taxes and restrain spending in order to save our economy and our country for future generations. She understands the importance of energy independence, pointing out the Obama administration is doing "everything in their power to stymie responsible domestic drilling." What America needs now is another Reagan. It is my sincere belief that the next Reagan is Sarah Palin.

Sarah Palin can easily establish a base of 40%-45% of the American people, despite the media's efforts to minimize and distort her. She can take her message directly to the American people, bypassing the liberal media, playing offense rather than defense in the political "super bowl." She will have the opportunity to enlighten the American people as to Barack Obama's past and relate his relationships to the policies he has established. Sarah Palin will win by speaking the truth and exposing the lies and dangers of another Obama term. Sarah Palin can bring a new vision of hope and excitement to America as a patriot who places America first. With her ethical and moral values that compliment her folksy and wisecracking appeal, Sarah Palin distinguishes herself beyond those same old typical unethical politicians who have disgusted the American people. Sarah Palin is a real American who has lived a real middle-class American life and understands the real needs of the American people. She and her husband were both union members and independent thinkers. She is forthright, honest and full of strength and endurance. She has a sincere and true love for America and refuses to offer any worldwide apologies for America. If Sarah Palin can persuade 10% of those Americans who voted for Barack Obama in 2008 to actually look at her and trust her honesty and vision for America, she will win; because many voters may vote against Barack Obama in 2012, just as they voted against Jimmy Carter in favor of Ronald Reagan in 1980.

In my personal opinion, America's best chance for survival is a presidential ticket of Governor Sarah Palin and Florida Republican Congressman Allen West, a retired U.S. Army Lieutenant Colonel who served in the Operation Desert Storm and Operation Iraqi Freedom combat zones. Congressman West understands firsthand international affairs and our enemies as he has fought to protect freedom and liberty in and beyond America. Together, Governor Palin and Congressman West would create the perfect team willing to battle and fight "tooth and nail" to save the country we and they love. Both are courageous and willing to fight the war against the socialist agenda of federal government control in a team effort to save America. Both Governor Palin and Congressman West have been underestimated by their opponents and have exceeded expectations, fighting through the pain and scars of their own individual battles and wars. On Tuesday, November 6, 2012, Sarah Palin will be announced as the next president of the United States of America, having achieved the victory of another battle to save "we the people" and our beloved America. On that day, the spirit of America will be alive and grateful, leaving many to wonder, once again, how Sarah Palin came "Out of Nowhere."

References

(1)   Kolawole, Emi, The Washington Post, 3/13/11.

(2)   Interview with George Sada, "Hannity & Colmes," 1/25/06.

(3)   "Saddam Regime Document: Saddam Ordered the Use of Chemical Weapons in Northern Iraq," Free Republic, 3/23/06.

(4)   Report following translation of video released by Al Zawahiri, CNN, 1/6/06.

(5)   "Al-Qaeda in Iraq taunts Bush, claims its winning war," Associated Press, 11/10/06.

(6)   Washington Post, 7/13/07.

(7)   Dick Durbin, Senate Floor, 6/14/05, as reported by Fox News, 6/22/05.

(8)   "Biden: Iraq Victory One of Obama Administration's Greatest Achievements," Yahoo News, 2/11/10.

(9)   "Palin Resigns from state oil and gas commission," Chambers, Mike, The Associated Press, 1/19/04.

(10)   "The Most Popular Governor," Barnes, Fred, The Weekly Standard, 7/16/07.

(11)   "Sarah Barracuda's 1982 State Championship," Inside Edition, 9/4/08.

(12) "Sarah Palin Biography," The Biography Channel.

(13) Sandpoint Magazine, Winter 2009.

(14) digitalalchemy.tv, 8/29/2008.

(15) "Little-Noticed College Student to Star Politician," Davey, Monica, New York Times, 10/23/08.

(16) Wikipedia.org/Sarah Palin.

(17) Wikipedia.org/Sarah Palin.

(18) Wikipedia.org/Sarah Palin.

(19) "The Faith of Sarah Palin," Lukins, Julian, Charisma Magazine, 1/1/09.

(20) "The Faith of Sarah Palin," Lukins, Julian, Charisma Magazine, 1/1/09.

(21) "The Faith of Sarah Palin," Lukins, Julian, Charisma Magazine, 1/1/09.

(22) "Sarah Palin Biography," The Biography Channel.

(23) "The Servant," Silk, Mark, Christianity Today.

(24) Armstrong, Ken and Bernton, Hal, The Seattle Times, 9/7/08.

(25) Wasilla Municipal Code §2.16.010, *et seq.*, 4/25/11.

(26) MacGillis, Alec, Washington Post, 9/14/08.

(27) Armstrong, Ken and Bernton, Hal, The Seattle Times, 9/7/08.

(28) "Sarah Palin Biography," The Biography Channel.

(29) "Going Rogue," Sarah Palin, p. 93.

(30) doa.alaska.gov/ogc/.

(31) "Palin Explains Her Actions in Ruedrich case," Mauer, Richard, Anchorage Daily News, 8/29/08.

(32) "Palin Resigns from state oil and gas commission," Chambers, Mike, The Associated Press, 1/18/04.

(33) *Op cit.,* Mauer and Chambers.

(34) "The Most Popular Governor," Barnes, Fred, The Weekly Standard, 7/16/07.

(35) Montanaro, Domenico, NBC News, 8/29/08.

(36) Wikipedia.org/Sarah Palin.

(37) Wikipedia.org/Sarah Palin.

(38) gasline.alaska.gov.

(39) "Denali—The Alaska Gas Pipeline," arcticgas.gov.

(40) "Exxon, State Continue to Battle Over Point Thomsen," Loy, Wesley, Anchorage Daily News.

(41) "Palin Has Long Experience Dealing With Big Oil in Home State," Gold, Russell, Wall Street Journal online, 8/30/08.

(42) "Little-Noticed College Student to Star Politician," Davey, Monica, New York Times, 10/23/08.

(43) MacGillis, Alec, Washington Post, 9/14/08.

(44) "Windfall tax lets Alaska rake in billions from Big Oil," Gonzalez, Angel and Hal Bernton, The Seattle Times, 8/10/08.

(45) "Alaska may give everyone $1200 to cover Fuel Costs," Marois, Michael, Bloomberg, 6/23/08.

(46) votesmart.org.

(47) bizcovering.com, 5/13/10.

(48) State of Alaska, Office of the Governor, Annual Report of Alaska Exports, 2007.

(49) "NAACP condemns racism in tea party," Hollingsworth, Heather, Associated Press, msnbc.com, 7/14/10.

(50) mediamatters.org.

(51) propublica.org/about/leadership#directors;   propublica.org/about/.

(52) "Giuliani Questions Obama's Qualifications," Cooper, Michael, New York Times, 9/3/08.

(53) whysarahpalin.com.

(54) "Obama Wanted Earmarks for Wife's Hospital, Fundraiser's Firm," Pitney, Nico, The Huffington Post, (huffingtonpost.com/2008/03/14/obama-wanted-earmarks-for_n_91546.html), 3/14/08.

(55) "Obama Lists His Earmarks, Asking Clinton For Hers," New York Times, 3/14/08.

(56) "NOW Slams Bill Maher for Sarah Palin Insult, Chides Media for Asking About It," FoxNews.com, 3/23/11.

(57) May, Caroline, The Daily Caller, 7/23/11.

(58) "Palin gets it right on birthers and Obama's faith," Capehart, Jonathan, The Washington Post, 2/17/11.

(59) glennbeck.com/content/articles/article/198/14530/?ck=1.

(60) glennbeck.com/content/articles/article/198/14530/?ck=1.

(61) "No Regrets," Coburn, Marcia Froelke, Chicago Magazine, August 2001.

(62) tv.breitbart.com/ayers-declares-very-open-marxist-leanings-week-before-event-with-obama/.

(63) Great-Quotes.com, Zell Miller, Gledhill Enterprises, 2011.

(64) "The Communist Manifesto, Marx, Karl and Engels, Frederich.

(65) cfnews.org/Alinksy-Lucifer.htm.

(66) hacer.org/usa/?p=424.

(67) gallup.com/poll/128042/americans-outlook-morality-remains-bleak.aspx.

(68) usconstitution.net/constnot.html#execord.

9876825R0022

Made in the USA
Charleston, SC
20 October 2011